HEART OF BUDDHA

HEART OF CHINA

HEART OF
BUDDHA

HEART OF
CHINA

The Life of Tanxu,
a Twentieth-Century Monk

James Carter

OXFORD
UNIVERSITY PRESS
2011

OXFORD
UNIVERSITY PRESS

Oxford University Press, Inc., publishes works that further
Oxford University's objective of excellence
in research, scholarship, and education.

Oxford   New York
Auckland   Cape Town   Dar es Salaam   Hong Kong   Karachi
Kuala Lumpur   Madrid   Melbourne   Mexico City   Nairobi
New Delhi   Shanghai   Taipei   Toronto

With offices in
Argentina   Austria   Brazil   Chile   Czech Republic   France   Greece
Guatemala   Hungary   Italy   Japan   Poland   Portugal   Singapore
South Korea   Switzerland   Thailand   Turkey   Ukraine   Vietnam

Copyright © 2011 by Oxford University Press, Inc.

Published by Oxford University Press, Inc.
198 Madison Avenue, New York, NY 10016

www.oup.com

Oxford is a registered trademark of Oxford University Press

Library of Congress Cataloging-in-Publication Data
Carter, James Hugh.
Heart of Buddha, heart of China : the life of Tanxu,
a twentieth-century monk / James Carter.
p.   cm.
ISBN 978-0-19-539885-4
1. Tanxu, da shi, 1875-1963.
2. Buddhist priests—China—Biography.
3. Buddhist priests—Taiwan—Biography. I. Title.
BQ990.A4897A3   2010
294.3′61092—dc22
[B]
2010009161

1 3 5 7 9 8 6 4 2
Printed in the United States of America
on acid-free paper

Frontispiece: Master Tanxu in Hong Kong, ca. 1960. With kind
permission of the Hong Kong Buddhist Library

Contents

Acknowledgments

Many people have been instrumental in bringing this book to fruition. To these, and many others I have omitted from this list from oversight or necessity, my sincere thanks.

Maura Cunningham read multiple drafts of the manuscript, and her insights and advice were invaluable. During the process of writing, Maura went from an impressive student to a valued colleague, and her comments and encouragement, more than any others, shaped this book. I hope and expect to return the favor one day.

Jonathan Spence not only read and commented on a complete manuscript, but taught me to trust my instincts, to think creatively about the past, to be thorough in following leads, and to tell the story I wanted to tell. In addition, Cecelia Cancellaro and Cynthia Read showed tremendous faith in the project, and their encouragement and hard work enabled this book to become reality. Keith Schoppa, Jeff Wasserstrom, and anonymous reviewers for Oxford University Press and California University Press provided important comments.

My friends and colleagues at Saint Joseph's University, Susan Liebell, Ian Petrie, and Richard Warren, all helped workshop numerous chapters of the book, and their comments were formative as I sought a voice and a direction for the book. Their support through several discouraging setbacks was also more important than they may know. David Carpenter shared sources and expertise on Buddhism. Also at St. Joe's, Naomi Cohen and Marjorie Rathbone provided library support and advice, working with interlibrary loan items from around the world. Sue McFadden provided crucial administrative support. A sabbatical leave permitted the time away from teaching to conduct the bulk of the research and writing.

Cynthia Paces supported and believed in this project from its inception, and enabled several of the research trips that made it possible. She, Karen Deaver, and Kit Hain read the first pages that eventually became this book.

Paul Buell, Bridie Minehan, and Yi-Li Wu answered questions about medical vocabulary.

As I tried to follow in Tanxu's footsteps, I had many guides. In Harbin, Duan Guangda, Rao Lianglun, and Jiang Dexiang helped point me on the path that first led me to Tanxu's story; in New York City, and throughout my journeys, Hoi Sang Yu and Master Lok To were indispensable guides to Tanxu's world and writings. On the road, Chin Yung, Master Fat Chee, Master Sing Wai, Master Yung Sheng, Master Chee Kai, Chin Yung, Ms. Ma, Mrs. Jie (Hong Kong); Master Mingzhe and his assistants and colleagues (Qingdao); and Yu Yuan (Tiantai Mountain), all facilitated my travels and arrangements.

Faculty, students, and audience members at presentations and colloquia at Yale University, Princeton University, Bryn Mawr College, Haverford College, Rutgers University–Camden, and Oregon State University all provided helpful feedback.

And thanks to Mariel and Charlotte, for being here.

Thanks to all of you. All errors, of omission and commission, remain my own.

HEART OF BUDDHA

HEART OF CHINA

Prologue: The Present Past

A man opens the door. He wears the saffron robes and prayer beads of a Buddhist monk, his smiling face framed by a shaved head and long eyebrows. The face is more youthful than I expect of an eighty-year-old man who has lived through war, revolution, and dislocation in China. Inside, brightly colored idols and the smell of incense contrast incongruously with the gray January streets of the Bronx outside.

I greet him in Chinese. He responds in English. This exchange, with neither speaking his native tongue, underlines the fact that we are between worlds—many worlds: China and New York City; present and past; religion and scholarship. He is Master Lok To, a senior Buddhist monk; indeed, a patriarch of the Tiantai sect. Born and raised in China, he has lived in New York for four decades. I was nervous about how he would receive me, a stanchly secular American scholar forty years his junior. He has endured occupation and exile for his faith, while I've lived most of my life in tranquil, leafy suburbs. But he immediately puts me at ease, continuing to smile as he shakes my hand (unusual for a Buddhist monk, who will usually press his palms together in greeting), and the distance between our two lives dwindles.

He leads me into the next room and we sit down at a low table before a window overlooking the streetscape of storefront Pentecostal churches and takeaway Caribbean restaurants. Sipping tea, we talk, still mixing languages. As I look around the room, through an archway I catch a glimpse of my reason for being here: behind an altar to the Buddha, Master Tanxu looks out at me from a large painting on the wall.

This book is about Tanxu's life; it is also about the history of modern China. At its core, though, it is about traveling between worlds. Tanxu, born in 1875 with the name Wang Shouchun, worked as a laborer, minor government official, fortune-teller, and pharmacist before leaving his family to become a monk and make a career founding Buddhist temples across China. Before his death in 1963, he witnessed and was part of a century of extraordinary change in China. Tanxu was constantly in motion, traveling throughout China by road, rail, river, and ocean. His travels took him from coastal North China, near Beijing, to the frontier of Manchuria. From there, he moved on to the heartlands of Chinese history and culture: the prosperous lower Yangzi Delta; the ancient capital of Xi'an; and Shandong, the home of Confucius. He left the mainland just twice: once to visit Japan, and then to the British colony of Hong Kong, where he spent the last years of his life. If we take him at his word, as a young man he even traversed the boundary between life and death, descending to the underworld and negotiating his return to the living.

To research this book I traveled Tanxu's itinerary, following him across China, living and working in many of the temples he founded. I also touched him through his dharma descendants, in New York City and Hong Kong. Along the way, what began as a strictly academic monograph became a different kind of story, one that illuminates twentieth-century China through the details of an extraordinary life. And although Tanxu is squarely at the center of the story, I resist the term "biography" because the details of Tanxu's life are a means to the end of understanding China's recent history rather than ends in themselves. To the extent that Tanxu is intended as an instrument with which to gauge broader trends, this book aspires to be "microhistory," a genre so eloquently described by historian Jill Lepore.[1]

My travels with Tanxu were only possible because of his memoir, *Yingchen huiyilu* (YCHYL). The title means literally "Recollections of Shadows and Dust," but is better translated as "Memories of the Material World." Tanxu dictated this record to students at his seminary in 1947, and its 540 pages (different editions vary slightly) contain insights and observations of Tanxu's personal journey, but also of China's travails as it moved from empire to republic, through war, famine, and revolution. Tanxu struggled deeply, and boldly, with his own identity as a human being, and at the same time he was one man among many seeking to define what it meant—or could mean—to be Chinese in the twentieth century.

The *Yingchen huiyilu* is invaluable as a source, but it is also frustrating. At times it is tremendously detailed, and many of its details can be cross-referenced with other accounts, building confidence in the reliability of Tanxu's account. Elsewhere, however, the text is maddeningly silent; Tanxu leaves essential characters voiceless. In places like these, the historian has a choice: to remain quiet or to apply what R. G. Collingwood called "the historical imagination." To build as complete a picture as possible, I have consulted other primary and secondary sources about the events, regions, and personalities that Tanxu describes, but also walked in his footsteps. The *Yingchen huiyilu* became a guidebook, leading me to more than a dozen cities across China. Often I found accommodation in the temples or monasteries that Tanxu helped found decades, and in some cases a century, earlier. I believe that sharing Tanxu's experience—to the extent it was possible—brought me closer to understanding the man and better equipped me to relate his story, even as it made balancing objectivity and intimacy more challenging.

Tanxu's memoir was not intended to provide an objective account of his life. He told his story to students seeking to understand where their master had come from and how his life had made him into the religious figure they knew. It is therefore prone to teleological explanations, often interpreting events as foreshadowing or pointing toward his eventual career as a monk. Occasionally, he describes as fact supernatural phenomena that are plainly impossible, according to secular, academic standards. I have chosen to present these events as Tanxu portrayed them, without evaluating their truth claims. Instead, by illuminating the cultural context surrounding these events, I use them to explicate the patterns of Chinese history and society over the past century.

The China of today, with its towering skyscrapers, high-speed trains and seemingly limitless economic potential, at first appears totally divorced from Tanxu's world of ghosts and visions. As I retraced Tanxu's steps, though, I found that the issues confronting China today are not so different from those that Tanxu observed one hundred years ago. Tanxu saw a weak and divided China, struggling to survive in the face of foreign invasion and internal division. Today, China is poised to be a world power, but the projection of strength disguises internal weakness. Dramatic changes to its economy, society, and culture threaten domestic stability, as coastal provinces develop rapidly but interior regions lag behind. In the past, Japanese invasions, European colonialism, and rural uprisings threatened social cohesion; today the threats are a frayed social safety net, masses of migrant workers, regional and ethnic tensions, and environmental degradation on an unprecedented scale. Now, as then, many Chinese find themselves wondering about their nation's identity and future.

Tanxu believed that China's material challenges had spiritual and intellectual roots and that China needed a stronger religious foundation if it was to survive and flourish. Today, the government fights "spiritual pollution" with internet firewalls and press censorship, but at the same time its elevation of greed and consumption to extraordinary levels (Deng Xiaoping, the architect of China's contemporary economic growth, famously argued that "To get rich is glorious" in the new China) has contributed to a spiritual vacuum. Many are dissatisfied as the social safety net has frayed, and that disaffection looms ominously in times of political or economic crisis. As Tanxu did a century ago, many in China today have turned to religion. Buddhism, Daoism, and Christianity are all growing rapidly. The government grapples with religious groups it considers cults or terrorists, including the banned Falun Gong sect and Muslim Uyghur separatists in Xinjiang Province. Moreover, Buddhism lies at the heart of Tibet's uneasy relationship with the Chinese authorities. Religion remains as powerful and as controversial in China today as it was in Tanxu's time.

Tanxu was born in the small coastal village of Beitang in 1875. War was his constant companion. His father died during the Sino-Japanese War of 1894–95. Artillery destroyed Beitang during the Boxer Uprising in 1900, forcing him to find a new home. Five years later, the

Russo-Japanese War made him a refugee once again. At the age of forty-two, he left home—without a word to his wife or children—to become a monk, but war continued to frame his life and work: for the next three decades Tanxu navigated feuding warlords, Japanese invasion and occupation, and the Chinese civil war. War drove him from his home one last time in 1949, when the Communist People's Liberation Army (PLA) chased him to Hong Kong, where he died.

I came across Tanxu while studying the role of Buddhist temples in the development of Chinese nationalism in the 1920s and 30s. In former colonies like Harbin and Qingdao, Tanxu's temples were the first prominent public buildings of traditional Chinese design, standing side by side with European churches, consulates, and office buildings. Even today, the cities in Tanxu's itinerary retain their unique character: Harbin, on the edge of Siberia, echoes with its Russian past; Shanghai celebrates hyper-modernism as some mourn its vanishing history; Ningbo and Yingkou are gently progressive coastal enclaves; and Qingdao retains its German heritage in beer and architecture.

A century ago, Tanxu used his temples to establish physical links between Buddhism and Chinese nationalism. At the same time, though, he was guided by the belief that the physical world was illusory. The title of his memoir, "Recollections of Shadows and Dust," uses a common Buddhist phrase meant to convey the impermanence and illusion of the material world, hardly the theological emphasis one might expect from a man who transformed cityscapes with his work in brick and mortar. I tried to understand this apparent paradox as I researched Tanxu's career, but my connection to him remained impersonal, even distant, and strictly academic.

This all changed with the unexpected series of events that led me to the Bronx. My research turned up a commentary that Tanxu had written on the Heart Sutra (a Buddhist sutra is a sacred text, usually purporting to record the spoken teachings of the historical Buddha). This brief and very popular text includes the famous construction "form is emptiness; emptiness is form." Tanxu's commentary was translated into English and widely read by Western Buddhists. One morning from my office in Philadelphia I emailed the Young Men's Buddhist Association (YMBA), in New York, to request a copy. They were happy to comply, but more interesting was this aside in their response: "By the way . . . [our] Master Lok To is a dharma heir disciple of Master Tanxu."

Lok To's name was completely new to me despite of all my research about Tanxu, and I wrote back quickly to learn more. A detailed message followed shortly:

> Master Lok To is a formal Dharma heir of Tan Hsu [Tanxu]. I heard from him that his transmission scroll (fa3 juan4), which I was shown once, was hand-written by Tan Hsu personally. . . . Now in his 80s, Master Lok To was the first president of the [Buddhist Association of the United States]. He is running a small temple consist[ing] of a group of three houses in the Bronx. If you have a chance, it will be good for you to visit him. I am sure you can dig up a whole lot of information about Tan Hsu from him. He is one of the most humble monks I know.

I was stunned. Trained as a historian, I was accustomed to knowing my subjects only through their documentary trail. A photograph, even, was rare. Suddenly it seemed possible that I could learn about Tanxu from someone who had worked closely with him. As if on cue, the telephone rang: Lok To's assistant was calling to find out more about me and to tell me more about Lok To and his relationship to Tanxu.

Lok To was also a traveler. He came to the United States from Hong Kong in 1962, just a few months before Tanxu passed away. He had lived in Buddhist monasteries since 1933, when he was ten years old. In 1941, he enrolled at Tanxu's Buddhist Seminary in Japanese-occupied Qingdao and soon became one of Tanxu's most trusted students, eventually helping his teacher flee the mainland for Hong Kong, ahead of the triumphant Communist armies.

Tanxu and Lok To worked together closely during the 1950s, and Lok To came to North America with Tanxu's encouragement. He settled in the Bronx at the invitation of local Buddhist laity, and established the Buddhist Association of the United States there in 1964. Ten years later, he moved to his current location, on Davidson Avenue, and founded the Young Men's Buddhist Association as a center for his translation work. There he has been for nearly forty years.

I was astounded that one of Tanxu's associates—perhaps his closest student and colleague for twenty years or more—lived less than two hours away from my home. Lok To seemed equally surprised to learn that an American scholar was interested in his master's career. In a series of telephone conversations and email exchanges, we assessed these unexpected opportunities. Lok To was at first concerned that I might actually be studying Taixu, a much more famous monk, roughly Tanxu's contemporary. When I said that I knew of Taixu but, no, I was interested in TANxu, he was very eager to share what he knew. He had for years hoped to write about the career of his teacher, but postponed this project for the more important task of spreading the words and teachings of the Buddha by translating texts into English. He was grateful to find someone who would tell Tanxu's story, and he and his associates implied—and sometimes stated explicitly—that fate had selected me to carry out this task. I was uncomfortable with this suggestion, both because I resisted the notion of fate and also because I wanted to maintain my scholarly objectivity. I could not deny, however, that a remarkable opportunity to tell this story lay before me, and I needed to pursue it. Soon I was arriving at the modest row house on Davidson Avenue.

Sitting with Lok To, Lu Bin (a young nun), and Hoi Sang Yu (a lay Buddhist who would become one of my most important guides through Tanxu's world), I share my interest in Tanxu, and what I know about him. I've been to Harbin, and Yingkou, and Changchun, places they've never visited. Had I been to Qingdao, they wanted to know? Not yet. But that was the Master's most important temple—I had to visit there: they could arrange it. They could coordinate my travels to most of the important stops on Tanxu's itinerary, including Ningbo, where Tanxu studied to become a monk, and Tiantai Mountain, where his sect of Buddhism was established 1,100 years ago. Lok To was formally the abbot of Chamshan Temple in Hong Kong, where Tanxu's remains were interred. I was welcome there anytime.

I was excited and a little nervous. My plan to write a scholarly book analyzing the role of Buddhism in the development of Chinese nationalism seemed obsolete. Now it appeared possible for me to travel in Tanxu's footsteps and write a very different book. Lok To gave me copies of Tanxu's writings. I had already gathered most of these, but when passed on to me by Tanxu's heir they seemed to gain added significance. I was familiar with the Buddhist notions of "conditioned causation," and "dependent arising," which in simplest terms explain that all events occur in relationship with other events. Now, as Lok To and the others talked of this, I produced pictures of Tanxu's temples in Yingkou and Harbin and soon found myself standing next to his dharma heir, posing for photographs in front of Tanxu's memorial shrine. These photos would serve as my "passport" into any of the monasteries I wished to visit.

The moment was exciting, but also unsettling. I am by training and disposition an academic: keen to observe, less eager to participate. Journalists are warned to report, not to become, the story. Was I not risking just this by accepting invitations to temples and posing before Tanxu's memorial shrine? And there was the question of faith. I make no claims for or against the beliefs that Tanxu, Lok To, and the other monks shared. Did I belong here?

Five months later, I stand in a mountainside clearing overlooking Clearwater Bay in Hong Kong's New Territories. A white stupa housing Tanxu's earthly remains gleams in the tropical sun. It is a beautiful scene of green cliffs plunging into the azure waters of the South China Sea. As I contemplate the view, a monkey emerges from the forest and, with barely a glance my way, walks to the plate of offerings on the altar in front of Tanxu's stupa. Taking an orange from the plate, it saunters casually back into the forest.

Just a few monks, and one nun, lived at the monastery. The only crowds were the insects that scurried out of my way when I emerged from my quarters. The only lights after sundown were dim fluorescent bulbs in the hallway, attracting a remarkable diversity of moths; the only sounds were frogs and crickets, and occasionally the barking of the nun's dog. Most nights, I was the only lodger in the monks' quarters: the posted prohibitions against idle talk in the temple were easy to observe.

The monks' quarters at Chamshan Monastery were in the main pavilion, which hosted most of the temple's important observances and services. Within its bright yellow walls, bells, gongs, and prayer mats surrounded the main altar. Statues and images of Buddhas, bodhisattvas, and arhats lined the walls. It was here that Chin Yung, the nun who oversaw the pavilion, began each day, ringing the bell at 4:30 AM to announce the morning service. The pavilion was built on a terrace carved out of the mountainside, protected from mud-slides and runoff by a tall concrete retaining wall, the base of which collected rainwater for use in the temple. The wall also sheltered a small trailer, which the temple staff used as a kitchen, and a dog-house (converted from a portable toilet). Adjacent to the temple was a Buddhist retirement home, hosting mainly elderly women (the segment of Hong Kong society most likely to be Buddhist). Each morning, as the sun began to illuminate High Junk Peak, a small procession of these retirees responded to Chin Yung's bell and tra-versed a narrow iron bridge to begin the day in chanting, prayer, and meditation.

These services started my day as well. My first morning at the temple, jetlagged, I opened my eyes at the call to prayer and peered out my window. The mountain across the valley peeked above the mist. As the gentle but insistent wooden bells and gongs mixed with the chirps of songbirds, I realized that this was a new kind of research trip. True, I spent hours each day conducting interviews and reading texts—but as important were these times when I im-mersed myself in Tanxu's world and his legacy. I struggled to under-stand how—if?—I fit into this environment. I was the only man and the only foreigner in the temple during these services. (The monks attended services in another part of the temple complex, I later learned.) Unwilling to intrude on the routine of the worship-pers, I observed the services from a dormitory loft, which was open to the hall below. Just above the head of the large Buddha statue, my perch permitted me to stay out of sight while I listened to the chant-ing, bells, wooden blocks, and gongs of the service. At first deeply unfamiliar, it soon became a comforting routine to start the day.

An example of Tanxu's calligraphy—an excerpt from the Heart Sutra—hung on the dormitory wall, and many mornings I would sit contemplating the characters while the music and chanting washed over me. I thought about how Tanxu's life had given rise to this place, and how the chanting of the women below carried on his work. I was often gripped by intense loneliness—friends and family were far away. I especially missed my young daughter, from whom I had never been away for more than a day or two. Tanxu's calligraphic rendering of the Heart Sutra—"emptiness is form, and form is emptiness"—emphasized the idea that breaking attachments like these was one of the essential messages of the Buddha for those seeking enlightenment, and my travels in search of Tanxu had underscored the power these attachments held for me.

Most days, Chin Yung took me to do more formal research into Tanxu's life. The Master's former students—Lok To's classmates—were scattered around Hong Kong. Frequently, these trips took us to Hong Kong Island, where the scene could not have been more different from Chamshan Monastery. Pico Iyer described Hong Kong as a "dream of Manhattan, arising out of the South China Sea," but Manhattan seems drab and orderly compared to the towering skyscrapers of Central sandwiched between green mountains and the brilliant blue water, or the dazzling neon of Tsimshatsui. Although the scene was far different in 1949, when Tanxu arrived here, it offered a similarly sharp contrast with his life in the monasteries and temples of China. Today, Hong Kong's reintegration with the mainland is a point of pride for Chinese nationalists who celebrate the end of colonialism in China, even as others worry about the fate of the territory's freedoms under PRC rule. Tanxu arrived after working for much of his career to promote Chinese cultural identity in foreign-dominated cities, yet the British colony gave him a freedom to practice his religion that he would not enjoy under the new Chinese government. Traveling between worlds highlighted the contradictions inherent in both.

My immersion in Tanxu's world is most complete as I follow the story of his ordination in the city of Ningbo, near Shanghai. Ningbo teems with an easygoing affluence. Centuries ago, it was one of the largest ports in Asia. Today, less hurried than Shanghai, less uncertain than Hong Kong, and less paranoid than Beijing, it is no longer one of China's great cities, but seems to have found a comfortable rhythm being past its prime. And, like almost all Chinese coastal cities, Ningbo is in the midst of an explosive construction boom.

A local monk drives me to Guanzong Temple, where Tanxu studied and later received the transmission scrolls as a forty-fourth-generation patriarch of the Tiantai sect. As we sit stalled in a massive traffic jam, I worry about what I will find. I had been assured that Guanzong Temple was still active, but the rapid pace of change in Chinese cities made it risky to rely on old addresses: my searches for some of Tanxu's temples in Shenyang and Changchun had yielded restaurants and an appliance store. Ningbo's development is not as frenzied as some cities, but I am skeptical when we arrive at the proper address and see only a storefront next to a narrow driveway. But at the end of the alley, though, I find myself standing in the same monastery courtyard where Tanxu arrived as a novice monk ninety years earlier.

The buildings at Guanzong Temple are less than a century old, but they wear their past heavily. The temple was closed during the Cultural Revolution, from 1966–76. During that time, Red Guards seeking to extinguish the "four olds" (old customs, old culture, old habits, and old ideas) shut down almost all religious institutions. Mao died, the Cultural Revolution ended, and gradually temples re-opened, especially famous temples that could generate revenue as tourist destinations. Guanzong Temple, though, was not a tourist draw, compared with other Buddhist sites in the Ningbo region, such as Tiantong Monastery (particularly sacred for Zen Buddhists), King Ashoka Temple (which houses a relic of the Buddha) or Putuoshan Island, one of Chinese Buddhism's holiest mountains. The temple re-opened but received very little attention. It thus remains much as it was during Tanxu's lifetime, although part of the compound had been converted into houses.

The day I arrive, the temple appears shabby and dark, but active. A handful of monks move among the pavilions. The temple's abbot, Master Yixing, less than five feet tall with a long gray beard, greets us. He did not know Tanxu personally, but he is familiar with one of the temple's most famous students, and he is happy to meet visitors who know about Tanxu, for it is a rare occurrence. He shows me where Tanxu prayed, studied, and slept. In the gathering twilight, the abbot leads us from these faded buildings to his office, where he brings out the architectural drawings for renovations to Guanzong Temple and the Ningbo Buddhist Association: it will be a grand, brightly colored compound with marble floors replacing the worn wood that creaks under my feet as I look over the plans. It will be an impressive complex, but I feel fortunate that I arrived before the renovations and can tread the very same boards that Tanxu walked decades before.

As Tanxu studied in this monastery in the 1910s, approaching his fiftieth birthday, he no doubt reflected on all the brutality and deprivation he had observed in his life. The first of Buddhism's Four Noble Truths declares, "All existence is suffering": Tanxu had suffered, and had dedicated much of his life to the path that would enable humans to transcend that suffering. My travels with Tanxu had taken me across the world, several times, but the only way to get to the start of the story was to travel back in time. This story begins neither in New York nor Hong Kong nor Ningbo, but in the poverty and political turmoil that was North China in the late nineteenth century.

CHAPTER 1

———✦———

Not Far from Anywhere

Tanxu's family had lived for generations in Beitang village, where the Jiyun River empties into the Bohai Gulf, the largest bay of the Yellow Sea. A small fishing community set amid the scrub brush, salt flats, and marshes east of Tianjin, Beitang was poor despite its location on the coast and near the capital. The Jiyun was a small river and heavily silted; as a result, the village could not serve as a harbor for seafaring vessels. Just a short distance inland, peasants grew winter wheat and other crops, but Beitang, like the rest of Ninghe County, could not produce enough to feed itself. The climate was mild, but the coastal soil was too salty for most crops. Its only significant exports were reed mats woven from marsh grasses. In Tanxu's time, Beitang village—today an outer suburb of Tianjin—relied on fishing for survival. In recent years, however, pollution has caused a dramatic drop in the fish harvest and fish that are caught are often too toxic to eat.

Vessels needing a harbor with a deeper draft went to Tanggu, twenty miles south of Beitang at the mouth of the Hai River, where ships arrived daily from nearby ports like Yingkou and Yantai. Larger ships steamed north from Shanghai or Hong Kong, both growing rapidly in the nineteenth century. Korea was just a day or two's sail, and Japan a day more. Most of the commerce that arrived at Tanggu was en route to Tianjin, the port of entry to Beijing and trade networks extending throughout inland North China.

There had been a port at this spot since at least the Song dynasty, in the tenth century, although the name Tianjin does not appear in the historical record until 1404. Its prosperity stemmed from its

13

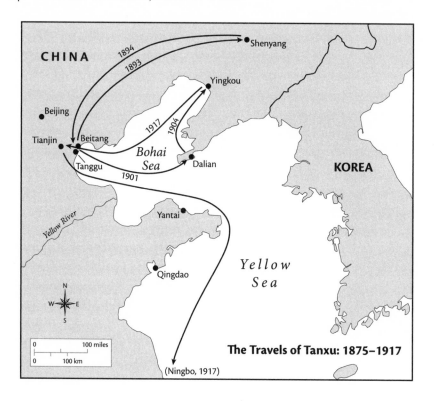

The Travels of Tanxu: 1875–1917

proximity to the sea, to Beijing (which became the Ming dynasty capital in the early 1400s), and also to the Grand Canal. Grain and goods traveled the canal between Beijing and the Yangzi Delta, and grain bound for the capital was stored at Tianjin. Merchants and mariners came to the city to tap into the regional trade network and to supply the capital. Especially important were the salt merchants, who built an industry from the salt pans dotting the flat coastal plain of Ninghe and neighboring counties, the same salt pans that made agriculture in coastal villages like Beitang difficult.

By the 1600s, Dutch merchants had arrived in Tianjin and found it to be a commercial city with few equals:

The city of *Tiencienwey* it self lies thirty Miles from *Singlo*, built also with strong Walls twenty five Foot high, full of Watch-Towers and Bulwarks, and the Place much set forth with Temples, very populous, and so full of Trade, that hardly the like Commerce is to be found in any other City in all China; for whatsoever Vessels are bound for *Peking* from any other part of China, must touch here, which occasions an extraordinary Traffick to Shipping which lie continually before this City. Here is also the Staple of all Commodities, this being a free Port, and no custom paid for any Goods Exported or Imported.[1]

By the middle of the nineteenth century, most of the city's population of thirty thousand made a living from commerce. Observers declared that "[i]n no other part of China was trade as lucrative as in this."[2] This prosperous trade attracted the European diplomats and merchants who would force China to change its relationship to Europe. The Opium Wars opened China to European trade on European terms, at treaty ports designated by the European powers. The first of these—Shanghai, Ningbo, Xiamen, Canton, and Fuzhou, along with the British colony at Hong Kong—were opened in 1842. A second war, in 1860, opened five more ports, including Tianjin.

Tianjin was a point of contact between maritime commerce and interior trade routes, and local events there manifested larger trends. French and English troops arrived in Tianjin in 1860 to enforce the new treaty provisions and establish concessions: mini-colonies ruled and administered by foreign governments with little regard for Chinese law. The British and French concessions were soon joined by an informal American concession and later by Japanese, German, Belgian, Italian, Russian, and Austro-Hungarian concessions. Each featured its own architectural style and competed with the others, and also with the adjacent walled Chinese city, to establish a visual identity. Along with Shanghai, Tianjin was one of the most cosmopolitan cities in China. Over the next half century, also like Shanghai, Tianjin flourished as an increasingly important international center.

Just sixty miles away, there was nothing cosmopolitan about Beitang village. When Tanxu was born, in 1875, Beitang saw few foreigners, indeed, few visitors of any kind. This isolation had been briefly interrupted during the hostilities surrounding the opening of Tianjin as a treaty port. British and French troops had landed at Beitang and occupied the town on August 1, 1860, and a local temple served as headquarters of the British 1st Division that summer.[3] But the British soon left, marching on to battles at Tanggu and Dagu en route to occupying Tianjin. Beitang resumed its isolation, but retained a seat at the window overlooking the growing involvement of foreign powers in China's fate.

Although oceangoing vessels needed larger ports like Tanggu or Yingkou, smaller ships could reach northern Hebei via the docks at Beitang, and likewise goods traveling between southern Manchuria and Tianjin could use Beitang as a port of entry to the river and canal network moving south.[4] Many men of Beitang worked these routes, crewing ships sailing between Yantai, Longkou, and Shidao, perhaps as far as Yingkou and Qingdao. Tanxu's father, Wang Deqing, made his living as a peddler, traveling on the junks that plied the Bohai Gulf, and buying and selling goods in the various ports along the way. He made little profit and spent few days at home.[5]

Tanxu's maternal family, surnamed Zhang, was religious, patronizing the half-dozen temples in and around Beitang village. In typical Chinese fashion, these temples—most nominally Buddhist—blended traditions, honoring local deities, Daoist gods, and a variety of Buddhas and bodhisattvas (benevolent beings who, on the cusp of achieving enlightenment, eschew nirvana and return to the mortal condition so that they can aid other beings in their quest for enlightenment). The Dragon King Temple offered protection from the fickle weather that jeopardized both the region's modest agriculture and the safe return of loved ones at sea.

There was also a temple to Guandi, the deification of Guan Yu, a general during the wars that followed the dissolution of China's first unified empire in 220 CE. Both Daoists and Buddhists came to worship Guandi as the protector of those who were righteous and loyal to their brotherhood, with the ironic result that he was worshipped by both police and organized crime. Guan Yu lived hundreds of years before Buddhism became prominent in China, but he converted posthumously to the Buddha's teaching. The monk Zhiyi (founder of the Tiantai school of Buddhism of which Tanxu would later become patriarch) encountered a vision of Guandi, decapitated and demanding that the monk return him his head. Instead, Zhiyi told him to contemplate the many men whom Guandi had himself killed. If he could progress from feeling only his own pain to understanding the universality of human suffering, he would gain much more than just his own head. Moved, Guandi sought instruction in the path of the Buddha.[6] Guandi's story and the temples dedicated to him illustrate the flexible boundaries among Buddhism, Daoism, Confucianism, and folk religions. Two other temples in the village, the San Guan Temple and the Xiaosheng Temple, were similarly versatile, serving both Buddhist and Daoist worshippers: to declare yourself one or the other would have been rare and unnecessary.[7]

When Tanxu's mother was in need of solace, though, she went first to the temple of the Buddha Amitabha. There she chanted Amitabha's name in the hope that he—or his spiritual assistant, the Bodhisattva Guanyin—would intercede on her behalf. She sought these beings' help to ease her grief: seven or eight children—we cannot be sure—born to the Wang family had died before 1873. Some had lived only a few years; others survived to be seven or eight years old, but the family was now childless and had lost hope of raising another generation. This was particularly tragic in the traditional Confucian social order, in which family was the measure of personal success in this world and the next. Without children to properly bury their bodies and revere their memory, the ghosts of Wang Deqing and his wife would haunt the land, denied nourishment at their ancestral altars. At the Hungry Ghost Festival each August, families set out food and drink for the Hungry Ghosts of their ancestors, who, once fed, could rest in peace for another year. Without a younger generation to provide for them, Wang and his wife risked a miserable eternity of hunger and thirst.

The fear of hunger was vivid, and not just beyond the grave. Famine was a constant threat; even without children to provide for, the family lived hand to mouth. Then, against her expectations, Zhang became pregnant and on July 3, 1875, gave birth to another son, whom she named Wang Shouchun (meaning "long-lived tree of heaven").[8] The baby revived the family's hopes for the future, but added another mouth to feed. Four generations were now living under one roof—a traditional goal—but reliant completely on Wang Deqing's erratic income, Zhang feared that this child, too, would never reach adulthood.

Tanxu insisted that from birth he was singled out as having a special fate, destined to be a Buddhist master. He was slow to speak as a child, and when he did utter his first words, they were not "mama" or "papa," but "chi zhai": to keep the strict vegetarian diet prescribed by Buddhism. Two, then three, years went by and still the boy said only, "Keep Vegetarian." Frustrated and concerned, his mother took him to a neighborhood woman with a reputation for wisdom. The woman declared that the child had taken Buddhist precepts in an earlier life and was attempting to keep them in this one.

Under the best of circumstances, keeping a toddler healthy with a vegetarian diet requires care and diligence; in a poor coastal village like Beitang, where fish and shellfish provided much of the protein, Zhang despaired of ever doing so. Furthermore, a large extended family lived in her household, and she was responsible for feeding it. How could she prepare a special meal for this child, avoiding meat and fish, in addition to her regular cooking? Following the Buddhist precepts would surely see this child—like his siblings before him—die before adolescence, but she took seriously the notion that the baby's convictions, as deduced by a village elder, were legitimate. She compromised, feeding the child vegetarian meals whenever she could, but remained anxious that the child was suffering, physically, spiritually, or both, and that this precious life would be cut short because of her inability to nourish him properly.[9]

Whether he was fated to be a Buddhist master or not, Wang Shouchun survived his childhood. He grew up knowing little of his father, who was usually away sailing with relatives among ports in northern China, the Liaodong and Shandong Peninsula, perhaps on his own boat. The boy grew up with little schooling. Few children in Beitang attended school. Most of the boys in the village spent their time along the rivers or the seashore, learning to fish and catch shrimp or shellfish. This was a way to pass the time, but it was also training for the future, since most families depended on seafood to live. Life for these children was dangerous. Every summer, several boys drowned in the rivers or the ocean. When those who survived turned nineteen, most went to sea, either as fishermen or working the junk trade like Wang Deqing. This too was dangerous.

Having failed so long and with such anguish to raise a child to adulthood, Wang Shouchun's parents insisted that he get an education, even though they could not afford to send him to school. When Wang was eleven years old, one of his uncles moved his family out of the communal home, establishing a new household on the other side of the village. With the household divided, it was easier to feed everyone and save some money, and Wang was at last able to attend school in a neighboring village in the summer of 1885. Upon entering school, or at the time of a similarly important transition toward adulthood, it was customary for Chinese men to adopt a "style name": Wang chose "Futing," meaning "Blessed Garden," or "Happy Home." Following standard practice, he was hereafter known as "Wang Futing" in all contexts (until he took his vows to become a Buddhist monk, thirty-two years later).

Wang Futing's first lessons were in the *Three-Character Classic*, a thirteenth-century text written entirely in lines with three characters. This primer taught students not only how to read the basic characters of written Chinese, but also introduced fundamental concepts of mathematics, Confucian philosophy, and history. Wang Futing was older than the other students, and the teacher soon began tutoring him individually on the *Great Learning*, an important part of the Confucian canon. He diligently memorized the text, but found little joy in the process and felt that he was a mediocre student. He looked forward to days when rain or snow prevented him from attending class and dreamed of running away to avoid school. He put aside this dream when he saw the severe beatings given out to students caught playing hooky, but even so, he was frequently "sick" to avoid classes and scraped by with barely passing marks for four years of school.[10]

Even during his struggles at school, Tanxu recalled in his memoir, he was surrounded by signs of a special destiny. One such sign appeared while visiting nearby relatives. These cousins lived in a rural area near the coast, and in the twilight after dinner, Wang had gone out of the courtyard to admire the view as night fell over the marshes. Sitting on a rock, wearing new robes he had just gotten for school, he was spotted by one of his aunts. Not recognizing the robed figure, she exclaimed that a great monk had come to visit them! Monks were not common visitors in Ninghe County, and when Wang Futing heard his aunt's exclamation, he rushed inside, eager to see the guest. Confused, the entire family went outside, looking for this mysterious monk who seemed to have vanished into the reeds, only to discover that the "great monk" in question was Wang Futing. Wang's mother took this as further confirmation of the village wise woman's words that Wang had taken Buddhist precepts in an earlier life.[11]

After four years of struggling at school, Wang Futing finally got his wish and was apprenticed to a cousin who operated a small store in Beitang village. This was a rare opportunity, for chances to study business were few. He soon found, however, that life at the store interested him even less than school. Wang Futing described his cousin, who was in his sixties and spent every moment in his store, as "miserly, mean, and arrogant." Business was slow, and the two cousins passed the days in silence, each observing the other for signs of what to do, with none forthcoming. Wang did receive basic training in accounting, a skill that he would call on throughout his career, but overall Tanxu recalled his time in the store as depressing: "I thought to myself that if I studied this business I would spend fifty or sixty years in a shop, and then I would die. This did not interest me. We watched each other, and the more we watched the less we saw, and the more I thought, the less happy I became." After six months in the shop, he left.[12]

Out of school and no longer apprenticed, Wang Futing was at loose ends. He spent much of his time alone, daydreaming about traditional adventure stories and romances. One of his favorites was the *Journey to the West*, a fictionalized account of the Buddhist monk Xuanzang's seventh-century travels to India to bring back sacred Buddhist texts. The book, written in 1590, was based on events of the Tang dynasty, nearly a thousand years earlier. In this novel, Wang Futing would have recognized the pantheon of Beitang village: Buddhas and bodhisattvas, demons and deities, all encounter and accompany Tripitaka (the name given Xuanzang in the story) on his trip. The Bodhisattva Guanyin sent Tripitaka on the journey. The third son of the Dragon King became his magical horse, carrying him over eighty-one obstacles set before him and his companions. Buddhas, Daoist immortals, and Chinese folk deities intermingled with humans in a world where the natural and the supernatural merged seamlessly.

The *Journey to the West* was appealing to an impressionable boy growing up with little guidance from his father, bored with village life, and convinced that he had a great destiny. It was also prophetic. Like Xuanzang, Wang Futing would become a monk, and like Xuanzang he would travel thousands of miles with the goal of reviving Buddhism in China. Along the way, he would encounter war and famine, and ghosts, demons, and bodhisattvas. For Chinese of Xuanzang's time, "The West" referred to India and Central Asia; when Wang Futing was born, the term implied European "Western Civilization." Though their destinations were different, Wang Futing, like Xuanzang, would journey to the West, making his home in Western colonies and concessions. Both men believed their journeys would strengthen Chinese culture and Buddhism in China.

Whether or not he was emulating Tripitaka, Wang Futing soon had a supernatural adventure of his own that would change his life and confirm his devotion to religious practice.

In the summer of 1892, cholera broke out in Beitang village. The epidemic coincided with exceptionally hot weather, and temperatures near 100 degrees Fahrenheit were blamed for the disease. Hundreds of people in the village became sick, and most died within a few days of the first symptoms. Coffins were stacked high along the side of the road, and everyone in Beitang worked constantly making coffins, burying the dead, and trying to keep the corpses from rotting in the stifling heat and further threatening public health.

In the midst of this epidemic, Wang Futing, now seventeen years old, was to be married. His mother had arranged the marriage, and the ceremony was to take place in early September, on the same day as the wedding of Wang Futing's neighbor and friend, Jin Desheng. Jin's family home was filled with friends and family from throughout the region, and the extended family celebrated the marriage and the start of a new generation.

Jin Desheng did not live to enjoy his marriage. He fell ill on the day of the wedding and died the next. Jin's young bride changed from the red bridal gown to the white dress of a new widow, and guests who had come to celebrate instead prepared to mourn. His mother's tears of joy quickly gave way to sobs of grief.

The funeral of his friend affected Wang Futing deeply. Gazing into the open casket, he was transfixed by Jin's body, bloated and discolored by the heat. This was the fate of all people, Wang reflected, as he looked at the blue, swollen face—wearing a cotton scholar's cap with a tassel—that just a few days before had been animated by love and friendship. Wang returned home from the funeral sad and thoughtful:

> After I saw him for the last time, at the funeral, my heart was as if stabbed. I returned to my home so grief-stricken I could barely stand it. I thought, people suffer because they never know at what moment they might die. My classmate Jin had been only two years older than me, with a new wife and good circumstances. Why had death come so quickly to him? Was there nothing we could do to protect ourselves from illness? Once we became sick, was there nothing we could do to stave off death? These thoughts dominated my mind. I was not happy.[13]

A few days later, Wang Futing thought that he was about to join his friend in death. Sharp pains stabbed at his stomach, and immediately he feared he had contracted the deadly illness. More than his own suffering, he worried what his death would do to his mother: after watching seven children die, how could she bear to see an eighth—seventeen years old, on the cusp of adulthood—die within a week of his wedding? Not wanting to alarm her, he retired to his room and fell into a fitful sleep, filled with nightmares.

And then he died.

In his memoir, Tanxu acknowledges that it must appear that he was hallucinating from the effects of fever, or having nightmares from the pain he suffered while he slept. These explanations, he insists, are plausible, but wrong. Wang died and embarked on a journey into the underworld. His memory of this experience, which is typical of Chinese conceptions of the afterlife, is also remarkable for the detail and emotion with which Wang recounts his journey:

> Everything looked muddled and unclear, as in a dream. Two ghosts appeared and took me flying across mountains and ponds and lakes, landing at the entrance of a courtyard, what appeared to be a Yamen (bureaucrat's office). Inside the gate were many buildings. The two ghosts brought me to one of these buildings

and said, "Go in!" I obeyed, and suddenly a fiendish face appeared before me, angrily shouting, "Wait here!"

At this point, I realized that I had died, and had come to the Underworld. I was heartbroken! I thought of my mother's words, her constant worrying that I had not been well nourished and cared for. She would blame herself for my death. I thought to myself that death was not so important to me—it was an inevitable and natural stage we all must endure—but my mother had only one child left: me. If I really were dead, she would cry herself to death. What could be done?

I waited—I don't know for how long, it seemed like a month—and heard not a sound. Looking around the room, I saw a man keeping accounts. He held a brush in his hand but I could not see what he was writing. There were no other people in the room. I walked slowly toward his desk, thinking of a way to make friends with him and his accounts. I called out "Sir!" and very politely asked, "For what crime am I to be tried?"

"I don't know!" he replied.

"Where is this trial?" I then asked.

"After a while, you will be taken from here to be tried."

"Whose court is this?" I asked again.

"Ah!" he exclaimed with surprise. "Do you feel that you are still in the land of the Sun? You are dead: a ghost. You are to be judged by the King of Hell—do you not already know this?" As he spoke, he continued writing in his ledger.

After this, I was deep in thought for a long time. I then asked, "Can I return to life?"

No response.

I repeated the question: "Can I return to life?"

"I don't know!" he replied impatiently. "When the court is adjourned all will be clear." As he spoke, he continued writing in the book, just as before.

I stood there for a moment, when I suddenly remembered some chants and incantations I had learned from my mother's trips to temples and shrines. I began to recite a chant that I had been told could call ghosts to return from the dead. I didn't know if the incantation was genuine or not. Perhaps it was just superstition? Would it be effective? I asked these questions to the gentleman.

He abruptly stopped writing and replied, "These are genuine. These are ways of calling people back from Underworld." He pointed to some wooden tablets on the wall. "The names on these wooden tags are people who have recently died but did not stay," he said. "The descendants they left behind recalled their spirits. It can be done, but if too much time passes, it is not easy to do."

I looked at the tablets he was indicating. Sure enough, there were many names, as well as coils of incense, papers and other items. I turned to him and asked what time the trial would be. He replied, "Wait! The King of Hell is in another room, having his head shaved." At this I began to feel like I would soon be seeing a play, starring the bearded and accursed King of Hell. It struck me as very odd that the King of Hell would have to wear the queue. Surely he was not a subject of the Qing Empire: why would the King of Hell here wear a ponytail and a shaved head—the hairstyle that indicated loyalty to the Manchu regime that had ruled China since 1644?

I waited in this room for a very long time until the two ghosts who had brought me here initially reappeared and took me out down a path and into a large pavilion. The ghosts pushed me hard through the entrance, and I stumbled into the hall. As my eyes struggled to adjust to the black and smoky interior, I could see nothing at all. In the darkness, a voice asked:

"Are you Wang Futing?"

This was a very strange and brusque voice I heard, and when it called me by my formal name, Wang Futing, I knew that this was Yanluo, the King of Hell, here to begin my trial. In a relaxed voice, I replied that I was Wang Futing.

"You have died!" Yanluo said. "Now, you are to be reincarnated."

I thought, if I were reincarnated, I would not know where I would go. Could I return home or not? Would my mother miss me? Was she already crying herself to death? I thought quickly, and asked again:

"Have I committed any crime?"

"You have not!"

I was heartened. "Since I am without crime," I asked, "could I not be returned to my current life? Why must I be reincarnated? I am my mother's only child, and ever since I was small she has feared I would die. If I do not return to her, she will forever believe that she failed me. She will constantly worry that no one will revere her memory and make offerings to the ancestral shrine. She will be overcome by grief. In my current life, I have just begun to study. If you force me to be reincarnated, my studies will have been wasted: would this not be a great insult?"

"Every life has its limits. It is not simply about you or your personal situation," the King of Hell replied.

"When I was on the earth, I heard that chanting sutras could extend one's life, and I have chanted many. Can this be taken into account?"

This was a practice I had started two years earlier, after I had seen my uncle die. I feared death, and so I sought ways to stave it off. The Wang family elders believed that reciting Buddhist sutras—texts that recounted the teachings of or stories about the Buddha—had the power to prevent catastrophe. After I learned this, I spent any free time I had reciting a few sutras, to stave off death.

The King of Hell said, "Reciting sutras is effective, but its power is limited. You are seventeen at this, the time of your death. If I grant you an additional five years of life—until you are twenty-two—would that demonstrate that your recitation of sutras has been effective?"

"Since reciting sutras is effective, couldn't you return me? I will continue to recite sutras, and thus continue to prolong my life—wouldn't this be acceptable?"

He gave me a disapproving look. "Simply reciting this kind of sutra is not sufficient!"

I thought hard. If it were not enough to recite these sutras, perhaps I could chant other sutras. In our village, there had been someone of the Shi family who had recited the Diamond Sutra for this kind of purpose. It was said that to memorize just four lines from this text was equivalent to making a shrine to the Buddha: I did not know the outcome of his chanting, or how many parts the sutra contained, or what its contents were like, but it was my only chance to return to my mother, so I spoke:

"If you let me return, every day I will chant ten chapters of the Diamond Sutra!"

The King of Hell heard my words and agreed to let me return.

After a short while, the two ghosts returned take me back. Soon, I was back in my village, and I saw the East-facing door of our South room. As I entered, I heard my mother crying bitterly. Our home had three rooms, one was light and two were dark. My family was all gathered in the middle room cooking. My corpse lay on the kang [a raised platform for sitting or sleeping that could be heated in winter by coal fires underneath], while my mother looked at my dead face, sobbing, not caring if she lived or died. The two ghosts took me to my old body, and pushed me from behind, saying, "Return to the light!"

Just then, it seemed as though I were awakening groggily from a dream, and I turned my head and saw outside that it was nearly noon.[14]

Wang Futing returned to the world of the living. Whether he had actually died, as he insisted, or dreamed or hallucinated his visit to the underworld, he was changed. He felt separated from his friends and family by his experience, which he did not share even with his mother, on whose behalf he had disputed with the King of Hell. Part of the reason he kept the story from her was that Yanluo had granted him just five more years on earth. Unless he held to the terms of the agreement, he would die—again—when he was twenty-two, still leaving his mother childless. Rather than demystifying death or diminishing its importance, Wang's experience heightened his awareness of mortality. He, like everyone else, would die, becoming a discolored corpse just like his neighbor Jin Desheng. Wang had bargained his way back to life, but it was only temporary. To satisfy Yanluo's demands, he found a copy of the Diamond Sutra and began reciting it every day.

The Diamond Sutra is one of the most commonly read texts in Mahayana Buddhism. It takes the name "Diamond" because its insights are said to be hard and sharp enough to direct the seeker straight to the most essential principles for attaining enlightenment. A copy of the Diamond Sutra, discovered in a Gobi Desert cave early in the twentieth century, is the oldest known printed book in the world, dating to 868 CE—nearly six hundred years before Gutenberg's bibles. The text runs about thirty pages in most English translations and can be recited in less than an hour.

For Wang Futing, recovering from his near-death experience, the message of the Diamond Sutra would have been helpful. It proclaims the principle of "non-abiding," the notion that one must be constantly aware of the trap created by one's own mind as it tries to make sense of the physical world. This trap—comprising the labels and descriptions and associations that our mind attaches to what it perceives—overwhelms our consciousness, distracting it and making progress toward enlightenment impossible. The non-abiding mind must constantly clear itself by attending to this web of mental constructs and recognizing them as just that: constructs of our own mind rather than things in themselves.

The Diamond Sutra is not nihilist. To live and work in the world—which includes living and working toward enlightenment for ourselves and others—we must make sense of the physical environment around us. The non-abiding seeker is aware of the mental constructs and their limitations and must step back from them and recognize them as labels; yet, to function in this world he or she cannot reject labels altogether. Even "the Buddha" is a label constructed by a mind, yet to deny the Buddha's existence would frustrate any attempt to follow his path. Non-abiding is thus a delicate balance between rejecting the mental constructs that govern our perception and making use of them. You cannot be bound by your perceptions, for that would distract you from the path to enlightenment; yet, neither can you let your mind wander without any regard to perception or the physical world, for that would lead to other distractions of daydream or fantasy. The teachings of the Buddha are themselves distractions, but without these teachings, achieving enlightenment is that much more difficult. The trappings of the physical world are neither real, nor not-real; they are both real and not-real. Within this contradiction we must strive to abide: non-abiding. The Diamond Sutra concludes:

> All conditioned phenomena
> Are like a dream, an illusion, a bubble, a shadow
> Like the dew, or like lightning
> You should discern them like this[15]

Or otherwise translated:

> Thus shall ye think of all this fleeting world:
> A star at dawn, a bubble in a stream;
> A flash of lightning in a summer cloud,
> A flickering lamp, a phantom, and a dream.[16]

The Diamond Sutra offered much for Wang Futing, but he faced a fundamental obstacle: he could not read it (at least not easily). He had received only four years of formal education and had been a mediocre, unmotivated student. So even when he obtained a copy of the text, and devoted every spare moment to reciting it, he still faced hundreds of characters he could not easily recognize. Slowed by the need to look up or recall unfamiliar characters, he could get through only two, sometimes three, chapters a day, not the ten he had promised. As the words of the sutra passed slowly across his lips, he felt the days of his life slipping by faster and faster; it seemed he would face the King of Hell again in just a few years.[17]

This made Wang's spiritual and religious quest even more urgent, and he cast his net widely. He consulted a master from a neighboring village—it is unclear whether he was a Buddhist or a Daoist, or if such a distinction was meaningful or important to either one of them—and was told that he could substitute for the Diamond Sutra the much shorter "Diamond Incantation." Wang could read this more easily and soon memorized it, chanting it whenever he could. But he also explored the full range of religion open to him, including Buddhism, Daoism, Chinese folk religion, and even Protestant and Roman Catholic Christianity.

Christian missionaries were common in the Tianjin region in the late nineteenth century. They had been banned from China by the Kangxi Emperor in 1721, but the 1842 Treaty of Nanjing, ending the First Opium War, re-opened China to legal missionary activity, and missionaries arrived with the soldiers and merchants who entered Tianjin in 1860. By the spring of 1861, Baptist, Methodist, and Anglican missionaries had set up churches in Tianjin to serve the growing foreign community as well as Chinese Christians. Roman Catholic missionaries came with the French troops at this same time, erecting the Cathédrale de Notre Dame des Victoires, completed in 1869.[18] The next year, this church was at the center of the "Tianjin Massacre," a violent encounter between local Chinese and French Catholics that resulted in the deaths of twenty-one foreigners and as many as forty Chinese Christians.

Underlying the massacre was a mixture of mistrust and arrogance. Gossip abounded in the city about the Christian missions. French Catholic nuns had been bringing children to the mission-run orphanage, sometimes giving payments to their families, and were implicated in a kidnapping ring. This combined with the high rate of mortality in the orphanage to fuel rumors that the nuns were buying children for use as human sacrifices or ingredients in stew (a jar of pickled onions, spotted in the church pantry, was apparently mistaken for human eyes). After the riot, apologies from the Chinese to the French court and the arrest and execution of sixteen Chinese officially resolved the incident, but mistrust toward Christians—both Chinese and foreign— would persist.

Remarkably, in this atmosphere of antipathy toward Christianity, Wang Futing sought out Christian churches as part of his religious quest. There is no record of a Christian church in Ninghe County prior to 1900, but there were several in Tianjin, and missionaries would have regularly traveled through Tanggu, just a few miles from Beitang village. Tanxu considered taking up Catholicism, Protestant Christianity, Daoism, and Buddhism. His home became a source of amusement and puzzlement for his friends: statues of Christian saints, Daoist immortals, folk deities, Buddhas and bodhisattvas, and icons from every religious tradition he could find were in evidence as he sought a way to avoid reencountering death.

Most religious traditions address the afterlife. But Wang Futing wanted to remain in *this* life, delaying death as long as possible, if not preventing it altogether. His mind was preoccupied with death, and he filled his spare moments with study of the occult. With immortality his goal, he turned to Daoist alchemy. At age nineteen, he sought out Wang Jieran, a Daoist master in the village, for instruction.

Their Western counterparts frequently sought ways to transmute base metals into gold, but Chinese alchemists focused almost exclusively on gaining eternal life. By the fourth century BCE, hopes for immortality focused on drugs and elixirs, and books to aid in their preparation spread accordingly. By Wang Futing's time, approximately one hundred such manuals offered alchemical instruction, usually preserved in Daoist texts.[19] Their prescriptions usually involved highly toxic compounds of lead or mercury. Not infrequently, practitioners succumbed to mercury and lead poisoning. Their deaths were not necessarily seen as evidence that their methods were wrong: some saw the elixirs as hastening the demise of one's physical form, and thus granting immortality in the world beyond. One such practitioner was Sun Simo, author of one of the most famous alchemical texts, *Essential Instructions from the Scripture on the Elixirs of the Great Purity (Taiqingjing danjing yaojue)*, which would have been available to Wang Futing.

In this text, based on a now-lost fourth- or fifth-century source, Sun Simo offers sixty-seven different elixirs for the seeker of immortality. In Sun's commentary, the first thirty-four recipes are said to be for "minor elixirs." These are presumably less efficacious than the next category, "great elixirs by which one leaves the world as an immortal." These potions, with names like the "Grand Concord Dragon Womb Elixir," the "Supernatural Flight Elixir of Grandee Chang," or the "Divine Dragon Elixir," are "not to be known at large. . . . all in all, they are not expeditiously come upon. Therefore, the methods of their preparation are not appended. Amateurs have a rough time of them." Following this category were "twenty elixirs not employed by the uninitiated."[20] The texts were not enough: to unlock the secrets of immortality required a teacher who was familiar with both the text and the tradition. Wang Futing sought Wang Jieran's help in this, but the older man was reluctant. Having dedicated most of his life to studying elixirs, he could not promise success and advised Wang Futing to wait a few years and see if his efforts yielded results. But Wang Futing was impatient; he concluded that alchemy, like the other teachings he had looked into, was a deception. Terrified of death, but finding no way to avoid it, he rejected religion.[21]

A branch of Wang Futing's family lived in Fengtian (now Shenyang, and sometimes referred to by its Manchu name, Mukden), the largest city in Manchuria, where his relatives worked as tobacco traders. They transported tobacco from Manchuria to

Hebei markets like Ninghe and Lutai. From there, they would go on to Tianjin and enter the broader North China market. Their tobacco sold, they bought reed mats—the regional specialty of the eastern Hebei marshlands—and returned to Fengtian to sell them.

Wang was not happy in Beitang. Although newly married, he does not mention his wife, only the traumatic death of his friend, Jin, and his own encounter with mortality. He was haunted by the fear that in just a few years he would face death once again if he could not find the right rituals to satisfy the judges of the underworld. He was eager to leave the village, but had few marketable skills. His limited education was inadequate to pass the civil-service examination for entry into the government bureaucracy. The size of the bureaucracy had not kept pace with the growing number of applicants, and by the late nineteenth century less than 5 percent of candidates were passing even the most basic of these tests. As a result, tens, or even hundreds, of thousands of young men without academic credentials were seeking employment in a struggling economy. Many of them were better educated than Wang Futing, but family ties made a difference, and in 1893, Wang Futing went to Fengtian to live with his cousins and join the family business. His wife stayed behind in Beitang.

The business was seasonal: in spring and summer, there was little to do but await the fall harvest when they would select and buy tobacco leaves, distribute them throughout the family, and make their trading trips to Hebei. Returning to Fengtian in the spring of 1894, with no prospect of work until fall, the family found Wang a position in a small shop owned by his grandfather's clan, working as an accountant and performing odd jobs. The business was steadier than tobacco trading, but it too was slow during the summer. Wang usually spent the morning at the shop, tending to the books and whatever tasks he was assigned, and then the afternoons were his own. Wang Futing welcomed this leisure and would wander the streets of the city with his cousins, enjoying having money to spend and eating and drinking as he pleased. Most afternoons, they would escape the heat of the city and retreat to the surrounding pine forests, sharing picnic lunches and intense discussions about religion and family. Though still affected by the traumatic events of the previous years, Wang felt free and happy.[22]

In the summer of 1894, while Wang Futing relaxed with his family and friends, Chinese and Japanese troops were preparing for war in Korea. Anticipating World War I, the war was both the product of and the catalyst for important political, technological, and economic changes. Since the middle of the nineteenth century, China and Japan had faced increasing pressure from Europe and the United States to open their economies to trade. In a span of twenty years, Western gunboats approached first China and then Japan, demanding access. China's ruling Qing dynasty hoped to maintain territorial integrity and stem the flow of opium, but it accomplished neither through wars with Britain in 1839 and again in 1858. Internal wars rocked the Qing Empire, including the massive Taiping Rebellion in which a failed Chinese scholar, believing himself to be the younger brother of Jesus Christ, led an uprising that left as many as thirty million dead. The ruling dynasty barely survived, and did so largely because of help from Western governments that were quietly pleased to have such a feeble government ruling China. Many Chinese attempted to reform their state, through both foreign and domestic initiatives, and by the 1890s there was hope that China had weathered the storm and would retain its place as the dominant power in East Asia. China's role as protector of Korea was a key element in this status.

Japan, for many reasons including its much smaller size, responded more effectively to the Western challenge than did China. When Commodore Perry sailed American ships into Tokyo Bay and insisted that Japan open its ports to Western trade in the 1850s, it provoked a period of military conflict and civil war. The Meiji Restoration of 1868 heralded a rapid period of change during which Japan developed and adapted Western-style military, industrial, and governmental institutions. By the 1890s, many in Japan felt that their nation had supplanted China as the dominant power in the region and deserved to be dealt with by Western nations as an equal. Korea was a useful opportunity to demonstrate these claims.

By the 1885 Treaty of Tianjin, Japan had forced China to recognize that Korea was a sovereign state. This was meant to deny China's traditional claims over the peninsula and also to facilitate Japanese commercial and military ambitions there. Both sides worked with Korean factions to advance their own interests on the peninsula, and by 1894 the conflicts within Korea had become a proxy war between their Japanese and Chinese patrons. Frustrated with the slow progress working behind the scenes, Japanese forces seized the Korean king in the summer of that year, holding him hostage to force Sino-Japanese negotiations over "reforms" in Korea. The Qing sent forces to respond. On July 25, Japanese ships attacked and sank a Chinese troop carrier en route to Korea, and a week later Japan declared war on the Qing Empire.[23]

Japanese troops defeated their Chinese counterparts decisively in the battles of Pyongyang and Yalu in September. These first engagements took place on Korean soil, but on October 25, 1894, Japan crossed the Yalu River into China and attacked the border city of Andong. Despite being severely outnumbered, the Japanese easily defeated the city's defenders, and one branch of the Japanese army moved north toward Fengtian, just 150 miles away. The news that Japanese troops were marching toward the city precipitated panic. Stores in the city closed, and many institutions sent their workers home in anticipation of an attack.

This was Wang Futing's first experience of war. Foreign troops had several times landed at his home village of Beitang and the surrounding region, but this had happened before Wang was born. The Japanese invasion fundamentally altered the Chinese view of the world. China had for centuries considered itself the center of regional—if not global—politics, culture, and economics. Now, the ease with which Japan destroyed China's most elite armies and navies underscored that times had changed: China was at great risk. For Wang Futing, already struggling with his own mortality, this realization must have weighed heavily as his employer in Fengtian gave him two pieces of silver and sent him home to Beitang.

There was no easy way to travel from Fengtian to Beitang in the fall of 1894. The war had disrupted rail service and the roads through Liaoning Province were dangerous, not so much because of the Japanese, but because of Chinese bandits. With a dozen other refugees, Wang set out on foot, heading southwest toward Shanhaiguan, the easternmost pass through the Great Wall where it meets the sea. Evading both armies and robbers for more than a month, Wang's group eventually made it through. Below Shanhaiguan the trains were running, and Wang was able to board one that would take him to Tianjin.

Wang was excited to be rejoining his family just a few weeks before the lunar New Year. New Year—the "Spring Festival"—was then as now the most important holiday in Chinese culture, and families expected to spend the two-week celebration together. But arriving back at Beitang, he was met by the unexpected news that his father had died. Wang's memoir shares no details about his death; he may not have known. During the summer and fall of 1894, naval battles between Chinese and Japanese forces in the Bohai Gulf disrupted the trade routes Wang's father sailed. He may have been a casualty of war, directly or indirectly, or the war may have been coincidental to his death: small sailing vessels were always at risk. His death may not have been related to his work; he was no longer a young man. But no matter how it came to be, Wang Futing arrived home to learn that he was now, at the age of nineteen, the head of the family.

Wang Futing had spent little time with his father, who was so often away, but he took the news hard, feeling it was "a blow to life and spirit." Resuming his education was no longer an option, nor was returning to apprentice with his cousins in Fengtian. He needed to replace his father's income and his options were limited. He took a job as an accountant in the county magistrate's office, keeping the books and managing the payroll until the war with Japan ended and the troops were demobilized. Wang then found a job in a local government office. The work was steady, but it was not enough to support his family, which now included two young daughters.

Wang maintained his interest in the occult even as he struggled to support his family. A man named Luo Tan, a practitioner of occult arts, astrology, prophecy, and medicine, persuaded him that medicine and astrology could be useful skills, always needed and requiring nothing more than a room in which to practice. This idea was doubly attractive to Wang Futing. Medicine and astrology could provide income that was stable and portable, and enable him to continue his research into spirituality and the occult.

The year was now 1896: the King of Hell's dispensation was to expire.[24] One would expect to encounter a sense of panic or dread in Wang's memoir about this period. Oddly, the memoir is silent on the approach of this dreaded date. War, dislocation, and family upheaval may have distracted Wang from remembering the significance of the year. Perhaps it was the sudden responsibility that fell upon him after his father's death, or perhaps his outlook on death had changed, but Wang Futing did not reflect at all on his turning twenty-two, a prospect that just a little while before had haunted him terribly.

By the time his mother became ill and died in 1898, Wang's circumstances had changed completely from what they were when he had negotiated his return to life. Four years before, he had celebrated the happiest times of his life, discussing philosophy in the forests near Fengtian. Since then he had been displaced by war, orphaned, and forced to be the primary income earner as head of his family. After his father's death, he had come to believe that his destiny lay outside the family structure. The words in Chinese for becoming a monk, *chu jia*, mean literally "leave the home" or "leave one's family." While his parents were alive, he would not consider becoming a monk. After all that his parents had endured to finally have a child survive to adulthood, Wang could not turn his back on his family. Now that his parents were gone, becoming a monk was a viable option, notwithstanding the fact that he was now himself a father and a husband.

In keeping with the syncretism of Chinese religious identity, Wang Futing was unsure about what kind of monk he ought to be. He visited all the temples in the region, both Buddhist and Daoist. He found that the Buddhist doctrine he encountered was simply too hard to understand: he resolved to become a Daoist monk. He sought out Wang Jieran, the Daoist master he had consulted several years before. Wang Futing again proposed that he become Wang Jieran's student and learn the ways of alchemy and elixirs of immortality.

As before, however, the master spoke skeptically about the quest for potions that would extend mortal life:

> You seem intent on studying with me, but I do not know if it is right or not, and I do not know if the elixirs will succeed or not. This seems a case of the blind leading the blind, perhaps leading you to jump in the river. Wait until I see if my elixir will work, and then I will find you again.[25]

Wang Futing believed that this was a trick to discourage him, but there was little he could do if the master refused to accept him as a student. Confused by Buddhism and rejected by Daoism, Wang Futing continued to work as an accountant.

The years following the Sino-Japanese War had been difficult for Wang Futing, and they had been no less so for China itself. Following victory in the 1894–95 war, Japan took possession of the Liaodong Peninsula. This prize was soon relinquished when European powers, leery of unchecked Japanese influence in the region, forced Japan to return the territory to China. Far from strengthening China, however, this action intensified competition among foreign empires in the process the Chinese called "the slicing of the melon."

Countering Japanese moves, and capitalizing on China's weakness, Great Britain, Germany, and Russia all obtained colonial concessions in the provinces surrounding the Bohai Gulf. In addition to treaty-port concessions in Yingkou and Tianjin, Great Britain obtained the port of Weihaiwei, on the north coast of the Shandong Peninsula just opposite Port Arthur. Germany was granted the colony of Jiaozhou Bay, surrounding the city of Qingdao, in southwestern Shandong, as well as a sphere of influence throughout the province. Russia leased the southern portion of the Liaodong Peninsula from China; combined with its concession in Harbin and its imperial designs on Port Arthur, the effect was not unlike a Russian annexation of Manchuria—a turn of events protested more strongly by Japan than by China. A century before, the Qing Empire had been among the most powerful states on earth. Now, it was being partitioned among rivals near and far.

Christianity came along with this European colonial expansion in the late nineteenth century. Since winning the right to proselytize freely in the "unequal treaties" (as the Chinese termed them) of the nineteenth century, Christian missionaries were active throughout Hebei and Shandong Provinces. Sometimes these missions were formally sponsored by foreign powers, but even if they were not, the missionaries were European citizens. Most foreigners in China enjoyed extraterritoriality, meaning they could not be prosecuted under Chinese law. Chinese Christians did not enjoy this immunity, but could generally evade punishment by seeking protection from churches or their imperial sponsors. Exploiting this situation, Chinese bandits sometimes declared themselves Christians to escape prosecution by the authorities, though the sincerity of their "conversion" was questionable. The two-tiered legal system and its abuses, real and perceived, bred resentment among Chinese non-Christians. In addition to this political conflict, many Chinese blamed Christianity for the frequency and intensity of famine and drought that afflicted North China in the late nineteenth century.

The events of the 1890s had prompted a spiritual crisis for Wang Futing, and he was not alone. Thousands of Chinese in Shandong, Hebei, and Liaoning Provinces were also facing threats to their families and livelihoods, and, like Wang Futing, many of these turned to traditional Chinese practices for support and solace.

"Boxers" is a collective term for a peasant movement, against foreign and Christian influences, that rose up in northeastern China at the very end of the nineteenth century. In his definitive history of the uprising, Joseph Esherick wrote that the Boxers "stood as a dramatic example of ordinary Chinese peasants rising up to rid China of the hated foreign presence."[26] The Boxers blamed foreigners for the ills afflicting their home provinces, including famine, drought, economic depression, and crop failure: the foreigners' religions, many Boxers believed, interfered with the proper order of things and disrupted the rainfall and other natural processes that sustained life. The Boxers received their name not from martial arts, but from movements they performed under the influence of spirit-possession. In these rituals, the Boxers called on heroes of popular literature, theater, and folk opera to possess their bodies. These included traditional deities who were worshipped in temples, such as Guandi, as well as fictional characters, like the Monkey King or Pigsy from the *Journey to the West*, and historical heroes immortalized in legend (rather as if in America today disaffected youth were to call on the spirits of Babe Ruth, George Washington, and Captain Ahab to help them fight the outsourcing of American jobs). While thus possessed, the Boxers were said to gain supernatural powers, including flight, invisibility, and imperviousness to bullets. These powers would enable them to defeat the evil influences of the foreigners.[27] Popular Boxer hymns give an idea of their mission and their tactics:

[Foreigners] proselytize their sect,
They believe in only one God,
The spirits and their ancestors
Are not even given a nod.

No rain is come from heaven.
The earth is parched and dry
And all because the churches
Have bottled up the sky.

The gods are very angry.
The spirits seek revenge.
En masse they come from Heaven
To teach the Way to men.

Spirits emerge from the grottos;
Gods come down from the hills,
Possessing the bodies of men,
Transmitting their boxing skills.

When their martial and magic techniques
Are all learned by each one of you,
Suppressing the Foreign Devils
Will not be a tough thing to do.[28]

Wang would have been a promising recruit for the Boxers: he was young (though older than the typical Boxers, most of whom were teenagers), with little education or property. But he was employed, and thus much better off than many of the young men who joined the group (and women, too, who joined the affiliated "Red Lanterns"). At the same time, he was curious about these people who sought a spiritual cure for China's ills. Wang Futing was clearly open to the idea of supernatural intervention in daily life. He believed he had died, argued with the King of Hell, and been returned to life; he had spent years studying Daoist alchemy and searching for immortality; and ghosts and spirits were regular parts of his world. Wang recalled that throughout Beitang and the surrounding villages, sixteen- and seventeen-year-old boys joined the Boxers, possessed by the spirits of cultural heroes. Some claimed immortality, exactly what Wang Futing had been seeking. Yet,

Wang rejected the Boxer movement. Perhaps it was because he found their methods inconsistent with his own study of the occult, or perhaps the Boxers' violent anti-foreignism repulsed him. He said that he found their intolerance unacceptable: those who joined them, they claimed, were guaranteed eternal life, while those who opposed them were doomed. Like many Chinese, Wang Futing navigated easily among Buddhist, Daoist, and other religious traditions, without insisting rigidly on any one faith or its practices. Whatever the precise cause, he concluded that the Boxers' ideology "made no sense."[29]

Although Wang Futing was not among them, the Boxers did gain tens of thousands of adherents. In 1899 they moved violently, killing thousands of people, primarily Chinese Christians (converts but also men and women whose families had been Christian for generations), as well as many Western missionaries. The Qing dynasty, desperate, supported the movement and declared war against the foreign powers. As the Boxers threatened Western missionaries and diplomats, warships gathered in the waters near Beitang, and by June 1900, more than a dozen foreign vessels were at anchor there. An "Eight-Nation Alliance" had formed to suppress the Boxers and protect foreign interests. On the night of June 16, after receiving word that the Boxers had besieged the legation quarter in Beijing, German, Russian, British, and French gunboats attacked and captured the Dagu forts guarding the entrance to the Hai River, leading to Tianjin. These forts—the same ones that had been overrun during the Arrow War of 1858— were just a few miles from Wang Futing's village of Beitang.[30]

The people of Beitang, many of whom still remembered that earlier war, were confused and frightened by the Boxer Uprising. It was not clear, even to combatants, whether the Boxers were in rebellion against the ruling Qing dynasty, in support of the Qing against foreign encroachment, or simply lashing out against any target that presented itself. The landscape around Beitang was heavily militarized: more than two thousand troops from Great Britain, Germany, France, Russia, the United States, Japan, Italy, and Austria were marching from Tanggu (seven miles away) toward Tianjin and then to Beijing. Thirteen thousand Qing troops were garrisoned at Lutai, less than twenty miles away, in the other direction. From mid-June on, Wang Futing recalled that artillery shells and fires in the distance kept the village constantly on edge.[31]

The villagers' fears were realized in August. Artillery shells landed in Beitang, setting fire to many homes, including Wang Futing's. Wang led a dozen villagers out of the burning village in a boat, but the attempt to escape brought the refugees into harm's way. Fleeing along the road, a few miles from Beitang, the earth was turned upside down by cannon fire. Wang Futing had faced death before. Once again, he felt that his time on earth was coming to an end:

> Artillery shells began to fall like rain, flying around our heads; we watched helplessly as the large cannons of the foreigners shot forth disaster. Wherever the shells landed, the land exploded and burned. Heaven and earth changed places, and neither dogs nor fowl were at rest. We had lost all our possessions and our homes, and now we began to see that our lives were slipping away.[32]

There is no record of an allied attack on Beitang, and the village does not lie along the path from Tanggu to Tianjin and then Beijing. However, allied soldiers were often confused as to just who their enemies were. The Chinese themselves were often construed as the enemy, and many young men in Beitang were sympathetic to the Boxers. It is not hard to believe that an artillery shell could have been directed at Beitang, either by accident or on purpose. Allied forces were also known to make punitive expeditions into the countryside, demonstrating their power without any specific military rationale.[33] At the beginning of August 1900, allied soldiers were marching north, skirmishing with Chinese villagers—Boxers or not—along the way. Wang Futing writes that he himself saw no one killed, but that refugees from other villages described corpses floating down the Hai River like paper lanterns set adrift during the lantern festival, a poignant image because those lanterns, floating downstream to the sea, represent souls finding their way to the afterlife. Crows and vultures perched on bodies bloated by the 110-degree heat. As they rotted, the corpses left an oily film on the surface of the river, already stained red with blood. These accounts match those of allied soldiers, who used these rivers for drinking and bathing until they became so fouled by corpses that this was no longer possible.[34]

Wang Futing and his small band survived these battles. Their escape plans foiled, they returned to Beitang. The scene was harrowing: much of the village had burned. Those villagers who had survived were dazed. Two scenes burned into Wang Futing's mind:

> I returned home to my street and saw a woman dressed in blue, carrying a small child, who had drowned in the water. Nearby, a woman had died on the side of the road, and her baby remained at her breast, nursing. How unendurable this world can be.[35]

These images lay bare the suffering of war: a woman refuses to part with a dead child, unable to accept that her worst fear has come true. An infant nurses from a corpse, the only source of nourishment it has ever known. Wang's observant eye for these details does not reflect on his own situation: he says nothing of his own family. He had two, and perhaps three, children by this time, but he is silent about their fate during the events he describes so vividly. We do not even know if his family accompanied him in the boat in which he fled Beitang. We learn later, in passing, that the entire family survived the attack, but it is difficult to understand how a man so sensitive to the suffering of mother and child can so utterly neglect the experience of his own wife and children. Perhaps, in the discipline he acquired as a monk, he forced himself to separate emotionally from his family, and reconnecting, even in memoir, was too painful. Or perhaps Wang Futing was strangely dissociated from his own family even as he felt acutely the suffering of humanity in general.

Troops raised the siege of the legation quarter, where foreign embassies in Beijing were located, a few weeks later, ending the immediate crisis of the Boxer Uprising for foreigners. The Boxer Protocol, as the peace treaty signed a year later was called, further weakened the Qing dynasty by forcing it to pay an indemnity of 450 million taels of silver—$330 million—over nearly forty years. The dynasty's credibility had crumbled as it first declared war against the foreign powers, then recanted, and finally agreed to peace under punitive terms in exchange for the support of those same powers. If there was surprise that the dynasty fell ten years later, it was only that it took so long.

For ordinary Chinese, especially those who, like Wang Futing, lived in the areas directly affected by the Boxers, the effects of the uprising lingered. Wang Futing's home and his job were both gone. To support his family, he needed to find work. So, with a handful of friends, he left Beitang and went toward Tanggu, where the larger port promised employment. Even this short trip was treacherous: landmines had been sown to stop foreign invaders during the Boxer Uprising. Foreign troops had relied on cows and sheep to show them the way, following the livestock's tracks to avoid the mines. Wang Futing and his companions followed in the same tracks. They also worked hard to evade Japanese troops—apparently more troublesome than the other foreign troops—with no money and little to eat.

As the six men approached Tanggu, a foreigner—Wang guessed him to be German—called out to the men: "Coolie!" He communicated that he was offering food and work, an appealing prospect to Wang Futing, who had not eaten a full meal for weeks. Soon, he was inside the mess tent, full of German soldiers and workers, enjoying beef, beans, steamed buns, and rice. The foreigners ate only with knives and forks, which Wang did not know how to use, so he ate with his hands. After eating, the Chinese men were told to wash the dishes, which they did, but not to the Germans' satisfaction (according to the memoir, this was because the water was cold and there was no soap). The Germans beat them for the poor work. After observing similar treatment of other Chinese working there, Wang Futing and his companions sneaked out of the camp and continued looking for work. A similar experience soon followed—this time Wang observed other Chinese being refused payment after working for a week. Rather than confront the same treatment, the men again moved on after getting a few meals.[36]

The men finally found steady work, and steady pay, working for a French company at a railroad depot, unloading ships' cargoes onto trains bound for Beijing and Tianjin. Wang Futing was eager to work, but soon found he had gotten in over his head:

The work they offered was loading and unloading railroad cars of rice, sugar, etc. Where they hired workers, there was a station for adults on one side, and children on the other side. There was also a place for doing heavy work, which paid better, and since I was not small, I went to the office where they were offering heavy work. In my heart I thought, "what a disaster!" because I was weak from having eaten little for weeks. Two men were expected to load 160 jin (80 kilos, 176 pounds) sacks of rice from steamers into the railroad cars. I was not strong enough to load these heavy sacks, but a Frenchman would stand alongside us with a steel baton, beating anyone who was not working well. What could be done!?

I continued to shakily unload the steamers and transfer the rice into the railroad cars, when one day I dropped a sack of rice, alongside the train. Slowly, I climbed down from the train. I was hidden from view, and I was also exhausted. . . . There under the railroad car, I lay for a long time, until the midday whistle blew. When he heard the whistle, the foreman called us all to eat, and then I climbed up from under the train.

We continued loading from ships to the trains bags of sugar, each sack weighed 80 jin (40 kilos), but that afternoon they did not seem so heavy. This I could manage, with difficulty . . . I worked day and night, just for my pay.[37]

After doing this work for some time, Wang Futing was able to save a string of cash that could be sent home to Beitang in the care of a cousin who lived in Tanggu. This cousin had been away on business when Wang had first arrived there, but now that he was back, Wang sought him out to deliver the money to his family, and also to discuss how he could make a living more reliably. The two men decided they could earn a better income in Dalian, a day's sail across the gulf, and found a ship that would take them there for 5 yuan each. Once there, Wang Futing's cousin found him a job loading and unloading railroad materials for a German company, with a salary of 30 yuan per month. Although he would return to his home village from time to time throughout his life, he never again called Hebei Province his home.

CHAPTER 2

Leaving Home

L ocated near the southern tip of the Liaodong Peninsula, Dalian in 1903 was a new city with an uncertain future. When the first treaty ports had been opened, in the 1840s, and again in the 1850s, the port at Dalian was not large enough to attract European interest. Yingkou, a hundred miles to the northwest, became the treaty port in southern Manchuria; forty miles to the south, Lüshun, commonly known as Port Arthur, became an important Chinese naval base as the country raced to modernize. Japan captured all three cities in the war of 1894–95, and used these ports to advance its interests in Manchuria.

European intervention, though, blocked Japanese ambitions. Russia—its border just a few hundred miles away—increased its presence in Manchuria, especially in the cities of Harbin, Shenyang, and Changchun. In 1898, Russia leased the southern tip of the Liaodong Peninsula from China, gaining Port Arthur as the ice-free port it had long sought and making the same territorial claims that Japan had attempted a few years earlier. Following the Boxer Uprising, Russia had stopped just short of outright annexation.

At Dalian, the Russians began to develop what was essentially a small fishing village into the southern terminal for their Manchurian rail network, itself integrated into the Trans-Siberian Railway linking European Russia and the Far East. Port Arthur served as the military base, as it had for Chinese forces in the past. Under the Russians, Dalian began to develop as an international port. When Wang Futing arrived in 1901, Dalian had already grown phenomenally. By 1903 its population was around forty thousand, and although it was administered by Russians, more than 95 percent of the population was Chinese.[1] Wang Futing worked in this mixed Chinese-Russian environment for three years, sending money home and making occasional visits. Wang would live in cities like these throughout his life: on Chinese soil, administered by foreigners, but populated predominantly by Chinese. These environments threw into sharp relief the differences between Chinese and Europeans and shaped Wang's views of nationalism, war, and culture.

As Russia expanded, Japan remained intolerant of Russian imperial dreams in Manchuria. In February 1904, a Japanese sneak attack on Port Arthur began a war for control of Manchuria that dragged on for two bitter years. Dalian, called by the Russians Dalny, was the most important civilian port in Russian Manchuria, but its defenses were compromised. Following the Battle of Nanshan, in May 1904, the Russian inhabitants of Dalny evacuated the city and moved to Port Arthur, which for the rest of the war was besieged by the Japanese navy. Wang Futing left Port Arthur sometime in the spring of 1904, and the city finally fell in January 1905. (The fact that a Chinese civilian was able to leave a blockaded city helps illustrate the fact that the conflict—though played out on Chinese territory—was between Russia and Japan.)

When the Russians evacuated Dalian, Chinese civilians looted much of what had been a prosperous port, according to the entering Japanese.[2] Wang Futing may have left along with the Russians, or he may have joined in the looting. Perhaps the looting led him to leave the city himself. All he reports in his memoir is that the war had left him unemployed, and he sought to leave Dalian. Wang found his way by boat to Yingkou, the largest port in southern Manchuria at the time and the center of European trade in the region. Wang Futing had relatives in Yingkou, and the city was a familiar part of his father's regular trade route around the Bohai Gulf. It seemed as sensible a place as any to wait out the war.

Wang Futing arrived in Yingkou in the summer of 1904, joining seventy-five thousand residents facing an uncertain future. He had fled Dalian to escape the fighting between Russian and Japanese troops, but Yingkou was hardly more stable; the Russian military authorities there had placed the city under martial law in March, but by the time Wang arrived the Russians were gone and Japanese forces occupied the city. European diplomats struggled to assess yet another new political situation, and Chinese citizens puzzled out the prospects of their dynasty and their nation.

Located at the mouth of the Liao River, Yingkou opened as part of the second batch of treaty ports that included Tianjin. It was misidentified by Europeans as Newchwang (Niuzhuang in today's pinyin romanization), a city about ten miles upriver that had been a harbor before it silted up. Starting around 1840, Yingkou—Niuzhuang—became the primary port for Manchuria, and the potential of Manchuria as both a market and a source for raw materials drew foreign investors to the city. Britain and the United States established consulates along the waterfront, and American companies like Standard Oil, Ford Motor Company, and International Harvester opened offices in the city. Traffic in the port increased steadily. Prior to 1890, passengers arriving at Yingkou never reached six thousand a year, but in 1890 they exceeded nine thousand, and a year later surpassed one hundred thousand. By 1893—the year before the Sino-Japanese War—nearly three hundred thousand passengers arrived, drawn by abundant farmland and employment opportunities in Manchuria. The flags of Great Britain, Germany, the United States, Japan, Norway, Russia, and the Netherlands all flew in the harbor.[3] According to the customs revenue, Yingkou ranked fifth among all Chinese ports in overall volume of trade.[4]

Yingkou was the closest of all the early treaty ports to Japan, and Japanese interests there grew steadily along with Japanese designs on Manchuria. By the start of war with China in 1894, Yingkou was Japan's primary source of soybeans. During the war, Japan occupied the city, and although it remained a treaty port with a foreign concession, Japan dominated. Eventually, the Japanese monopoly on trade compromised Yingkou's role as an international entrepôt, and the Russian development of Dalian, along with the political and military instability of the region, sent Yingkou into decline. It also placed it at the center of Russo-Japanese conflict.

All but helpless in the face of this war being fought on its territory, the Qing government declared that land west of the Liao River was not involved in the conflict; east of the Liao River—including Yingkou—was considered a theater of war. Western relief organizations including the Red Cross established themselves in Yingkou, preparing for refugees, and the Japanese consul in the city arranged for Japanese civilians displaced by the war to be taken to Tianjin for safety. Battles were fought outside the city, but Russian troops evacuated Yingkou before fighting spread to the city itself. Japanese forces took control of the city and the port on July 25.[5]

When Wang Futing arrived in Yingkou in the wake of the Japanese occupation, there was much confusion, not much comfort, and little work to be found. The American consul, Henry Miller, summarized the situation: "Considerable devastation of crops and villages has been occasioned by the war, and the absence of a firm hand of government has caused robber bands to be more active than usual.... The change from Russian to Japanese administration took place in this city without a great deal of disorder although the looting of public places was severe." Miller was hopeful that order would soon be restored: "The district now covered by the Japanese seems to be quiet," he observed, "and the harmony . . . seems to indicate a peaceful occupation so far as Chinese and Japanese are concerned."[6]

Wang Futing was safe, living with his cousin, but idle and in need of money. His vocational training was of no use: no one was looking to hire an accountant in a sea of refugees and soldiers. But Wang had other skills that could be of use to a population unsure of its prospects. During his spiritual search in the 1890s he had studied both astrology and alchemy with a Daoist master, and although he ultimately rejected Daoist claims about immortality, he was now in a position to hang out a shingle as a fortune-teller and apothecary:

> Originally, when I had studied the occult sciences, it had not seemed like a legitimate use of my time, but now it was useful. Every day, people asked me what their future held, whether they would be able to find food because of the war. They had lost their jobs, and many of them had these kinds of questions. I gave each of them a prophecy, and a plan. Most of the time, they worked, and so business was not bad. It was enough to support myself.[7]

Wang set up shop on the sidewalk, as fortune-tellers throughout China had for centuries. The sidewalks of late-imperial Chinese cities could be frenzied bazaars, thronged with fortune-tellers, barbers, storytellers, merchants, matchmakers, and old men playing chess, tending caged songbirds, or fighting crickets. On these busy streets, clients sought out Wang to determine auspicious days for important events and assess their prospects for personal and professional success. Fortune-tellers used several methods. Some emphasized physiognomy, reading a client's fate in palms, facial features, and body type. Wang Futing favored astrological methods, plotting the year, month, day, and sometimes hour of a client's birth on a series of axes, to produce a spiderweb design indicating the influence of stars, planets, and the moon. Employment, health, marriage, children, wealth, happiness, and longevity were just some of the topics that a reading would address.[8]

Like most fortune-tellers, Wang did most of his readings in public. Wealthier clients might receive private, written readings, but conversation was the substance of the fortune-teller's art, a chance to establish credibility and to persuade the client to heed the advice given, to return for more readings, and to spread the word. Wang Futing was a good prognosticator, a good conversationalist, or both: within a few months he established a reputation for insight and foresight, and also for producing efficacious elixirs and medicines. He had a regular clientele and even took on a student, a local merchant who was so pleased with Wang's prognostications that he asked to study fortune-telling with him. His success enabled him to move into a more permanent establishment. In 1906, he opened a traditional Chinese medicine shop, where he saw patients, diagnosed illnesses, prescribed, prepared, and sold remedies, while continuing to offer his services as a fortune-teller.

In addition to paying the bills, Wang Futing's fortune-telling practice enabled him to continue his quest for religious fulfillment. Astrology blended Buddhism, Daoism, and other folk religions until they were all but indistinguishable. Wang began attending lectures regularly at a local institution known as the Lecture Hall. This organization represented a broad range of Chinese religious experience, in keeping with Wang's eclectic interests: Confucian texts, Daoist elixirs, Buddhist sutras, séances, and charitable campaigns were all at home there. Wang spent as much time as he could at the Lecture Hall, studying and listening. Eventually, he himself was asked to speak on important topics. Since childhood,

Wang had felt called to a spiritual journey, but determining the right path repeatedly frustrated him. He studied Daoism, Buddhism, the occult, and even Christianity, but was unsure at every turn whether he was following his true calling. At the Lecture Hall, he explored all of these traditions, but increasingly focused on Buddhism. His turn to Buddhism was not unique to him: the number of both lay Buddhists and clergy was growing during this time of "Buddhist revival." One of Wang Futing's close friends in Yingkou, a man named Liu Wenhua, offers an example.

Liu Wenhua, like Wang, had been touched by personal loss. Alcohol abuse played a role in his inability to hold a job, and his wife and young daughter both died under unclear circumstances. Liu blamed himself for their deaths because his lack of work had left the family poor and vulnerable. Bereaved and depressed, without work or family to occupy him, Liu spent most of his time in Wang Futing's medicine shop reading Buddhist texts. As a younger man, Liu had cast a broad net seeking spiritual guidance, trying any tradition that seemed practical in the moment, but his grief focused his energy on Buddhism, and he went into the hills surrounding Yingkou where he approached a Buddhist monk in a small temple. The monk rebuked Liu's dilettantism, insisting that the teachings of the Buddha could not be casually combined with a dozen other teachings and practices. On the monk's advice, Liu left Yingkou for the Jiaxing Temple in Beijing, engaging in intense sutra readings there. Soon, Liu began collecting sutras and other sacred texts and bringing them to the Lecture Hall in Yingkou, helping to establish a library. Wang Futing and others nicknamed him "Xuanzang," after the Tang-dynasty monk who had gone to India to collect sutras and bring them back to China.

Liu Wenhua's religion postulated a porous divide between life and death, which Wang Futing would have recognized from his own childhood experiences. Liu's encounters with spirits and the afterlife, like Wang's, challenge modern sensibilities. One night, for example, while he was up late in the medicine shop reading sutras, Liu was dazzled by a bright light emanating from the center of the room. The light revealed an enormous map of the world. As Liu struggled to understand what was going on, two ghosts approached him: the spirits of former friends with whom he'd had a legal dispute. After the two men had died, the judges of the underworld deemed their lawsuit frivolous and sentenced them to suffer for a time before they could be reincarnated or ascend to heaven. To shorten their waiting period in hell, they had returned to ask Liu's forgiveness. When Liu assented, the power of his forgiveness was made plain: the ghosts, overjoyed at their release from purgatory, called upon the spirits of Liu's wife and daughter. Liu's gesture had freed them, too, from further suffering in the underworld. With a bow of thanks they ascended to heaven. Liu's parents appeared next, smiling and happy that Liu's act of forgiveness would enable him to ascend to heaven after he died, reuniting the family.[9]

To Wang Futing, this story illustrated the power of Buddhism and the importance of diligent study. Liu Wenhua gained power when he rejected the informal, syncretic approach to religion that was typical of Chinese culture and instead studied Buddhist texts exclusively and intensely. Inspired, Wang Futing followed his example. Although he felt that all the religious traditions being practiced and studied at the Lecture Hall were worthy—they all promoted good over evil and encouraged adherents to cultivate their minds and souls—Buddhism's attitude to reality and to suffering attracted him. The first texts he approached, the Surangama, Diamond, and Lotus Sutras, all emphasized that this world, and the suffering in it, is but an illusion, distracting our minds from the true nature of the universe and the work that we must do to attain enlightenment. For Wang Futing, the chance to believe that there was more to the world than the war and disease that had framed his own life for twenty years was appealing.

Wang Futing found another element in Liu Wenhua's story less compelling: the importance of family. Wang's relationship to his family was complex. He had lived mainly apart from his wife for more than fifteen years and had never lived with any of his children (two daughters had been born in the late 1890s, and a son in 1905; four more sons would be born in the next ten years). As his business flourished, Wang could afford to return home to visit his wife and children, and he brought them to Yingkou to live in 1908, just before Liu Wenhua's vision.

Liu Wenhua found proof of Buddhism's power in the redemptive vision of his dead family—all the more potent because of his feelings of guilt over his role in their deaths. Wang Futing took the message of Buddhism's power to heart as well: within a few years he would devote himself to becoming a monk. But the other message, that one's family on earth was a fleeting thing, to be treasured for its brief duration, was lost on him. Instead, Wang moved in the opposite direction, rejecting family as irrelevant—or worse, an obstacle—to gaining enlightenment. Feeling called to be a Buddhist monk, he prepared to leave his wife and children.

By the summer of 1914, Wang Futing had studied the Surangama Sutra intensely for nearly ten years, and he felt there was little more he could learn without entering a monastery. News reached him that a Buddhist master was lecturing on the Surangama and Lotus Sutras at Zifu Temple on Red Snail Mountain, near Beijing. Wang left his home and traveled to the temple, where he spent a week attending lectures by Master Baoyi. During this time, he was befriended by Qingchi, the monk in charge of accommodating the many pilgrims who came to the temple. The two men discussed the significance of the sutras, and of the Buddha's teachings in general, for a world in crisis. For Wang Futing, the sutras revealed a world in which the teachings of the Buddha could transform lives. These teachings had resonated with the Buddha's disciples, leading them to enlightenment, and also to enlighten others.

China in 1914, Wang believed, lacked the moral and spiritual foundation to understand these teachings. The world had become too selfish; only when people abandoned petty self-interest and resolved to care for the "Great Self" could China, and the world, be saved. The "Great Self" was the community of all sentient beings—not just humans—who could gain enlightenment via the Buddha's teachings. Wang Futing had grown up surrounded by the suffering caused by war, famine, dislocation, and disease; the promise of these teachings to alleviate the suffering of the world was very powerful to him. Committed to transcend the petty self, Wang decided to join a monastery.[10] This was his chance to follow the destiny he had perceived since childhood, and he hoped in this way he could achieve betterment not just for himself but for China.

Wang Futing believed that China's survival as a culture and as a nation depended on its spiritual revival. His experience in three wars had revealed China's weakness. He saw British, French, Japanese, Russian, and American troops march across Chinese soil—across his own doorstep. China's armies and industry lagged behind these other countries, and unless it could strengthen itself, China surely faced extinction.

Wang Futing was just one among many seeking to rescue and renew China in the face of Western and Japanese imperialism. Many of the solutions proposed were themselves imported from the West, and called for China to modernize along Western lines. Theories of social Darwinism, suggesting that human societies were pitted against one another in an ongoing process of natural selection, were first translated into Chinese in 1896. Yan Fu, who read and translated Thomas Huxley's *Evolution and Ethics* in the aftermath of the Sino-Japanese War, stressed in his translation the nationalist and prescriptive elements of Huxley's theories, the processes by which one nation would dominate another. Chinese intellectuals like Liang Qichao saw in social Darwinism the prescription for strengthening the Chinese nation through education and heredity. China could reform itself, but if it did not, it would perish.[11] Many of these hopes were frustrated in the failed reform movement of 1898, but the movement continued into the nineteenth century, culminating—apparently—in the 1911 Revolution that overthrew the Qing dynasty. However, the Republic of China that replaced the Qing showed little sign of political innovation; the Republic's first president, Yuan Shikai, was inaugurated in January 1912, but his administration never fulfilled the revolutionary hopes that accompanied the end of two thousand years of imperial rule. Yuan was a military man, and his power derived from the loyalty of his troops, not a commitment to republican government. Sun Yat-sen, the ideological force behind the revolution, wisely avoided challenging Yuan's power. Those who did threaten Yuan, like the promising politician Song Jiaoren, found that he did not tolerate dissent: Song was assassinated at a Shanghai railway station in 1913, and Yuan was rumored to be behind the killing. If Yuan hoped to secure his power by eliminating a rival, he was mistaken. Support for his presidency weakened with the realization that he cared little for democracy and would stop at nothing to silence opponents. Memorial services for Song were held throughout the country, some with as many as ten thousand people in attendance, and there were threats of vengeance against Yuan.[12]

Economically, there were moments of opportunity. Chinese entrepreneurs flourished by filling many of the roles vacated by their European and American competitors, who withdrew as Europe descended into the "War to End All Wars." At the same time, the war in Europe increased global demand for raw materials, demand that China could help meet. The economy of coastal China flourished, and a new class of Chinese business owners asserted themselves. Because of Yuan's authoritarianism, there was, however, no political voice for this new class as they ushered in the "golden age of the Chinese bourgeoisie."[13]

Japan saw the withdrawal of the Europeans as a chance to further its own interests in China, and in 1915 presented Yuan's government with "21 Demands" that would make China a virtual Japanese colony. The Chinese government managed to resist the most egregious of these demands, but Japan's bullying undermined the regime still further. In the fall of 1915, desperate to restore the nation's prestige—or his own—Yuan declared China once again to be an empire and laid plans to install himself as emperor. Widespread opposition forced Yuan to rescind the plan and he never assumed the throne; the debacle accelerated China's political disintegration. Yuan Shikai died, humiliated, in 1916.

In response to the Republic's failure, young Chinese, especially in the cities, sought to bring about cultural renewal through art and literature. This New Culture Movement gave rise to some of China's best known authors, including Lu Xun, Ba Jin, and Ding Ling. It also gave birth to the Chinese Communist Party. In 1915—the year after Wang Futing attended lectures at Red Snail Mountain—the leaders of the New Culture Movement founded the journal *New Youth* as a forum to discuss and spread Western ideas about class, gender, art, and politics. For these young men and women, the failure of the 1911 Revolution was its inability to make a clean break with China's traditional past, as epitomized by Yuan Shikai's attempt to restore the monarchy. The word "new" dominates the institutions and processes of these reformers and revolutionaries: China needed to modernize, and to move away from its traditional past.

Wang Futing's ideas were different. He, too, felt that China's future was in jeopardy, but the problem was not that China was straitjacketed by conservative thinking; the problem was that China had failed to follow its own moral standards. The solution lay in spiritual regeneration based on China's traditions. Wang made up his mind to live a monastic life, to follow the Buddha's teachings and in turn spread them throughout China so the nation might be strengthened from within. He was not alone in this movement: estimates show that the population of Chinese monasteries was growing during the early twentieth century, although the extent of the growth is difficult to quantify.[14] This trend, ironically, frustrated Wang Futing's ambitions. Dozens—perhaps hundreds—of men had come to Red Snail Mountain to join the monastery. When the lectures ended, there were a limited number of spaces available, and Wang Futing was unable to secure one of them. Disappointed, he returned home to Yingkou. Two years passed.

Now in his forties, Wang Futing was a respected member of the community, a successful apothecary and fortune-teller. Every day, he diagnosed patients and dispensed medicine, charging patients on a sliding scale: wealthy patients subsidized those who were less able to pay. In the port city of Yingkou, Chinese merchants flourished in the absence of their European competitors. This meant that there were many wealthy local families in need of medicine, diagnoses, and astrological readings. In the summer of 1917, while Wang was making a house call to one of his wealthy patients, a young Buddhist monk stopped in at his medicine shop and left his name card at the counter.

When Wang returned to the store, he found the card and the note written on the back: "Living at Qingxiu Temple, in the southeast corner of Tianjin—Qingchi." Wang was elated; it had been three years since he had befriended Qingchi during his summer at Red Snail Mountain. His desire to enter a monastery had not diminished, and now he saw an opportunity to fulfill his destiny. Sewing the name card into the sleeve of his gown, he went home and contemplated how to proceed.[15]

For three days, he told no one of his plans, remaining alone with his thoughts and emotions swirling around this decision. Though the choice to become a monk was intensely personal, the decision would affect his wife and seven children as profoundly as it would himself. Wang Futing and his medicine shop provided the family its sole means of financial support. His oldest two children, daughters, were already married; by Chinese custom, they were now part of their husbands' families and no longer Wang's responsibility. However, his five sons ranged in age from fourteen to less than two years old, and they relied completely on Wang's income.

Options for his wife—tellingly unnamed in the memoir—were few. Divorce and remarriage were difficult. The Republic of China had drafted a new civil law code granting women much easier access to divorce, including in the event of a husband's disappearance for three years or more, but the code was controversial and not implemented until 1931. Wang and his wife were still subject to the Qing legal code, under which divorce was nearly impossible unless the husband sought it. A wife could not even sue for divorce on her own behalf: any suit would have to be initiated by her birth family (in Madam Wang's case, it is not known where, or even if, the members of her natal family were living). The grounds on which a wife's family could seek divorce were extremely limited. Even in cases where a husband abandoned his wife for three years or more, or beat her causing permanent injury, divorce still required the husband's consent. (In contrast, a husband could gain divorce for many causes, including that his wife talked too much.)[16]

Even if Madam Wang could obtain a divorce, her prospects would be bleak. With no family to provide a dowry—not to mention five mouths to feed—there was no economic incentive for a man to marry her. The most likely candidate would be a man desperate for a male heir, and if she failed to bear a son, her new husband might beat her (and unless he actually killed her, or close to it, the law would not consider him guilty of a crime) or abandon her (just as Wang had already done). If she did bear a son, her utility would be gone, exposing her to the same risks. There were few options for a woman whose husband left her, none of them good.

And it is unlikely that Wang Futing would want her to remarry. Chinese Buddhism graphically depicts the suffering of souls being punished in the underworld for their transgressions in the life just ended. These images, borrowing heavily from Chinese folk religion, can be found in many Buddhist temples, including several that Wang Futing would later found. Among the most lurid scenes are those showing the torments reserved for women who remarried, which is seen as a violation of the marriage vow. Some are thrown into boiling cauldrons. Others are dismembered: stripped naked and taken by demons, who hold the woman by her feet and turn her upside down, legs spread apart. Two devils grasp a large two-handled saw. With a grim air of duty, they place the saw between the woman's legs and proceed to cut her in half, from crotch to head. Her husbands, aggrieved by her failure to observe her vows, watch contemptuously. She promised herself to both of them, and each man waits for his half, in fulfillment of her promise.

Images like this would have been familiar to Wang Futing. He would not have wished his wife to suffer this fate; he understood that he was leaving her alone to raise their children. "I have not had a moment to save any money, and we depend completely on this small medicine shop to eat. After I have gone, there will be no one to manage the apothecary; it will surely close. The entire family will be hungry, destitute, and homeless."[17] Yet, despite this, he believed himself called, not only to become a monk, but to help China and all humanity receive the teachings of the Buddha.

It would certainly be better for his family if he stayed. Or would it? They would have food to eat, shelter, and clothing, but were these the kinds of nourishment that were truly needed? His neighbor, Jin Desheng, had belonged to one of the wealthiest families in Beitang village. At his wedding he was surrounded by family and friends. Yet, he died the very next day, and his widow was left without wealth or wisdom, to mourn a life that had barely begun. What would happen, he wondered, if he were to die tomorrow? Would his family then be provided for? No, he decided—they would still be poor and alone. At least as a monk, he could learn the ways of the Buddha and make some sense of the suffering. With his spiritual work, he could help them overcome and transcend the bitterness of the world.

As Wang Futing contemplated leaving his family to become a monk, he confronted questions that the Buddha himself had grappled with 2,500 years earlier. Many religious traditions, including Buddhism, see human society as a distraction or a temptation, holding one back from enlightenment, or divine inspiration, or wisdom, or the righteous life that leads to salvation. For millennia, men and women have withdrawn from normal social relations to seek higher callings, as priests, nuns, monks, and shamans. Like the Buddha, who left his family at the age of thirty-five, Wang Futing lived a long time in secular society before dedicating himself to a clerical religious life. The Buddha, in his last incarnation before his enlightenment, had been a prince, Gautama Siddhartha. Like Wang Futing, he had a wife and a child. In some versions of the story, his son is born on the very night Siddhartha resolves to leave home to seek enlightenment, and on hearing of his birth the Buddha is not overjoyed, but declares that a new obstacle has been placed before him (the son, in recognition of this, is named Rahula, or "fetter").

This irony, in which the birth of a child—normally among the most joyous of human events—is seen as a burden, is at the core of Wang Futing's choice. In deciding to abandon home and family, Wang contemplated the Four Noble Truths, the Buddha's first teachings after attaining enlightenment. The first of these insists that "existence is suffering." The Buddha pointed to the physical and emotional sufferings that dominate human existence, including birth, old age, sickness, death, separation from loved ones, the company of loathed ones, and being denied one's desires.

The Buddha does not deny that the world contains great beauty and joy, for it is beauty that ensnares the mind to chase after joy, to constantly seek pleasure. This beauty, though, and the pleasure it begets, is temporary; any pleasurable act, if continued long enough, will become painful. The reverse is not true; that which causes pain continues to cause pain unless steps are taken to ameliorate it. Buddhist scholar Donald Lopez has drawn the analogy that pleasure in this world is like carrying a heavy burden on one shoulder. Eventually, it becomes unbearable. Shifting the load to the other shoulder brings relief, but this temporary pleasure soon leads to a new, different, pain . . . in the other shoulder. There is no physical act that does not result, ultimately, in suffering.[18]

This first realization leads to the second noble truth: desire, or craving, causes the suffering that is existence. This includes desire for material comforts and luxuries, but also the desire to simply go on living and partake of all that the world offers. The experience of joy in this world leads us, ironically, to suffer from its absence. The only absolute truth is that the beauty and goodness in the world— *because* it is in the world—will come to an end. The most intense desire, the one that causes the greatest suffering, is the desire for permanence, which is impossible. All human relationships are fleeting. The love of parents, spouses, children, and friends will all be ended by disease, old age, and death. Anyone who has mourned the loss of a loved one knows the pain that it causes; an infant, separated from its parents for just a moment, expresses agony, crying as though she will never again see her mother, until with time she learns that the separation is only temporary. Yet, can we really say that the child's fears are unjustified? It is not the separation that is temporary, but the reunion.

This ignorance of reality's true nature is an even more fundamental cause of human suffering. It leads humans to believe that physical comfort and pleasure can be maintained, and thus to desire these things. This leads to another basic delusion, that of the self. The desire to seek comfort and pleasure relies on the belief that every individual is a separate, physical entity inhabiting the world, accruing karma. One of the most complex and frustrating notions in Buddhist thought is the "no-self." Most religious traditions see the key to salvation or enlightenment in the recognition of a soul or self that survives the material body and thus can reap rewards for virtuous behavior in a world beyond this one. This soul is often depicted as immortal, transcending the confines of the physical body and the world it inhabits. The Buddha taught the contrary, that belief in an immortal soul tied one to a false notion of reality. It is wrong to think of a self or soul that transcends the physical world because this entails that there is something real to transcend. The soul, the self, and physical reality are a series of constantly changing circumstances, none lasting more than an instant. Our consciousness deludes itself into believing in its permanence by perceiving and interacting with other apparent consciousnesses. The interaction confirms for us that we are real, that our self today is the same self as it was an hour, or a day, or a year ago. Yet, according the Buddha, the self cannot be said to exist, because it is just a temporary aggregation of circumstances, but neither can it be said not to exist, because that would imply that it is less permanent than anything else. Everything is fleeting.

Ignorance of the transitory nature of *everything* leads humans to crave permanence. The knowledge that all physical phenomena are transitory—not just rain showers and crashing waves, but mountain ranges and continents as well—is unsettling. In response, we seek strong, stable structures that suggest permanence and fear their loss as they inevitably change. Human relationships can operate in the same way: many parents weep as their child grows up, happy that he or she is thriving, but mourning the loss of the infant, then the toddler, then the schoolchild, and so on, as each phase of life moves past. Here again, the greatest joys are accompanied, and at times overshadowed, by grief.

Having addressed the suffering of the world and its causes, the third and fourth noble truths show the way to escape it: by eliminating desire, one can eliminate suffering, and to eliminate desire, one must follow the eightfold path toward enlightenment, as the Buddha taught. Wang Futing decided to pursue this path, and decided also that this would be best for his family, not because of how it would affect them in this life—there was no doubt they would suffer hardships in his absence—but because of the lifetimes upon lifetimes to come:

> If I go without saying a word, leaving her alone to raise five children, her life will undoubtedly be very difficult. [But] if I am truly concerned about my wife's situation, or the implications on my own life, it is, in fact, about much more than one life. I fear for lives and lives, and generations and generations, eternally sinking down, further and further from enlightenment! If I could become a monk and focus all my energy on the Buddhist scriptures, and truly follow the path of the Buddha, then, in the future I could meet them again and encourage them to revere the Buddha and believe in his teachings. When this body passed away, would they not find a world twice as beautiful?
>
> And yet. . . .

He continued to wrestle with the implications of the path ahead, but finally decided to see it through:

Give it up! Give it all up!

Although my heart was absolutely committed, my thoughts still wavered, tempted by the corrupting influences of material comforts and customs. The indecision was unbearable, torn as I was between the many reasons in my head to stay in my old life, and the reasons in my heart and soul to continue along this new path. When I finally made the decision to leave, I felt as though I had not a care in the world.[19]

Three days after receiving Qingchi's note, Wang Futing told his wife that he was going to the cemetery to tend to his relatives' graves. Instead, he set out for Tianjin, forsaking his family life to become a Buddhist monk. He was forty-one years old. He had been married for twenty-five years and had seven children, five of whom still lived at home.

It is not easy to make sense of Wang Futing's decision to leave his family. There is no escaping the fact that he knowingly abandoned his wife and sons without any apparent means of support. If the most fundamental of human obligations is to care for one's children, then it is hard to forgive his decision, leaving his family to rely on charity. Had she still been in Beitang, his wife might have had a safety net of friends and family to fall back on, but now she lived hundred of miles away. Other than her children, Wang Futing's cousins were her only relatives in Yingkou.

Wang Futing justified his decision as both altruism and destiny: altruism because as a monk he would work for the enlightenment of all beings; destiny because his early life had shown that he was fated to be a great monk. He was giving up a comfortable life that he had worked hard to establish, renouncing worldly comforts. He would do this for his own enlightenment, but also for the good of China, for the good of humanity, even specifically for the good of his wife and children, who would suffer more now but ultimately be rewarded with a clearer path toward enlightenment. He may have chosen a path that would help his family toward a greater good, but he did so without consulting them, without even telling them that he was leaving and they were soon to be completely self-reliant. Perhaps he was merely rationalizing his desire to be free from domestic responsibility (although he had been married for twenty-five years, he had shared a roof with his wife for less than half of that time). Wang Futing's career as a monk would benefit many people, but his children and his wife suffered.

Whatever the ethics of his choice, Wang Futing left his home in the spring of 1917 and set out for Qingxiu Temple in Tianjin. Qingchi was there; it was three years since Wang Futing had confided in the monk at Red Snail Mountain, and the two men became reacquainted over tea. Wang Futing expected to be warmly welcomed and encouraged to join monastic life—had he not been invited to come to Tianjin? But Qingchi smiled at his request, and then laughed:

> The last time I saw you, you said you wanted to become a monk, but did not succeed because of the crowd. Now, you say again that you want to become a monk. You still have many people in your home, you should not let your imagination run wild and simply decide to enter a monastery! You can stay with me for a few days. When you have had enough, return home and stop your family's worrying! I have seen many people who have at one time thought about becoming a monk, and then afterward they have missed their family and regretted their decision. I cannot tell you how many people who left home in this circumstance later decide to go back.[20]

Wang Futing was annoyed at being dismissed like this; he resolved to convince Qingchi of his commitment by immersing himself in temple life. He passed several days in prayer, and each evening he talked with Qingchi about becoming a monk. He emphasized the depth of his conviction and his vision for the future:

> I am not one of those men who decides to become a monk on an impulse and then changes his mind! I have studied the Buddhist sutras for many years. . . . I am a businessman, in the upper levels of society; my goal in becoming a monk is not to obtain clothing, shelter, and food, nor is it to escape my present situation. My goal is to study the sutras, which I have done on my own for seven or eight years. . . . In the future, when I have the opportunity, I will expound the Dharma, and revere the sutras, and spread

knowledge of the Buddha throughout the world. The world's morals are in decline; the people are losing their traditions, and they have no way of saving themselves. I myself, when I was young, studied other faiths and the occult sciences. Eventually, I came to study the Buddhist sutras, and I felt that their teachings were superior to the others, so I have decided to become a monk. This motivation comes from deep within my soul. . . .

Some may think that I have left home so that I can find a small temple in which to live with warm food and clothing, enjoying peace and tranquility. This is absolutely not my intention! I hope to find a master who will train me to become a monk. Leading a happy life is finished; suffering is also finished: nothing will distract me from my master's teaching! In the future, if my luck is good, I will travel far and wide spreading the word of the Buddha; if my luck is not good, then I will still be a diligent, hardworking Buddhist.[21]

Wang Futing asked Qingchi to serve as his master, but the monk declined, saying that his temple was too small and his knowledge too limited. Instead, he wrote on wooden sticks the names of four eminent monks who would be suitable teachers. After burning incense and praying for guidance before a statue of the Buddha, Wang Futing drew lots and selected the name of Yinkui, the abbot of a temple in Nanjing. Complicating matters, seemingly, they found that Yinkui had very recently passed away: Wang Futing had not yet become a monk, and already his master had died! Qingchi, though, did not take this as a discouraging sign. Master Yinkui had died without someone to carry on his line. It was auspicious that now, before Yinkui's funeral had even been held, Wang had selected his name. In a few days, Wang would travel to a temple in Hebei Province, run by one of Yinkui's students. There he would take the tonsure—have his head shaved as part of the ritual of ordination—to begin life as a novice monk.

Qingchi worked to ensure that Wang Futing was prepared for the life ahead of him. All the status Wang had accumulated throughout his life was gone. He had been a father and a husband; this was irrelevant now. His age had earned him the respect of his juniors; this too was now irrelevant. Whereas he had previously been a successful fortune-teller and apothecary with many wealthy clients, he was now just a novice monk. He enjoyed no status outside the *sangha* (the community of monks and nuns). Even within that community he was a novice, inferior to everyone:

> No matter where you take your vows, or how old you are, all others are now master to you. If two monks meet on the road, and one is a novice, he must stand aside to let the other pass. . . . It does not matter at all what your relative ages are, you must bow to your superiors. If someone comes to lodge overnight, you must carry his water bucket and his belongings and bring them to his room. Afterwards, you must do the washing, and when you have finished you must very reverently bow to your guest. When everyone eats together, you must allow everyone else to finish eating first. When you are walking, you must follow behind. In the morning, you must arise to beat the drum and ring the bells, and maintain the Buddha hall, and sweep the temple grounds. All of these duties are the obligations of the novice. Consider carefully whether you can endure these sufferings. Can you do it?[22]

Wang Futing assured him that he could. He was prepared to pursue a life that saw even death as an illusion to be overcome through study, practice, and dedication. Rising before dawn or emptying chamber pots was of little consequence. Wang Futing declared that he would do whatever was necessary to follow the path of the Buddha. Whatever hardship or suffering had to be endured, he would endure it. If something absolutely could not be endured, he still would endure it. If patience were impossible, he would be patient. Wang Futing had unlimited confidence in his ability to succeed as a monk because, as he put it, it required no special skills—only commitment.

> The ways of the monk require no cunning or skill. They are not magical or mysterious. They are achievable by all people. Even if, in society, reverence for the Buddha ceases; even if reverence for the gods and spirits ceases; even if all knowledge and handicrafts cease, and you are left with only your own ability to practice and study, you will still, always, be able to succeed.[23]

After a few days, Qingchi and Wang Futing left Tianjin by train, bound for Gaoming Temple in Laishui County, Hebei. They intended to change trains at Gaobeidian, but arrived late and missed the last train for the day. Qingchi decided to test Wang Futing's commitment: the two men walked the remaining several miles through the mountains to Gaoming Temple. They arrived, exhausted, in the middle of the night and knocked on the door.

Chunkui, the abbot of the temple, answered the door and asked what brought these two wanderers to this isolated temple so late at night. Qingchi, gasping for breath, declared that he had brought Wang Futing to be initiated into the sangha as an acolyte of Master Yinkui. Chunkui welcomed them and immediately prepared for the ceremony.

In addition to having his head shaved, Wang Futing had to be assigned a dharma name. To become a monk is to be born again; just as one is given a name at birth, one's rebirth must also come with a new name. Together with the two monks, Wang Futing selected the characters "Longxian," meaning "profound status" to be his new name. As his hair fell to the floor, Wang Futing ceased to exist. Chunkui told him:

> When you leave family life, you are born again. You are transformed into a different person. For all that has happened in your past, it as if you died yesterday; for everything to come, it as if you are born today. From this time forward, everything is utterly changed.[24]

Longxian, as Wang was now called, remained at the temple for three days. He changed into the simple robes of a monk and learned the proper procedures for praying and making offerings to the Buddha. On the second day, the ceremony was completed. He was now a novice monk, and he passed the day in reflection. He had a great deal to think about. He was much older than most novices. He had lived a full life—indeed, he had already exceeded his statistical life expectancy—by the time he was re-born as a monk. Did he think of his children, or his wife, and how they were faring in his absence? By this time they must have realized that they would have to make a life without him. Did he remember his mother, or the old women in Beitang village who had predicted that he would become a monk?

Perhaps he thought of the years he had spent studying sutras in Yingkou, all guiding him toward this moment. Or, perhaps he thought only of the path ahead and the new life he had chosen. In any case, on the third day, he returned to Qingxiu Temple in Tianjin, to begin life as a monk (though still without a master), declaring, "From this time forward I walk in the steps of the Buddha."

Longxian spent six months as a novice monk. It is unclear why he returned to Qingxiu Temple, since Qingchi had already refused to serve as his master, but during this time he became familiar with the routine of monastery life. He fetched water for the monastery, swept the pavilions and the grounds, and washed the floors of the Buddha hall. He arose before 4:00 AM to ring the bells to call the other monks to prayer. When wandering monks arrived to stay at the temple, he tended to their needs.

His journey to a new life, though, was not yet complete.

In the fall of 1917, Master Dixian—one of the most eminent monks in China—visited Tianjin on the occasion of his sixtieth birthday; the sixtieth birthday is auspicious in Chinese cosmology because the traditional calendar is arranged into a series of five Earthly Stems and twelve Heavenly Branches. Each year can thus be identified as part of a sixty-year cycle. So, the sixtieth birthday marks the point at which one has lived through all of the stems and branches. Dixian (1858–1932) was a leading figure in what historian Holmes Welch termed the "Buddhist revival in China," and he had been spreading and promoting Buddhism for years as a means of strengthening China. He had served as Dean of Students—the only monk on the faculty—of a new school for training Buddhist missionaries that opened in Nanjing in 1906.[25] There were even stories that he had led an army of monks in the Battle of Nanjing, during the 1911 Revolution that overthrew the Qing dynasty.[26] Dixian was very well-connected politically and had won the Republican government's support for a bill (which ultimately proved ineffectual) that would have made his temple—Guanzong Temple in Ningbo—the only place in China where Buddhist monks could receive a certificate of ordination, so that Dixian would be the only man in China capable of ordaining them. Acts like this made Dixian controversial; Taixu, the most prominent Buddhist reformer in twentieth-century China, declared Dixian a "traitor to Buddhism."[27] For his part, Dixian—and most other Chinese Buddhists—felt that Taixu's "reforms" were dangerously radical. Taixu advocated a broad array of changes to Buddhist organization, education, and administration that would emphasize modernization over traditional practice. Men like Dixian feared "that if [Buddhism] were made into something as new as Taixu seemed to be proposing, it would no longer be Buddhism."[28]

Although he favored political change in China, Dixian emphasized traditional Buddhist practice and was considered a conservative monk. While Taixu pushed for new Buddhist schools that would include modern scientific education, Dixian wanted to repair the infrastructure of temples and monasteries. He had long been eager to restore the prominence of Buddhism in North China, where there were few important temples, and observers had lamented the sad state of Buddhism since the fifteenth century.[29] For his sixtieth birthday, he went on a tour of the north, culminating with a series of lectures at important temples in Beijing.

The arrival of such a prominent monk was celebrated among all the temples of the region. For Longxian, it held special significance. Dixian had been one of the four monks presented to Wang Futing as possible masters. Now that Dixian had come to visit the temple, Qingchi called Longxian aside and told him that the master's arrival was an extraordinary sign. It was generally very difficult to change masters, but the special occasion of Dixian's birthday might make it possible for Longxian to make another new beginning.

Qingchi went on to share with Longxian the details of a recent dream in which a novice monk came from the north to stay at his temple.

> His name was Tanxu—a very unusual name. He stayed at the temple for a few days and then suddenly died. We cremated the body, but when I set the funeral pyre alight, the monk sat upright, and exclaimed a few sentences no one could understand. Then, in a flash of light, he vanished! Startled by this scene I awoke and immediately realized that it applied to you. You arrived from the north, with the goal of becoming a novice, and my introduction card was analogous to igniting the funeral pyre: you should be called by this name.[30]

Wang Futing agreed, but with one change: the character "Tan" (埃) used for the name in the dream contained within it the radical "土"meaning "earth." (A radical is a component of each Chinese character that categorizes it and gives a clue to its meaning and/or pronunciation.) Since he had left family life before taking this new name, he asked that it be removed to symbolize that he had already left behind earthly concerns, replacing it with the character "倓," also pronounced "Tan." Everyone agreed, and the name Tanxu was conferred as part of a second tonsure ceremony. The process could not be completed until Tanxu went to Dixian's home temple in Ningbo, several hundred miles to the south. To get there, Tanxu would embark from Tanggu—the port of Tianjin—just a few miles from his birthplace in Beitang village. As a boy with the name Wang Shouchun, he watched his father sail off on the waters of the Bohai Gulf from Tanggu. As a young man, with the name Wang Futing, he found work at these docks after the devastation of the Boxer Uprising and had sailed from here to Dalian and then Yingkou. Now, as Tanxu, he found a steamer bound for Shanghai, a day's journey south. From there, it was just a short ferry ride to Ningbo, where he would continue to craft his new life.

CHAPTER 3

New Worlds

When Tanxu—no longer Wang Futing—arrived there in 1917, Ningbo, once one of the busiest ports in Asia, had been in decline for some time. As he made his way from the ferry dock to Guanzong Temple, much was unfamiliar; Tanxu had moved frequently during his youth, but here he felt alienated by the accents and languages of people talking on the street, smells of food cooking, the local vegetation, and the climate. Although he had been a refugee, an orphan, and a fugitive, he felt more out of place on this trip taken of his own will than he had in all his previous flights.

With three other novices, Tanxu enrolled at Guanzong Temple seminary, founded by Dixian to train a new generation of monks. Dixian was particularly happy to have northerners at his seminary: he had long aspired to revive Buddhism in North China. The seminaries in the north were neither numerous, rigorous, nor prestigious enough to train monks effectively, so revival would depend on northerners coming south to train. Northerners were therefore particularly valued at the seminary and even received special treatment: the discipline in the temple was very strict, and even small lapses of etiquette could result in beatings or expulsion. However, Tanxu and other northerners were often forgiven slight breaches, both because their importance to Dixian's plans and because their "northern temperament" was presumed to be coarser then that of their southern counterparts.

Tanxu soon found, however, that these indulgences did not eliminate the difficulties of studying in the south. To begin with, he could not understand what his teachers were saying! The notion that regional language differences in China are "dialects" under-states the difficulties in communicating across the empire. Although the common written language helps unify China, many of the native tongues spoken across the country are mutually unintelligible: speaking with people from another region was not, usually, simply a matter of understanding an unfamiliar accent, but of learning a new spoken language. Many of the monks at Guanzong Temple lectured in the local language, the Wu dialect, which Tanxu—a native speaker of Mandarin—could not understand at all. Wu dialect (the second most widely spoken language in China, after Mandarin) is the native language throughout much of the Yangzi Delta, including the major cities of Zhejiang and Jiangsu Provinces, and is comprehensible to neither Mandarin nor Cantonese speakers. This language difference was part of what made northerners so valuable, but it also was an obstacle to their success at the seminary. Even the monks who did lecture in Mandarin spoke with thick regional accents that he could barely understand.

The language was just one challenge. Ningbo's climate was much milder than his home in the north, but the buildings in the south were not heated, and at night they became much colder than the stove-heated accommodations to which he was accustomed. (This situation remains today: although northern cities can be frigid in winter, central heating makes them comfortable and warm inside. South of the Yangzi River, most buildings are unheated, and this can make the cool, damp southern winters less pleasant to endure than the much colder north.) The food, too, was radically different. Despite his insistence that he would bear any suffering to follow the Buddha, Tanxu found himself unable to cope. After just a month, homesick and disappointed, he listed reasons why he wished to leave the seminary:

1. In Ningbo they eat disgusting food.
2. The nights are too cold for me to sleep.
3. The language is unfamiliar: I cannot understand anything I hear in class.[1]

The language issue was the most serious, but Tanxu was too embar-rassed to tell the teachers that he could not understand their lectures.

Instead, he told the monk in charge of accommodations that it was too cold at night for him to sleep, jeopardizing his health. Instead of permitting him to transfer to another temple, the monk taught him how to fold his quilt to better keep warm. The food and language remained foreign to him, but at least he could sleep at night.

The situation soon improved. During Tanxu's first months at Guanzong Temple, Master Dixian had been away, lecturing and presiding over ceremonies throughout the region. When he returned, he took over some of the lecturing duties, speaking in Mandarin without much of an accent. Suddenly able to understand the lectures, Tanxu found himself revisiting materials familiar from years of studying sutras in Yingkou. Thoughts of leaving Ningbo dissipated, and he settled into the routine of Guanzong Temple, rising each morning at 3:00 AM and chanting with the other monks in the main hall until 5:30, when breakfast was eaten. After a short rest, he recited sutras starting at 8:00, followed by the midday meal at 11:30. This meal was followed by "free time," which might be used for study or sleep. (Perhaps because of this limited free time, Buddhist monks eat, in my observation, faster than anyone I have ever seen!) At 1:00 PM, the school day began, and Master Dixian lectured on sutras. Sutra lectures alternated with meditation periods, and some rest, until about 6:30 and the evening meal. After dinner, time was available to study, until 9:00 PM, followed by a short meditation session, after which no lamps could be lit. Six hours of sleep, and the cycle would repeat.

While Tanxu adapted to the new lifestyle of the monastery, China struggled with its new identity as a republic. China's first President, Yuan Shikai, who had first forced the assembly (by the skepticism-inducing vote of 1,993–0) to ask him to assume the title of Emperor and then backed down amid widespread disapproval, had died in 1916. The New Culture Movement was redefining what it meant, or could mean, to be Chinese, as the country slid toward political chaos. Little of lasting benefit came from Yuan's administration, but for Buddhists, his presidency opened new avenues to political power. Several lay Buddhists took positions in the new government, among them Ye Gong-chuo, who became head of the Communication and Transport Ministry. Ye was a devout and learned believer. As part of Yuan's initiative to establish a Buddhist education society with government support, Ye invited Dixian to lecture in Beijing. Dixian eagerly agreed; the invitation fit perfectly with his ambitions to revitalize Buddhism in North China, but he was already in his sixties and could not depend upon his health to manage the long journey north. It was decided that two or three students should accompany him, capable of lecturing in Dixian's place should he need to rest.

The first companion selected was Master Renshan, a former student of Dixian and the abbot of a temple in Yangzhou. Experienced and renowned as an interpreter of scriptures, he was an easy choice. Choosing a second companion was harder. One by one, top students who had been at the seminary for many years approached Dixian and asked to go with him to Beijing. All were refused, either on the grounds that they were too inexperienced, or did not speak standard Mandarin, or without any reason at all.

Tanxu anxiously observed Dixian's preparations to go north. Recalling his struggles to understand the monks who had lectured in Dixian's absence, he resolved that rather than endure this again he would ask to be released from Guanzong Temple and seek a more suitable monastery at which to continue his training. He struggled with this decision, and with nothing to lose he decided to ask Dixian to take him on the journey as one of his assistants. Dixian astonished him by replying simply, "OK," adding that because his own speech might be hard for northerners to understand, Tanxu could serve as an interpreter when needed. Other students resented and questioned the decision, but in a few days Tanxu and Dixian departed by ferry for Shanghai. From there, Dixian and his entourage—Tanxu, Renshan, and a lay Buddhist sent from Beijing to escort them north—set out on a ship bound for Tianjin.

After two days' sail across the Yellow Sea and around the Shandong Peninsula, the ship docked at Yantai, one of the ports Tanxu's father had frequented as a merchant sailor. There, Dixian disembarked to rest and recover from the wearying sea voyage. The master and his companions were welcomed into the home of a local official, Wu Yong, who put them up for the night. Magistrate Wu was a Buddhist, and his wife was especially devout. Dixian, though, found her to be a dilettante, trying a variety of beliefs in the hopes that one might prove profitable. After sharing the midday meal, the group conversed over tea. Dixian used these opportunities to teach his companions about the Buddha and his message, usually by sharing stories. Sometimes these stories were Buddhist parables, reflecting on the power of the sutras or the wisdom of the Buddha. Others were popular legends or unusual news stories of the day.

This first afternoon in Yantai, Dixian asked their hosts if they had heard of the strange goings-on in Shanghai recently. The official replied that he had heard no such stories, but was very eager to hear the tale. Dixian sat silently for a few moments, and then began to tell the story of Madame Cheng, a wealthy Shanghai widow whose husband had just died. "Madame Cheng was utterly devoted to her husband," Dixian began. "After his death, she was inconsolable, wanting nothing other than to see her husband again.

At the time in Shanghai there was a Frenchman who was versed in "ghost studies." He was reputedly able to summon the ghosts of the recently deceased and performed séances for 1,000 yuan. Cost was no concern for the Cheng family, and so they hired the Frenchman.

He came to their house one evening, arranged an altar, and began to perform rites and recite chants. This went on for about an hour, but no ghost appeared. The medium, frustrated and exhausted, spoke:

"This person is very difficult to find! I searched for him in the afterlife for a long time. Eventually, I spotted him, condemned by the judges of the underworld to serve a long sentence to atone for his crimes on earth. No matter how urgently I called, he could not come out."

Mrs. Cheng had been devastated since the death of her husband, unable even to eat. Her only reason for going on was to see her husband once more and to talk with him. As the foreigner told the story of her husband in hell, she became angry.

"This ghost game you are playing is a fraud!" she said angrily. "My husband's life was happy and virtuous. He helped hold the community together: worshipping at temples and paying for bridges to be built. He never wronged anyone, so why would he be condemned to hell? You made up this story to humiliate us."

As Mrs. Cheng blustered furiously, the Frenchman proposed a solution, offering to find someone else in the afterworld as proof of his skills. Mrs. Cheng's daughter-in-law spoke up. Her husband had died a few days before, so with a heavy heart she asked if he might be summoned to verify the Frenchman's honesty.

It was agreed. Preparations were made and the foreigner readied the altar and the lamps.

This time was not at all like the last time. There was no need for incantations or rituals at all: the ghost simply appeared in the middle of the room! On seeing his wife, his tears fell upon the table. After they had talked for a while, the ghost's widow asked him about his existence in the afterlife. He replied,

"Because I have only recently died, I am still a wandering ghost; I have not yet been taken for judgment—the worst part is the waiting! During my life I did so many things wrong. Now I am gone and there is nothing I can do but beg you all to redeem me, through your merit and good deeds and chanting sutras. In my clothes, I still have a check—you can take it to the bank and use it for things for the house, things that you need, things to better care for our child."

In his coat pocket the family indeed found a check, just as the ghost had said. Standing nearby, the man's son asked, "Are you my father?"

"Yes, dear child! You listen to what your mother says!"

The ghost began to cry again, as did the family. In the midst of all this grief, the daughter-in-law suddenly remembered the question they had come to ask:

"When we earlier called on your father, why did he not come?"

The ghost stopped his crying long enough to choke out, "He has already been condemned to hell," and with these words he resumed crying, even harder than before. Mrs. Cheng, standing nearby, interrupted:

"Your father spent his entire life doing good work. How can it be that he has been condemned to hell?!" She absolutely refused to believe it.

"I asked him this very same question," the ghost answered. "It seems that long ago, when he was an official in Beijing, my father had been in desperate financial straits. During this time, the crops in Shanxi Province failed, leading to famine. The emperor dispatched father to Shanxi to manage the relief effort, but instead of distributing the relief coupons, father kept 600,000 taels of silver for his private purse. Because of father's actions, tens of thousands of people died. When the imperial court sent an official to investigate, father bribed him, and the whole incident was covered up. . . . When he got to the afterlife, he did not wait a few days, but went directly to hell."

"Your father spent his whole life doing good works!" Mrs. Cheng cried. "He made amends for his crimes, but he still went directly to hell?!"

"Of course, he did many good deeds, but they did not outweigh his crimes. In the future his charitable deeds might let him ascend to heaven and prosper, but in this life he is responsible for thousands of deaths, and he has not yet made up for it."

When Mrs. Cheng heard these words, she became enraged!

"If all his good works did no good, why should we continue to do good works . . . what good are they? Quickly! Send people to some Buddhist temple and tear it down, and chase off all the monks!"

In the midst of all this discussion, the ghost simply disappeared. In the end, they went to a Buddhist temple, but disturbed neither the buildings nor its occupants.[2]

Dixian finished the story and then turned to Magistrate Wu: "This story has been around Shanghai for many days, and almost everyone knows it. You and this Cheng are distant relatives, right? Is this really his story?"

Magistrate Wu thought for a long while. Embarrassed, he said that Cheng had been an official in Beijing, and that he had been poor, but more he could not say for certain. The conversation ended here, for no one seemed willing to speak.

Dixian and Tanxu shared tales like this with different audiences throughout their trip to Beijing. Tanxu recorded these stories to demonstrate the power of karma and the importance of one's actions: "What is the point of all these unrelated stories I have told?" he asked in his memoir. "To persuade everyone that ghosts and spirits do really exist! Hell is real! Karma is real!" Evil acts would result in suffering, whether it was in the current life or the next life.

The stories illustrate important Buddhist beliefs about fate and justice. First, they show that all actions have consequences. The official in the first story was perceived by society to be upright and honest, but as a younger man he had accumulated bad karma that could not be erased by good deeds. Despite the incredulity of his wife and family, he was condemned to hell to repent for his sins, while his son, who had been neither famous nor important, seemed to enjoy a better fate in the afterlife.

The Abrahamic religions of Judaism, Christianity, and Islam tend toward absolutes. The first commandment, that you shall worship no other god, depicts a jealous and exclusive deity that would be unfamiliar to most Asian religions; in this story, for instance, Buddhism and Daoism mix freely, along with "popular religions" that are not formally part of either tradition. In the Abrahamic religions, heaven and hell are final judgments, eternal paradise or never-ending suffering. Paradise and damnation are both present in Chinese religions as well, but they are not final. Hell is a punishment to be endured, a price to be paid before the sufferer can be reborn. Heaven, too, is temporary: one's actions in paradise determine your future fate, just as actions on earth do. In the West, heaven is bliss without end, not a reward that can be withdrawn; in the Chinese view, misdeeds or transgressions committed in the afterlife can result in rebirth back on earth or even in a hell.[3]

This time in paradise can also be an opportunity to cultivate virtue before gaining final enlightenment. As Tanxu would develop in his later lectures on Pure Land practice, the intermediate step of a heaven or "Pure Land," presided over by a Buddha or bodhisattva, provided a chance to hear the teachings directly from one who had attained, or was on the cusp of, enlightenment, free from earthly distractions.

These ideas about the afterlife exemplify the syncretism found in Chinese religion. They show just how intimately different religious and spiritual traditions were entwined: the network of judges, bureaucrats, ghosts, and demons in the afterlife are distinctively Chinese—they often replicate power structures and relationships found on earth—not the Buddhism that developed in India. Many elements of Daoism and popular religion are present, as are parts of the Confucian state system. Dixian's parables, and Tanxu's own story, show the extent to which Buddhism had become Chinese, and also the way in which the Chinese spiritual tradition defied easy categorization.

Dixian's stories also criticize the dilettantism common in Chinese tradition—the official's wife in the first story is shown to be foolish, misunderstanding her husband's life and fate, and taking her anger out on the medium, her family, and the local Buddhist clergy. Perhaps the message was intended for Magistrate Wu's wife, whom Dixian saw as a dabbler, not a serious seeker. His message was consistent: dedication to Buddhism would yield enlightenment, but a scattershot, undisciplined approach to enlightenment was unproductive. It is, perhaps, surprising that Tanxu would so earnestly accept this narrow interpretation of Buddhism. He had spent many hours studying and practicing Daoist alchemy and fortune-telling, and during his time at the Lecture Hall in Yingkou he had embraced a variety of faiths. But he came to believe that single-minded attention to Buddhism was the most productive way forward.

Dixian and his entourage concluded their sea voyage in Tianjin— just a few miles from Tanxu's birthplace—and continued to Beijing by train. After a few days' rest, Dixian began his lectures on the Lotus Sutra. The lectures took place at the Jiangxi *huiguan*—a lodge constructed by migrants from Jiangxi Province that served as a community center. This lodge may have been chosen because it could accommodate the hundreds who thronged the hall to hear Dixian speak.

The Lotus Sutra is one of the most important and widely revered Mahayana texts. It is unclear when and where it was first written, but it relates a sermon the Buddha preached near the city of Rajagriha, in northern India, in the fifth or sixth century BCE. It is not even known in what language the sutra was originally composed. Translator Burton Watson suggests that it was first written in a Central Asian language, and then translated into Sanskrit—the classical language of Indian religions—to give it gravitas. The text was first translated into Chinese in 255 CE, but only gained wide readership following Kumarajiva's translation in 406. Most subsequent translations into other languages have been based on Kumarajiva's classical Chinese translation.[4]

The Lotus was well-suited to Dixian's love of parables. Many of its most famous passages are parables: analogies to help seekers better understand the Buddha's message. Perhaps the most famous of these parables is the Burning House.

In this story, the Buddha describes the enormous house of a wealthy family, with hundreds of rooms and elaborate grounds. The house, though opulent at first glance, is dangerously run-down, with rotting staircases and leaking roofs. The extended family lives inside the house, including the owner's three young sons, who entertain themselves with toys and sweets.

Returning home one day, the man sees that his house is on fire. He runs inside to rescue his children, telling them that they are in terrible danger and must leave the house, but he cannot convince them because they will not part with their toys. He tells them that the house is burning and that they will not escape if they do not come with him, but they do not believe him because they cannot see the flames, which have not yet reached their room. The father is panicked, not least because the house has only one exit, and the warren-like nature of the house will make it impossible for the children to find their own way out if and when they realize the danger.

Assessing the situation, the father changes his approach. He tells his sons that outside they will find the most wonderful surprises. Rather than toy carts, he promises them real carts, drawn by livestock and covered with jewels and silks, if only they will come outside. Excited at this prospect, the boys follow their father through the burning house and outside to safety. Their father is overjoyed and fulfills his promise by purchasing bejeweled carriages for his children, complete with drivers and footmen.

After relating the story, the Buddha asks his followers if the father should be censured for lying because he lured the children out by promising a reward that did not yet exist. They answered that the father should not be punished because he saved the boys' lives. So it is, the Buddha said, with his own teachings. He tells the seeker that a paradise awaits those who follow the eightfold path toward enlightenment, and that he or she may be reborn in a "Pure Land," or paradise. Actually, there is no such paradise; neither is there not such a paradise. The true nature of reality is that the void and substance are one and the same, everything that is said to exist in the world, including ourselves, is undifferentiated. Even that which we believe to be our self does not exist; on achieving enlightenment, we do not achieve paradise, we realize that we are undifferentiated from the rest of the universe: we do not exist as individuals. This is the ultimate message of the Buddha, yet it contradicts the promises of rebirth in paradise of the Buddha's earlier teachings: if we, as individuals, do not exist, what is there to be reborn? Does this contradiction make the Buddha a liar? No; it is done in the pursuit of enlightenment and so may be justified.

The same message accompanies the parable of the Phantom City, also found in the Lotus Sutra. In this story, the Buddha tells of a city filled with the most fabulous of treasures: delights and riches beyond the most outlandish fantasies. But this treasure trove is located in an inaccessible region, high in the mountains, over many hundred miles of treacherous and poorly marked road. Only one man knew the way to this treasure, and a group of treasure hunters hired him to lead them there. The treasure seekers set out, promising to endure any hardships on the way to this ultimate treasure, but after weeks of travel, suffering cold and hunger and danger, they decided they could not go on. Even though the treasure would be great, they could no longer stand the struggle to achieve it, and told their guide that they must turn back.

The leader was very disappointed, for he knew that the treasure they sought was worth any suffering. He told them that around the next bend in the path lay a wonderful city where they could eat and rest before resuming their journey. The group continued a bit further and, indeed, a city appeared, just as their guide had promised. The travelers were elated; after the struggles of their journey, this place was paradise indeed. They lay down their burdens and rested.

After some days, the city suddenly vanished. In fact, it had never existed at all, but had been an illusion conjured by the guide, who possessed magical abilities. He told his charges that he could not bear the thought of them turning back when they had worked so hard to achieve their goal, so he deceived them by creating the illusion of this city to give them some rest and some reward—or at least the illusion of rest and reward. Without this, they would not have gone on. So, even though he had deceived them all, he had done so with the purest of motives. Thanks to their leader's trick, they were able to achieve their goal.

The Buddha, too, employed this kind of tactic. The path to enlightenment is long and difficult; it will almost certainly take many lifetimes to achieve and very few have the ability to persevere all the way. For this reason, the Buddha creates intermediate goals and rewards, in which the seeker may find rest and encouragement. These rewards are the paradises into which we may be reborn, but they are no more real than the physical world we seek to overcome. They may be said to be deceptions, but because they are aids on the road to enlightenment, without which we might not succeed, the deception is justified.

Using parables like these to explain and demonstrate the power of the Buddha's teachings, Dixian remained in Beijing for six months. The greatest challenge he faced was unifying, or at least coordinating, the many Buddhist temples and shrines in the capital. According to Tanxu, there were thousands of temples in Beijing— some of them very large—but none of them would invite Dixian to lecture there. Dixian could not even find accommodations in a temple. Instead, lay Buddhists quartered the group at a tobacco warehouse in the city. Tanxu attributed this antipathy among local monks to the deep divisions between northern and southern sects of Buddhism, but more than this he blamed the lack of commitment and expertise of many northern monks. Monks in the north, separated from the active centers of Buddhism in the south, lacked the rigor or knowledge of their southern counterparts. Tanxu described several of these monks who discouraged their colleagues from attending Dixian's lectures for fear they would reveal the shortcomings in their own understanding of the sutras.

Tanxu asserted that many of these men became monks to escape commitments or obligations in secular society. If so, these monks reinforced and exemplified a motif in Chinese history that depicted monks as shady characters, living at the edges of society. Monks were viewed with suspicion because they rejected many of the traditional structures that ordered society, including work, family, and government. The prohibition on work and reliance on alms encouraged a popular image of monks as lazy and parasitic. Monks' vows of celibacy defied not only basic human desires, but Confucian norms that emphasized family obligations and raising a new generation. Charges of hypocrisy were common, as were stereotypes of monks who flouted their vow of celibacy with numerous "devotees."

Their association with a spirit-world of ghosts, demons, and spirits made monks popular targets for accusations of sorcery and witchcraft. Unexplained illness or erratic weather patterns might be blamed on dark magic. Governments often questioned the loyalty of monks—especially Buddhist monks—because their devotion to transcending the material world denigrated obedience to political authority. In the Manchu Qing dynasty, suspicions of monks intensified because by shaving their heads monks avoided the queue: the shaven forehead and long braid that the Manchus insisted all men adopt to demonstrate their loyalty to the dynasty. Failure to adopt this hairstyle would condemn a layman to death, but monks were exempt. Many Manchus practiced Buddhism, in both its Chinese and Mongol/Tibetan varieties, and so monks were in principle venerated and respected. However, Qing authorities were well aware that a political dissident under investigation might simply shave his head and don robes, claiming his hairstyle was religious in motivation.[5]

A major challenge for Dixian and his entourage in Beijing was combating this image of monks as suspicious and untrustworthy. Fortunately, according to Tanxu, although the clergy in Beijing was weak, the Buddhist laity in the city was numerous and enthusiastic. Tanxu himself also may have helped the cause by the diversity of his own training, which incorporated elements of Daoism and other traditions. When Dixian fell ill during his visit, Tanxu diagnosed him, relying on his training as a pharmacist. He took Dixian to an astrologer, Bai Chenghuang, one of the most famous fortune-tellers in Beijing, who had attended many of Dixian's lectures. Although some of Dixian's company opposed "tainting" him with the superstition of fortune-telling, Tanxu insisted. The resulting exchange led both men to a new understanding of the other's tradition and practice (both, for instance, emphasized rites that would free the Hungry Ghosts of those who died without the proper burial or funeral rites). Bai Chenghuang even summoned one of these ghosts, a general who lamented that he could find no rest although he had been dead for many years. Dixian responded that such suffering could only be overcome through attention to the Buddha's message:

"What you need is hard work. When you free yourself of vain hopes, [only] then you can feel shame, and repent your sins. . . . In this way, your suffering can be eliminated."[6]

When word spread that Dixian and Bai Chenghuang had cooperated on these rites, and that Dixian had succeeded in easing the ghost's pain, the crowds at his sutra lectures grew. Most of the laity in Beijing did not care whether a practitioner was labeled Buddhist, Daoist, or something else, but Dixian's demonstrated power showed that his teachings were efficacious and, therefore, worth following. Here, he tapped into a centuries-old tradition: from the earliest arrival of Buddhism in China, gods and goddesses had competed with Buddhas and bodhisattvas, often merging and adapting with one another to produce new cults and sects. These sects gained—or lost—adherents based on their *ling*, or efficacy. A god, practitioner, or teaching that was efficacious was likely to spread and thrive. Historian Valerie Hansen, describing the religious landscape of twelfth-century China, put it this way: "Lay people chose among practitioners and gods on the basis of efficacy. . . . The very supple nature of Chinese popular religion granted devotees and practitioners ample room for innovation: whoever provided the most compelling explanation could persuade others of the power of the god he (or she) worshipped." This flexibility made religion sensitive to changes in social and economic conditions: as peoples' lives changed, religion could adapt to help them meet new challenges, and those gods or practitioners or traditions that adapted most effectively were bound to win support.[7] This was particularly true in times of political and social instability, such as the Southern Song dynasty that Hansen describes, or the Republican era of the early twentieth century.

Dixian and Tanxu, by demonstrating the power of Buddhism, its compatibility with other traditions, and that they, as monks, were worthy of trust and respect, laid a foundation for reviving Buddhism in Beijing. Ye Gongchuo, along with some other lay Buddhists, urged Dixian to establish a seminary in Beijing. Dixian declined, saying that he was too old and tired to undertake so ambitious a project, but these same laymen raised funds to assist Dixian in expanding the seminary in Ningbo, with the understanding that the monks trained there would eventually come north and help to improve the situation of Buddhism in Beijing and other northern

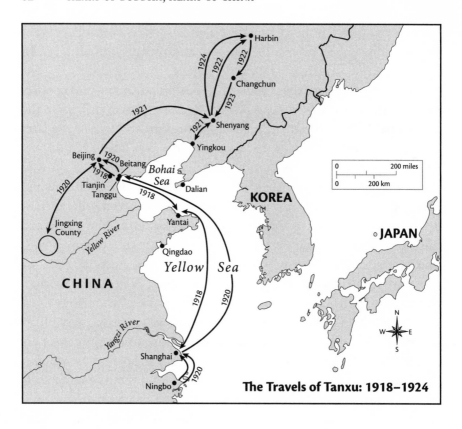

The Travels of Tanxu: 1918–1924

cities. Dixian and Tanxu returned to Ningbo that fall. Tanxu passed
the next year, 1919, at Guanzong Temple, studying but also attending to the monks' medical needs because of his background as an
apothecary.

The year 1919 is a watershed in modern Chinese history because
of the events that accompanied the end of World War I. For Tanxu,
though he was not directly involved in these events, 1919 was crucial as well. During the run-up to the Boxer Uprising, Germany
had gained territory in China's Shandong Province—primarily the
colony of Jiaozhou Bay, centered on the city of Qingdao; part of
China's motivation for supporting the Allied war effort, including
by sending laborers to Europe, was the restitution of these lands.
Emboldened by Wilson's principles of national self-determination,
China expected that the colony would be returned when Germany
was defeated. Instead, the Versailles Treaty that ended the war

ceded the German claims in Shandong to Japan. When news of the betrayal reached China, protests erupted in many cities, especially in Beijing.

The New Culture Movement, which had been gathering momentum since 1915, now took on the alternate name of the May Fourth Movement, after the date in 1919 of the first protests over the Shandong decision, and its participants became known as the May Fourth Generation. To these men and women, China faced an even more difficult road than their revolutionary or reformist forbears, with their unqualified confidence in the virtues of Western civilization, had perceived. The events of 1919 had shown the peril of blindly following the West; even when China became a republic, joined the family of nations, and supported the Western powers in war, the Europeans sided with imperialist powers against China's territorial integrity. Frustrated by both Chinese tradition and Western imperialism, the May Fourth Generation plotted a course for China to modernize, but warily. Many in the movement adopted more radical Western ideologies, like socialism and anarchism, which rejected both tradition and imperialism. For most reformers, China needed to move boldly so that it could confront the West as a modern nation.

Tanxu, however, still believed that China's foremost need was spiritual renewal. This was why he had left his family and become a monk. He believed that Buddhism could strengthen the country by providing a moral foundation for society that would enable China to compete successfully. This suggests that Tanxu was a cultural conservative, but he was no xenophobe. He believed strongly in China's traditional cultural legacies, but he had lived his whole life surrounded by foreigners and had not rejected them. He had included Christianity in his spiritual search, and as he watched foreign troops overrun China's armies, he saw a force to learn from, not to flee. The religious convictions he saw among the foreign soldiers and merchants—whether Japanese, German, Russian, or French; Buddhist, Protestant, Orthodox, or Catholic—persuaded him that China had been beaten as much by spiritual conviction as by superior technology. Buddhism in China, especially in the north, was weak, and he felt called to revive it. He was certain that spiritual renewal was essential to China's survival, and furthermore that the teachings of the Buddha could save humanity from the sufferings that he had confronted in his own life. The Buddha could show the way to transcend these sufferings, and he felt called to spread these teachings throughout China, not simply to cultivate his own learning behind the walls of the monastery.

In the spring of 1920, Tanxu was frustrated, and he began to think it was time for him to leave the monastery. Dixian had taken ill while lecturing at a nearby temple and could not conduct classes. His replacement was dull and uninspiring, and lectured in a thick regional accent that Tanxu could not understand. Tanxu had never intended to stay in seminary long; he wanted to be out spreading the Buddha's teachings and working to strengthen the heart of China. Without Dixian's lectures, Tanxu felt he was wasting time, all the more precious because he had become a monk so late in life. The weather also was a factor; after the relative cool of Beijing, Tanxu found Ningbo's heat and humidity—not to mention its mosquitoes—oppressive. He approached Dixian to ask for leave from Guanzong Temple, but Dixian refused, saying that his training was not complete, and that he was relying on Tanxu to help him revive Buddhism in the north.

Determined to leave, Tanxu resorted to a lie. He told Dixian that a former teacher was very ill, and that he needed urgently to go pay his respects. Dixian was suspicious, but could not easily refuse such a request. He granted Tanxu twenty days' leave, insisting that he return as soon as possible. Tanxu gathered his belongings, wrapped in a mosquito-net bundle, and walked toward the main gate of the temple. Other students gathered around, asking where he was going. He repeated his story about going to see his former teacher, and then moved out of the crowd and through the main gate. As he walked out, he reflected on the time he had spent at the temple:

> This was the place where I became a monk, where I had taken the tonsure, and where my Buddhist life had commenced. I had taken classes, and meditated. Master Di had been very benevolent toward me, and had taught me well. My classmates had welcomed me, and the entire community was very close. Suddenly, I did not want to leave. I walked through the gate, went a few steps, and then turned my head to look back; walked a few steps more, and

then turned to look back again. However, this had been just a short period of my life—I was already more than forty years old, and my goal in leaving family life had never been to study: I wanted to understand the meaning of life and death, and I wanted to spread the word of the Buddha. And, since I would always be a student of Guanzong Temple, I was in a sense not leaving it.[8]

Tanxu arrived at the ferry dock in the morning, but the next boat did not depart until the afternoon, and so he passed a few hours at a nearby teahouse. Eventually the ferry came and Tanxu boarded it. He carried few material possessions, but was burdened with the knowledge that, for the second time in his life, he was lying to those closest to him and leaving a commitment under false pretenses. A few hours later, he disembarked in Shanghai, a world away from the monastery where he had lived for the last three years.

Tanxu did not take this step away from his master, in defiance of his instructions, lightly. The bond between teacher and student, canonized in Confucian thought, is powerful in Chinese culture, and the devotion of a Buddhist novice toward his master is deeper still. For Tanxu to break this bond required both personal and professional sacrifice. Throughout his life, though, Tanxu showed himself willing to challenge or disobey rules—even fundamental laws of nature and society. As a boy he had defied death itself, rejecting the judgment of the King of Hell and insisting to be returned to his previous life to ease his mother's pain. He had broken his marriage vows and his commitment to his children to become a monk, believing that he could better serve humanity by spreading the Buddha's teachings. Now, he was disobeying the command of his master so that he could work to spread the dharma in the north. Before he could proceed, however, he first found it necessary to reconcile his new life with the family he had left behind.

CHAPTER 4

——————

Family

Guanzong Temple had frustrated Tanxu. The isolation of the monastery was at odds with the more public role he sought for spreading the Buddha's teachings. But after leaving the temple and resuming his travels, he was alone and often melancholy, pondering the path he had chosen. He had become a monk to help China, and all of humanity, along a path toward enlightenment, but in the process he had violated many ethical principles. He had lied to his wife and abandoned his family; he had deceived his master and deserted his temple. He had even transgressed against his parents: as their only surviving child—especially as their only surviving son—Wang Futing was expected to uphold the traditions of ancestor worship, maintaining their graves and their memories. As a monk, Tanxu lacked the financial resources to ensure these observances. Moreover, although Tanxu did have several sons, born before he took the tonsure, they were left without financial support when he became a monk, throwing the long-term survival of the lineage into question. Feeling isolated and guilty after leaving Guanzong Temple, Tanxu sought reconciliation with his past. He returned to his birthplace, Beitang, and then to Yingkou, where his wife still lived.

In Beitang, there was little evidence of his past. Foreign soldiers fighting the Boxers in 1900 had destroyed his home and any family altars or records it contained. None of his relatives were left. Only the graves of his parents in the village cemetery remained, and he went there to conduct a memorial service. Walking to the gravesite, he recalled a letter that a friend had received from his grandfather, shortly after he had left to become a monk. The grandfather wrote:

You and I have been bound together for a long time, beginning with the great love we shared for your mother. Before you were born, we prayed to the Buddha that a son would be born, and when the child was born, our prayers were answered! You were a cherished treasure. We nursed you tirelessly, and labored hard. When you became an adult, we sent you to school. When, after a short time, you did not return home, our hopes for your future turned to worry. Your father died, but your mother lived, your older brother was weak, your younger brother was poor, and I had nothing to fall back on. Your mother's heart was broken, for her son had forgotten his mother; she cried day and night, longing for your return. Now we know the truth and can give up hope that you will return. Your mother is consigned to the loneliest of existences.[1]

Tanxu felt close to his mother and responsible for her well-being. He had challenged the judgment of the underworld in order to remain with her on earth. It is no wonder that the sentiments expressed in this letter haunted him as he prepared to visit her grave for the first time since he had become a monk. Carrying these thoughts, he walked the half mile from the village center to the gravesite, where he stood and recited Buddhist sutras. Fingering prayer beads, he tried to honor his mother, as a son and a monk, alone with his thoughts and her memory. Nothing else of his family remained in Beitang, and Tanxu soon traveled on.

One of Tanxu's justifications—or rationalizations—for his decision to leave his family had been that after his education as a Buddhist, he would be able to return to his wife and lead her on the path toward enlightenment. This would be of greater benefit than the financial or emotional support he could provide as a husband. Even if he believed this deeply, it would still be painful and difficult for Tanxu to face his wife, but this is what he resolved to do. Nearly four years after abandoning her, he stopped in Yingkou on his way to Manchuria, gathering support for the publication of sutras.

Tanxu's detachment from—and perhaps discomfort with—family life may be inferred from what his memoir does not say. Despite his eye for detail, he gives no details about his children, not even their names or the years of their birth. This frustrating silence about his domestic life is understandable; details about family life were unlikely to be important to his audience: men who had taken vows of celibacy. The silence on family matters is also consistent with Tanxu's desire to cast the material world as a distraction from the important issues of enlightenment and the dharma. Nonetheless, despite his discomfort he would go to his wife, to reassure her that he was alive, to explain why he had left her, and, he hoped, to help her accept the wisdom of the Buddha.

Arriving in Yingkou by train from Beijing, Tanxu went directly to the Lecture Hall, where he had first studied Buddhist sutras and lectured on the Buddha's teachings. His friends there were astonished to see him. They told him how the entire neighborhood had searched for him after he disappeared. His wife had waited for him, desperately, and even now held out hope that one day he would return. They did not know how she would handle the revelation that he had at last returned, but no longer as her husband. Tanxu stayed the night at the Lecture Hall, discussing what had become of him since he had left Yingkou, and explaining why he had left and why he was now returning. Tanxu's friends envied his position as a monk; although they had continued reading the sutras and studying the dharma, their knowledge had advanced little. There were few monks in the area and no temples where they could go for answers to difficult questions. They brought up the idea of building a temple in Yingkou, but Tanxu quickly dismissed such talk as idle and ignorant of the commitment that building a temple demanded.

The next day, accompanied by two friends, Tanxu returned to the home where his wife was living with their sons. Even as he approached the door he had last walked through years before, Tanxu considered turning away, dreading the pain he would soon face, pain that he had created. But before he could act on his second thoughts, his friends called out to his wife, who invited them in. The three men walked inside; Tanxu stood in the doorway.

Madam Wang sat on the *kang* in the living room. When she saw her husband, she did not speak, but turned her head away from him and began to cry. Tanxu did nothing at first, merely stood by and watched as the woman with whom he had spent twenty years and raised seven children wept, overcome by a mixture of grief, anger, relief, and confusion. Tanxu's monk's robe told her some of what had happened but many questions remained unanswered. When her tears subsided a bit, Tanxu spoke: "Do not cry. I have returned: you ought to be happy."

Tanxu's first words to his wife, more than three years after abandoning her to raise five children on her own, seem more than a little insensitive. Not surprisingly, this speech did little to calm her. She began to weep again. As word of the reunion spread, several of her friends came from nearby houses to comfort her. With their support, she mustered strength to speak:

"You left without a word, without saying anything!"

"If I had said anything to you, would you have let me go?"

"You left us! What was your family to do?"

The reunion upset Tanxu. Even though the events are self-reported, Tanxu reveals himself as very human. He becomes defensive. His attempts to comfort his wife would be laughable were they not so hurtful. He continued:

"In the three or four years since I left, I have received no messages about you, and is it not true that you are still alive, that you have not starved to death? Have you been unable to survive?"

She did not reply.

He continued, "I went away to become a monk, and today I have come here to see you. Imagine that I had died of disease: then I would never have been able to come back, and then what would you have done? You would still have needed to live, still have needed to find a way?"

"How are you able to be so quick and happy?" she retorted. "How are you able to be so clever? If you die you simply die: you have no choice in the matter. You *chose* to leave."

"No one chooses," Tanxu responded. "There are no guarantees. When I was seventeen, and had just married you, I was dead for four days, and at that time you weren't sobbing over me with your nose running, were you? Happily, I was able to return, to live again. You have not had to live in widowhood all these years; you have not had to remarry. Classmate Jin, who lived across from us and married that same day, died the very next day. His bride changed from her red wedding dress to the white mourning dress. Have you not seen these circumstances? Who will not die? Who is able to guarantee that you will not die soon? Among all our friends and family, there are many who lived long lives, but just as many who died young—much younger than us. I fear that you are not appreciating the life you have been given, and tomorrow you could die!"

Tanxu seemed more comfortable on metaphysical ground. Life and death, fate and circumstance, were easier for him to contemplate, and perhaps understand, than his personal role in the fate of the woman facing him now. She remained unmoved.

"So what?" she said.

Tanxu seemed flustered that his existential arguments had failed. He changed tactics, claiming that he had left home to help her, by enabling her to be free from the entanglements that accompanied family life:

"Have you not seen how officials are acting now? After they gain the wealth of office, they take concubines, steal and conceal houses of gold and other secrets. Many men leave their families behind to seek fortune, and then squirrel that fortune away, helping their families not at all. In my case, I left home to help you escape family life!"

"In what way was your becoming a monk and deserting your family for my benefit?"

"In order to help you alleviate suffering and find happiness!"

Tanxu went on to lecture her about the eight sufferings taught by the Buddha in the Lotus Sutra: birth, old age, sickness, death, separation from loved ones, encounters with enemies, and not getting what one desires. These sufferings afflict the lives of all humans, and indeed of all sentient beings. Had he remained at home, Tanxu might have made this life more comfortable and secure for his wife and children, but they would still have been trapped with these sufferings—the suffering that is life on earth. Now, Tanxu insisted, he offered a way for his family to transcend these sufferings, by teaching them about the path of the Buddha. He even urged Madam Wang to become a nun herself and bring the boys to become monks. He could use his many contacts to introduce her to an appropriate teacher. Tanxu saw this as the best way forward for all of them: if his family were to join the sangha, they would be looked after, and he could feel that he was still responsible, indirectly, for caring for them.

Madam Wang's world was turned upside down, again. For three years she had held out hope that her husband might return to her. Somehow, she had maintained her family—probably with help from relatives and perhaps wealthy clients of Tanxu's medicine shop. Now, he had returned, but he was no longer her husband, and instead of offering to support her and their children, he proposed that she become a nun.

This was more than she could commit to, but she did agree to learn more about the Buddha. Tanxu introduced her to the master who had first taught him in Yingkou. In Tanxu's account, her decision was a tribute to the persuasive power of the Buddha's teachings. Tanxu's position as a Buddhist monk may have enabled him to provide some support for his family through the local temple. It seems likely that her connection to the Buddhist community in Yingkou improved the quality of Wang's life. She never left the city and did not remarry—which suggests that she was able to live comfortably enough, at least, to continue as she was. Given the options available to a middle-aged widow with no obvious skills, this may be seen as success. One can only speculate on her feelings.

Tanxu was pleased. From this time forward, he remained in regular contact with his family. His children grew up in a Buddhist household, and his wife became an active lay Buddhist. Two of his sons became Buddhist monks, so they must have viewed Buddhism as a positive force, rather than as a home-wrecking institution that had taken their father away. (Tanxu does not say what became of his three other sons.) He passed through Yingkou regularly for years to come, raising money for and overseeing the construction of the Surangama Temple there. He saw his family on some of these visits, though he does not mention it often in his memoir.

Tanxu writes that, as she lay dying, on the eve of her death, his wife thanked him for introducing her to the path of the Buddha, and she died reciting the names of the Bodhisattva Guanyin and the Maitreya Buddha. This certainly would have set Tanxu's mind at ease, knowing that his decision to leave home had indeed benefited his wife, even in this life. We have no other evidence to compare with this. Surely, the transition was not as neat as it appears in Tanxu's account, but it does appear that much of his family followed him into Buddhism.

Tanxu's journey from Tianjin to Ningbo and back seemed to set his mind at rest about the decisions he had made. He now turned to the future, entering fully into his career as a monk. Almost immediately, he faced challenges to his faith. On the train back to Beijing, a Chinese Christian chastised Tanxu for wasting his time on prayers to the Buddha. The two men continued to argue for much of the journey, attracting a crowd of onlookers as they debated reincarnation, resurrection, and the nature of God. Following hard on the heels of his stay at Yingkou, where he had lectured before becoming a monk, this public disputation encouraged Tanxu in his career as a public speaker.

Tanxu's career now took off rapidly. Once he was back in Beijing, a Buddhist relief organization sent him on his first mission. Jingxing County, an area northwest of Beijing, had been hit repeatedly by drought and famine. Food and other supplies were being distributed, but someone who could preach the dharma and tend to the people's spiritual needs was also needed. As one of the few Buddhist monks who could speak the right dialect, Tanxu filled the bill, and in the spring of 1921 he was sent to lecture in Jingxing.

The short train ride to Jingxing illuminated the seriousness of the crisis in the county. Along the railway siding, Tanxu saw people eating leaves and bark from trees (indicators of a famine's severity as measured by Chinese governments for centuries). In other places starving families dug grass and roots from the earth to make their only meal of the day. Water was so scarce that it was almost never used for bathing—locals joked that they bathed only three times: when they were born, when they married, and when they died.

Tanxu's mission was to teach these people that the Buddha's path could help them transcend the suffering of this world. While relief workers provided food to keep the body alive, Tanxu preached that the physical world was not the ultimate reality. The eightfold path offered a way to eradicate hunger and thirst forever and completely.

Tanxu had competition. The local monks, like many throughout China, practiced a blend of Buddhism, Daoism, and folk religion. To alleviate the suffering of the people, they had focused on developing supernatural and superhuman powers, chants and incantations for the endurance of cold, hunger, and other types of deprivation. They did not object to Tanxu's preaching sutras, but felt that he was unnecessarily limiting the scope of their activities.

For his part, Tanxu saw these "heterodox beliefs" as distractions that held the people back from attaining enlightenment. He dismissed the monks' "magical" techniques. Far from being spiritual, he saw them as mere physical tricks: the camel can live for days without water, yet this does not make it magical. It is good for people to learn to endure hardship, but it was deceitful to claim it was magic. Perhaps you could learn to go seven days without food, but would you not then have to resume eating? It was not magic; it was bound by the rules of the physical world. More important, no matter how one managed in a particular physical environment, this world can never lead to a good end. The only way to achieve enlightenment was to transcend the material world through meditation and practice, following the path of the Buddha. Learning tricks to survive a cold winter's day without a coat was just a waste of time.

Tanxu continued this struggle for half a year. Near the end of this period, a former classmate arrived in the town to visit him. This old friend was now the manager of a watch shop. Watches and timepieces were recent arrivals in China, having come into general use only in the late nineteenth and early twentieth centuries. By the time Tanxu arrived in Jingxing, wristwatches were, according to historian Frank Dikötter, "the ultimate object of desire." Dikötter notes that watches were widespread throughout China at this time, particularly among the wealthy, who favored imported models. By 1930, less expensive Chinese-made watches were available to at least some workers, even in smaller inland cities. In Beijing—the nearest large city to Jingxing—there were more than a hundred watch sellers. Tanxu's friend appears to have been one of them.[2]

On the face of it, the two men inhabited very different worlds: one sold instruments of advanced technology that offered a framework for organizing life in the physical world; the other denied the physical world altogether. The watches were probably of foreign design, and the watch shop would have been part of a long process of purchasing, importing, and retailing the timepieces. Tanxu, on the other hand, rejected the notion of time itself as part of the material world that wrapped us in such deception and suffering. Yet, despite these differences, the two men were both committed to China's future. Their conversation illuminates Tanxu's views on nationalism and his role in it. His friend dismissed Tanxu's lifestyle as unpatriotic: "You monks! Nothing you say is of the least use. You consume, yet you don't support national products. If we all became monks, what kind of world would be left?" Tanxu defended himself, "If we all opened watch stores, then what kind of world would we have?" The debate went on:

> "People who live in the world—do they not have need of watches?"
> "The world has need of all sorts of people: monks, professors, laborers, steelworkers, . . ."
> "We need professions that contribute to the good of the nation. What contribution do monks make? It is not that I am saying it is bad to become a monk. It is just that since monks sit and eat [and] do not work, they are depleting the national resources— and this leads to slander from people who do not understand Buddhism."
> "To spread the dharma and improve society . . . this is the work of the monk! If everyone would become a monk, the war and suffering of the world would end. My only fear is that everyone not become a monk!"[3]

In Tanxu's vision, the Buddha and all those who followed his path constituted an axle around which China, and the world, turned. The monk provided support and stability to the system. To the watch-seller, Tanxu presented the monks' role in society as an arbor: the central axle around which the gears and mechanisms of the watch rotated. All of the expense and energy that went into designing and assembling the watch would be wasted without this fundamental stability at its core. The analogy moved naturally to a wheeled vehicle—without an axle, it could not move forward. This analogy applied neatly to Buddhism. Chinese Buddhists belonged to the Mahayana school—the "greater vehicle" which differentiated itself from earlier schools by emphasizing the role of bodhisattvas, beings who would work to ensure the enlightenment of all sentient beings in the universe before achieving nirvana for themselves. Whether in the vehicle of the nation or the vehicle of humanity Tanxu believed that he, as a monk, played an essential role. Did he see himself as first a servant to the nation or to humanity? It is hard to say. It appears that he saw these roles as compatible. The same teachings that would serve China would serve all of humanity. Yet he explicitly states that China's national prosperity—in physical *and* spiritual terms—depended on a community of monks at its core, stabilizing and supporting the rest of China. In the next phase of Tanxu's career, he would take on increasingly public roles, attain the title of master, and exert an influence on culture, society, and politics in many Chinese cities.

CHAPTER 5

Conditioned Arising

For a Buddhist, each human action, through the karma it generates, brings us closer to, or further from, enlightenment. The idea of karma entails that the decisions, choices, and actions of the individual determine what choices are subsequently available. Our actions create the future, or at least limit the range of futures that might come to pass. Though he would have rejected the religious underpinnings of karma, Karl Marx seemed to endorse a similar idea when he wrote, "Men make their own history, but they do not make it as they please; they do not make it under self-selected circumstances, but under circumstances existing already, given and transmitted from the past."[1]

When Tanxu returned to Beijing from Jingxing County, his opportunities sat—like the strange juxtaposition of Marx and Buddhism—at the intersection of politics and religion. These forces had long been in tension in China. In 1898, the Guangxu emperor had called for the conversion of many Buddhist and Daoist temples into schools as part of a program to modernize China's educational system. The destruction of temples would serve two agendas implicit in Guangxu's edict and espoused by intellectuals like Kang Youwei. It would provide buildings for the new schools, but it would also help reduce the influence of religion at a time when it was considered antithetical to modernization. Religion was presumed to be conservative and anti-modern, at odds with the progressive reform movements that hoped to bring about national renewal.[2]

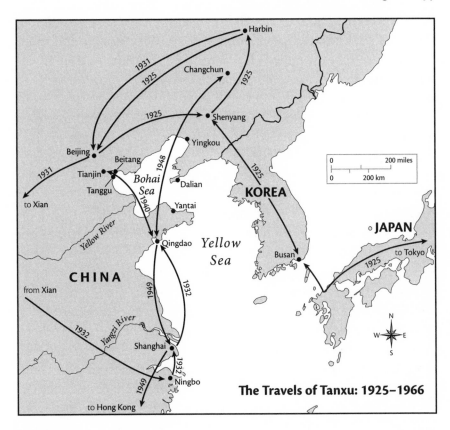

The Travels of Tanxu: 1925–1966

Though delayed by the conservative backlash in the Qing court that brought down the emperor himself, within a few years the movement to convert temples to schools took root throughout the country. Soon, the government was seizing temples throughout China, though the seizures varied depending on the disposition and strength of local civil and religious leaders. The fall of the Qing dynasty in 1911—the end of imperial China—left a complex and challenging environment for religions. The new republic had a vague commitment to modernize China, and rejected many religious or supernatural concepts like the Mandate of Heaven and did not patronize the state cults as emperors had for centuries. Buddhism, which had a sometimes-tense relationship with the state, was simultaneously freed by the removal of state orthodoxy (with which it was often at odds) and burdened by the possibility that modernity might not have room for religion of any kind.

As different visions of the Chinese nation competed throughout the 1910s and into the 1920s, advocates of more secular and modernizing approaches came to dominate the government, strengthening the anti-clerical movement that included the temples-to-schools policy. China was implementing a new educational system; Buddhist and Daoist temples (many of which were sparsely enrolled and short of funds) appeared contrary to the image the government wished to project. For a state seeking both to find space for modern schools and to diminish the profile of religious institutions, temples were tempting targets.

China, though, remained fragmented, and the temples-to-schools policy was not uniformly implemented. The decline of Buddhism during the nineteenth century left many temples empty or underutilized, and these were the first to be confiscated. When the government targeted more prosperous temples for conversion, controversy arose, and the results were uneven. In some places, powerful temple patrons blocked seizure altogether, while in others, zealous reformers evicted monks and gutted monasteries. Some temples chose to introduce schools themselves. Such schools could retain a religious element, as long as certain standards of curriculum and assessment were met (and these, too, varied greatly from place to place). To save themselves from dissolution, many temples quickly opened their own schools.

Once again Tanxu's status as a northerner made him valuable, and many temples invited him to lecture to attract students for new schools. His first invitation was to the Longevity Temple (Wanshousi) in Shenyang. In 1894, Tanxu (then Wang Futing) had passed some of his happiest days in this same city, working in his relatives' shop and discussing important events over picnics with his cousins. That summer had ended with the outbreak of war with Japan, and Tanxu had fled, beginning the series of journeys that brought him, ten years and three wars later, to Yingkou, where he began his study of Buddhism. The journey to Shenyang required Tanxu to pass through Yingkou once again.

During his previous visit to Yingkou, when he had re-encountered his wife, Tanxu had dismissed suggestions to establish a temple there. The small handful of lay Buddhists in Yingkou had neither the financial resources nor the social connections to take on such an ambitious project. When he returned in 1921, Tanxu found that the intervening years had done nothing to dampen their enthusiasm. Over lunch, they talked of the day when their new monastery would be complete. Tanxu again tried to dissuade them: "If you want to build a small temple for meditation, perhaps we can do that, but a large monastery is too difficult."

Lu Bingnan, the most determined among the group, argued that there was no doubt they would succeed, particularly with Tanxu spearheading the campaign, because they were all committed to the cause. Tanxu, though, continued to dismiss the idea: these five friends had no idea what they were getting into. Furthermore, they seemed to believe that Tanxu would live at the monastery they were planning to erect. He would not commit to this. He was devoted to traveling and spreading the dharma: this was the reason he had become a monk, and why he had left Guanzong Temple against his master's wishes. Nevertheless, the topic would not go away. Tanxu recalled their conversation:

> After lunch, discussion turned once more to this idea of founding a temple, but the children playing made too much commotion, and we couldn't talk easily. I thought that this might enable us to forget the topic, but instead, Lu Bingnan took us to the back of the Lecture Hall, and pointed out a parcel of land, one or two acres:
> "Master! Look at this piece of land. It is level and well situated, it is not far from the Lecture Hall."
> I looked at the piece of land very carefully, and pressed my palms together to indicate that it was a very good place. I saw that there was a vegetable garden on the land, and asked Lu Bingnan to whom it belonged. When he replied that he didn't know, my frustrations returned. I said, "You all have a vain hope. First of all, you don't have any money. You don't know who owns the land, yet you just intend to build a temple in the middle of someone's field. This is just a dream!"
> But no matter what else I would say, it was clear that they intended to build a temple. Wang Zhiyi right away got a blank scroll. On it, he drew a map of the temple they planned. He gave it to me as an invitation.

The situation then took an unlikely turn. Just as I was beginning to think about building this temple, Zhao Zhenhou arrived at the Lecture Hall to look around, and he spotted the drawing, and asked what it depicted.

Lu Bingnan replied, "We are planning to build a temple, on the piece of land behind the Lecture Hall." He added that they did not, however, know who owned the land.

Zhao laughed. "You really are dreaming, planning to build a temple and you don't even know who owns the land! But, you may be in luck: I know whose land this is! It is a Japanese named Tanabe. He had been the Japanese consul, and bought this land to build a home. Later, Tanabe was recalled to Japan and sold the land to the Tanaka Company for 20,000 yuan. They have been trying to sell the land to me for three years, but they are asking too high a price. I can see, though, that this land would be good for constructing a temple. I will go and see if they will lower their price."

Zhao Zhenhou went to talk to the Tanaka Company, and discussed the possibility of building a temple on the land. Because Tanaka was Japanese, he believed very deeply in Buddhism, and was delighted that the land be used for constructing a temple. He wired Tanabe, who was also delighted at the prospect. They agreed to reduce the price from 20,000 yuan to 15,000 yuan if it were to be used for constructing a temple. They required 6,000 yuan up-front. We all began to raise money right away, but even with all that had transpired, I knew that much work remained to be done. "It seems that your dream has begun to run wild," I said. "We still don't know how much money it will take to build this temple, but even to get the 6,000 yuan that you need now, you will need to begin turning rocks into gold!"

Mr. Zhao knew that these men had no wherewithal, but he did not discourage them, but instead told them not to worry about the money, that the Buddhas and bodhisattvas would help them.[3]

The next morning at daybreak, Lu Bingnan burst into Tanxu's room, laughing uncontrollably. Eventually, he managed explain that the previous night he had dreamed that a man had arrived at the Lecture Hall, waving a banner. The man asked for help planting the flag in the field behind the Lecture Hall. Lu helped him do this, and then woke up. As he related the dream to Tanxu, he identified the man with the banner as Jiang Yi'an.

Lu continued to smile excitedly, but Tanxu was confused and asked to know the meaning of this dream. Most importantly, who was Jiang Yi'an?

Jiang Yi'an was a wealthy industrialist from Shandong. He owned factories throughout northeast China, and put much of his profit into philanthropy. Traveling back and forth between Manchuria and his home in Shandong, he frequently passed through Yingkou and visited the Lecture Hall. He had told the five friends that he could be counted on to support philanthropic projects that might arise. Lu felt sure that he would support the construction of a temple; sponsoring a temple would promote virtue and also accrue good karma for the sponsor.

When Lu shared his dream with the others, everyone agreed that Jiang Yi'an was just the kind of supporter they needed. They made plans to write to Jiang at his factory in Harbin. As Lu Bingnan was dreaming of his role in founding the new temple, however, Jiang was not in Harbin, but in Yingkou, waiting to catch a train on his return from visiting family in Shandong Province. His plan was to spend just a few hours in Yingkou, but a problem with the tracks forced him to stay there for a few days. So, improbably, just as plans to find Jiang were developing, he actually arrived at the Lecture Hall. Lu Bingnan and the other men were stunned to see him— they had not even written yet, and already he had come to answer their prayers! Jiang Yi'an saw them all laughing and smiling and, realizing something was up, asked why everyone was so giddy. They sat down at a table, and explained to him their plan to erect a new temple.

First they talked about politics. For the most part, though, they spoke informally about the purchase of this land for the temple. Jiang said that he had done well that year, making more than 30,000 yuan in profit. Much of this he had reinvested, and he had also financed his brother in a business venture, but he still had 10,000 yuan or more that was not spoken for.

This seemed to fit perfectly into Lu Bingnan's hope that Jiang would contribute money for the purchase of the land, but he was embarrassed to ask directly. He continued to circle around the topic, Finally, he pointed to the land behind the Lecture Hall: "You see this piece of land?" he asked. "It is so flat it appears that it has been smoothed by hand. It belongs to the Japanese, but they are prepared to sell it, very cheap."

"How much money do they want?"

"Very inexpensive! The fair price is 12,000 yuan, but since the owner is a very devout Buddhist, and he knows that we want the land to build a temple, he is willing to sell it to us for just 6,000 yuan. Right now, we are trying to buy it, but we simply do not have this much money"

"OK, then: Buy it! I have the money. I am returning to Harbin tonight by train. After you have agreed on the terms to buy the land, send me a telegram telling me the amount and I will wire you the money."

Jiang left. The sale was negotiated, and Tanaka even agreed to contribute to the construction of the temple with a gift of 500 yuan. The next day, Lu Bingnan and Tanxu sent a telegram to Jiang in Harbin, and that afternoon they received 6,000 yuan at the Western Union office in Yingkou.

The sale was completed once the owner of the adjoining parcel— an Englishman named Finnessey—was persuaded to accept the agreement. By Chinese law, neighboring landowners had a right of first refusal when land was sold out of the family, and Finnessey at first objected that he wanted to buy the land himself. Eventually, he was persuaded—perhaps bought off—and the land was obtained for building the Surangama Temple.[4]

For Tanxu, events like these demonstrated the importance of "conditioned arising." In the Buddhist conception of the universe, nothing exists independently. Objects, ideas, and phenomena of all kinds are only momentary convergences of factors, themselves constantly coming into and out of existence, depending on the conditioning events that surround them. Because we are ourselves part of this network of causes, our perception itself is always dependent. Abstractly, we create the universe around us—although the universe is not created by ourselves alone. In practical terms, this idea suggests that every act depends upon a set of circumstances that make it possible.

Tanxu claimed that his own career founding temples and schools and preaching the dharma was successful, not because of his own skill or hard work, but because of conditioned arising. The temple project in Yingkou demonstrated this. Conditions arose, permitting certain events and processes to come into being. These included the attributes that he brought with him, as well as the attributes that enabled *those* attributes to come into being. In this way, every event in the universe is a product—and a cause—of every other event in the universe.

The Buddhist principle of "expedient means" helps explain Tanxu's career as well. At first glance, it seems contradictory that he would invest so much time and energy on physical institutions. Tanxu used architectural forms and specific locations to make spiritual and political points. According to the sutras, these kinds of material gestures are ultimately empty: the material world is but an illusion, as is our physical self. However, for practical purposes, it is important to provide incentives that will lead people along the way to enlightenment, providing short-term rewards or encouragement. Just as in the parables of the Phantom City or the Burning House, about which Dixian had lectured in Beijing, it is sometimes more important to satisfy temporary needs than to be completely honest or consistent about the nature of reality. A temple in Yingkou, where people could study and meditate, would be such an incentive.

The land for the Surangama Temple had been purchased, but the temple's future was far from assured. The idea to build the temple had arisen quite suddenly, and the opportunity to acquire the land for it had followed with even greater speed. No fundraising or other development work had been undertaken. Building the temple would cost much more than the price of the land, and all the obstacles that Tanxu had foreseen still stood in the way.

A few days after the land had been purchased, Tanxu resumed his journey north to Shenyang to take up a position as head lecturer at the Longevity Temple school. Tanxu met an old friend in Shenyang, He Yutang, a manager for the British-American Tobacco Company, the largest tobacco company in China. He introduced Tanxu to his boss, Lü Fuchen. Like Jiang Yi'an, Lü was from

Shandong and had businesses throughout the northeast. And he was a devout Buddhist. Lü and Tanxu talked over a meal, and it emerged that Lü had no male heir and was looking for worthy causes to support. The new temple in Yingkou was ideal, and Lu agreed to give 50,000 yuan over the course of several years, provided his business continued to go well.

The project still faced many challenges. The men in Yingkou had three main goals. First, they wanted a place where they could continue and advance their own studies of the Surangama Sutra, which they had been studying for many years. Second, they wanted to commemorate Tanxu, and celebrate a man from Yingkou who had gone on to become an eminent monk. Third, they hoped to found a monastery, so that they could themselves follow Tanxu's path and become monks.

Tanxu worried about these motives. He believed that one should never become a monk for any reason other than commitment to the Buddha's path. Pledging to do so for money—even money that would construct a temple—violated that principle. Furthermore, using the temple to celebrate his own career was troublesome, especially in Yingkou. Although he was the most prominent monk to have come from the region, many did not consider him truly local, since Yingkou was neither his birthplace nor his ancestral home. Also, the circumstances in which he had left his wife and children were controversial. Some felt that he betrayed his family by deserting them. Others felt that he had shown a lack of integrity in lying about his departure. (Tanxu himself was sensitive about how he had misrepresented himself both to his wife and to Master Dixian.) Furthermore, Tanxu's departure had confirmed for many in the city their view of monks as untrustworthy. With a monastery in the town, how many other men might be lured to abandon their families in the same way?

For all these reasons—as well as his desire to move around to spread the dharma—Tanxu insisted that another monk be found to oversee the temple-construction campaign. He offered the position to Chanding, his partner in collecting and publishing sutras, who turned down the position on account of his age, fearing that he would not live to see the project completed. Unable to think of a replacement, Tanxu urged him to reconsider. The two men went together to Shenyang to begin collecting the money from Lü Fuchen. Tanxu may have hoped that Lü's enthusiasm for the project would rub off on Chanding and persuade him to take on the responsibility. Instead, they found that Lü's businesses had faltered: three of his enterprises had failed completely and he had lost tens of thousands of yuan: he could no longer contribute to the project.

Tanxu was depressed by the loss of this enormous gift. Together, he and Chanding worked their connections in Shenyang to find other donors, but raised only 2,000 yuan. It was just a fraction of the original promise but it enabled them to keep the momentum going. They were introduced to the manager of a lumberyard near Yingkou, who donated wood to build the temple. Construction began soon after the Spring Festival in 1922. Within a few months, money ran out and construction was halted, but another donor (Pang Mutang, a businessman from Dalian) was found, and his gift of more than 10,000 yuan assured the project's success. The Great Pavilion began to rise from the field behind the Lecture Hall.[5]

With the Yingkou temple underway, Tanxu continued on to Shenyang, where he devoted himself to his role as the head lecturer at the Longevity Temple school. The school had opened in the spring of 1921, and Tanxu began his lectures shortly thereafter. The school was popular, attracting students from throughout the region. Tanxu's lectures—on the Surangama, Heart, Lotus, and Diamond Sutras—were well attended. Local companies asked him to lecture for their employees, and groups of lay Buddhists asked for help with their studies. He gained a reputation as an important and effective monk, spreading the dharma and working to revive Buddhism in the region. From Shenyang, Tanxu traveled across Manchuria, lecturing in cities from Haicheng and Yingkou in the south, to northern cities like Changchun, Suihua, and Harbin.

Up to this point, in 1922, Tanxu had arrived in Yingkou three times. The first was as a refugee, fleeing war between Japan and Russia. The city had given him the opportunity to develop his business as a fortune-teller, and provided the space to explore his political and spiritual identity. The second time, he arrived in the city as a monk making his first trip into the world after his time in the monastery in Ningbo. He re-encountered his wife and attempted to explain (and perhaps to understand) the ethics and consequences of his decision to become a monk. This third time, Tanxu came to Yingkou as an established monk—not yet a master—and used his influence and position to found a temple in his adopted hometown. He left Yingkou as a cultural patriot, sought out by local and regional political leaders for his ability to use Buddhism to promote and strengthen the Chinese nation. This would be his identity during the most active phase of his career.

CHAPTER 6

Ice and Fire

The symbol of Harbin today is an onion-domed Russian Orthodox church, St. Sofia. Featured on promotional literature,
websites, and even the logo of the city's television station, the image
of the church evokes the city's roots as a Russian colony, built by the
Tsar's government in the 1890s as it pushed a railroad across
Manchuria to its new port on the Pacific, Vladivostok. The Church
of St. Sofia was actually built during the 1930s, when Harbin was
under Japanese control, in an attempt by the Russian community to
define and retain its identity. This makes the church an even more
appropriate symbol not just of the city, but for all of Manchuria in
that it lies at the crossroads of three of the modern world's great
empires: China, Russia, and Japan.

Today, St. Sofia is no longer a church, but a museum to Harbin's
Russian past, housing historical photos, including some showing
half-a-dozen Christian churches that were destroyed in the Cultural
Revolution of the 1960s. St. Sofia is also a mandatory backdrop for
local couples' wedding portraits. Once night falls, floodlights illuminate the building, making it an even more prominent landmark.
Between St. Sofia and the Sungari River lies Harbin's European
quarter, remarkably intact after a century of upheaval. Cobblestone
streets and art nouveau storefronts have been newly restored, giving
the city a walkable downtown with a European feel.

Harbin's tourist board promotes this architectural legacy, along
with other remnants of Harbin's colonial past, including a Jewish
cemetery and a riverside promenade. Today regarded as tourist
attractions, these non-Chinese elements were formerly seen as

threats to the city's Chinese identity. As recently as the 1990s, St. Sofia was derelict and almost impossible to find down a warren of tiny alleys. The Russian cemetery was removed and made into a fairground, with the grave markers broken up and used as path stones. The suggestion that Harbin was a Russian city with nineteenth-century roots was "refuted" with evidence from archeological digs showing the existence of an ancient settlement within the current city limits. Never mind that these ruins were not Chinese— they were created by the Jurchens, a Northeast Asian people whose Jin dynasty overran much of what is now northern China in the twelfth century—they were sufficiently non-European for the purpose.

Tanxu first visited Harbin in the early 1920s, fundraising for his temple projects in Yingkou, Changchun, and Shenyang and working to promote Buddhism in China's northernmost major city. The city he found combined foreign and Chinese elements, but with respect to Buddhism, there was little to satisfy him:

> Harbin is in China's Northeast, lying on the South bank of the Sungari River. Originally it was a remote and desolate village, but with the completion of the Chinese Eastern Railway it became a commercial port, and grew more prosperous with each day. In the world of business Chinese and foreign elements mixed freely. At the beginning of the Republican era, other religions flourished, but regretfully, even though Harbin was a Chinese place, there was absolutely no Chinese Buddhism, not a single decent temple.[1]

The battle for Harbin's identity heated up in the 1920s, just as Tanxu's career in Manchuria was prospering. Although largely Chinese in population, Harbin had been administered by Russians from the time of its founding in the 1890s until the Russian Revolution of 1917. The Republic of China did not recognize the Bolshevik government, and all Russian rights in the city were reclaimed by China. Over the next decade the new Chinese rulers set about remaking Harbin in their own image.[2]

Chen Feiqing, a lay Buddhist from Jiangsu, played a crucial role in this project. Chen was appointed to the city government in 1921 as head of the railroad customs bureau. Because Harbin was largely funded by income from the railway, this was a powerful position, especially now that control of the railroad was up for grabs because of the fluid situation surrounding the Russian government. Contractually, the railroad was a joint Chinese-Russian operation, but for most of its existence the Russians had actually run it. With the downfall of the tsar's government, the Russian side of the partnership was in disarray and China became the dominant partner. Ambitious Chinese officials used the opportunity to pursue their vision of what Harbin should be. For Chen Feiqing, this meant—among other initiatives—constructing Buddhist and Confucian temples to challenge the Orthodox, Catholic, and Protestant churches, and also synagogues, that lined Harbin's boulevards.

Throughout China, and especially in intellectual circles, religion of all sorts—particularly Buddhism and Daoism—was under assault as anti-modern "superstition." When the Nationalist Party unified the country in the late 1920s, it engaged in a systematic (although only marginally successful) campaign to eliminate "superstition" in the form of temple festivals from the center of Chinese cultural life.[3] In Harbin, however, the dynamic was different. Contestation over what it meant to be Chinese was less crucial than a clear assertion of Chinese identity to stand in contrast to the Russian and European buildings that dominated the city. Approval for the construction of the temples was granted, and Chen Feiqing was looking for a monk to spearhead the project.

Ma Jiping, a government minister in Beijing, had heard Tanxu lecture in Jingxing County a few years earlier and recommended him for the task. Ma wrote inviting Tanxu to discuss establishing a temple in Harbin, and Chen delivered the letter to Longevity Temple in Shenyang. In the first week of February 1922, with nighttime temperatures falling to −40 degrees, Tanxu traveled to Harbin to lecture on sutras and meet with Chen Feiqing and other local leaders.

Tanxu welcomed the chance to found a temple in Harbin. Dixian, Tanxu's master, had long emphasized the importance of reviving Buddhism in North China, and this desire also motivated Tanxu, who had spent most of his life there. The lack of Buddhist facilities in the north had frustrated him as a younger man trying to learn about the sutras, eventually driving him south to study. More northern monks were needed if Buddhism were to thrive here, and monasteries and temples had to be built. Harbin, one of the largest and most important cities in Manchuria, was a perfect location. Furthermore, the struggle over Harbin's political and cultural identity resonated with Tanxu's own observation of China's place in the world. Like Manchuria in general, Harbin was a crossroads for many nationalities: Chinese, Russians, and Japanese, but also Americans and other Europeans. Tanxu had seen the conflicts among these nations since childhood, always seeing China on the losing end. The new temple—to be named Paradise Temple (Jilesi)— would be not just a religious edifice, but a marker of the Chinese identity Harbin's new rulers were promoting.

For the greatest symbolic effect, the temple needed a highly visible location, where foreigners as well as Chinese would see it and understand its message. At the first meeting about the temple, in February 1922, it was decided to purchase land with government money (from the railroad ministry), at a location chosen for maximum impact. Harbin's original Russian layout was in the form of a cross. At the intersection of the two axes was the ornate, wooden Cathedral of Saint Nicholas, constructed in 1898. (This church was the most visible casualty of the Cultural Revolution in Harbin, burning to the ground in 1966.) At the base of the cross were the city's foreign cemeteries, primarily Orthodox Christian and Jewish. A wide avenue, Bolshoi Prospekt, connected the cathedral with the graveyards, past most of the city's other important churches, including Catholic, Protestant and Orthodox sites that remain active today.

Paradise Temple was to be built on Bolshoi Prospekt, just outside the entrance to the cemeteries, its pagodas and pavilions literally overshadowing the paths of mourners and celebrants traveling between the churches and the graveyards. Scholars may debate to what extent Buddhism can be considered Chinese, but Russian mourners passing by the bright yellow temple walls with their large Chinese inscriptions understood that they were not in Russia. The new temple was part of a broader campaign to mark public spaces with Chinese architecture, including a school that opened opposite the main entrance to the train station and a Confucian temple across from the Paradise Temple, also near the entrance to the European cemetery.

While the builders of Paradise Temple worked to promote their vision of Chinese identity, China itself remained contested. Shortly after the decision to build the temple was made, war broke out between two rival warlord cliques. The outcome of the war changed the power dynamics in the government. Song Xiaolian, the superintendent of the railroad (effectively the mayor of Harbin) lost his post and was replaced by Wang Jingchun—a Christian. Wang was unhappy with the decision to use government money to construct a Buddhist temple and attempted to rescind the approvals. The project was delayed for more than a year as Chen and Tanxu tried to persuade Wang to release the promised funds.

While Harbin bureaucrats wrangled over the fate of Paradise Temple, Tanxu returned to Shenyang to complete his commitment to the temple school there. While in Shenyang, Tanxu undertook another project, the revival of a long-dormant temple. The impetus for this project came from a local lay Buddhist, Wang Langchuan, who was politically well connected. After attending Tanxu's lectures as the Longevity Temple, Wang sought a place where he could deepen his understanding of the sutras. The Expansive Wisdom Temple (Boruosi) in Shenyang had been founded in the seventeenth century, but had fallen into disrepair over the years. Wang decided to renovate and expand it. He persuaded Tanxu to oversee the project and used his political connections to secure contributions from many local officials and politicians, including the governor of Fengtian Province. Tanxu was not actively involved in daily activities at this temple, but his name conferred legitimacy, and he continued to lecture there whenever he was in Shenyang, until the Japanese invasion of 1931.[4]

The situation in Harbin did not change until the arrival of General Zhu Qinglan as regional administrator and head of the local militia. Zhu was from Zhejiang Province, in the Yangzi Delta (where Tanxu had studied in Ningbo) and had made a successful career in business and politics, holding numerous regional and provincial offices. He arrived in Harbin without any particular religious conviction. In fact, in previous postings he had advocated destroying temples in order to advance his own political agenda. In Harbin, however, Chen Feiqing persuaded him of the value of Paradise Temple and also of establishing a Buddhist Association. Zhu and Chen moved quickly, encouraging men in the government to join the Buddhist Association. Eager to overcome Wang Jingchun's resistance and move the project forward, Zhu arranged a meeting between Wang and other members of the government. Tanxu came as well, at Zhu's special invitation.

In previous meetings, Wang Jingchun had dismissed Tanxu as a heathen, telling him that he was fundamentally opposed to Buddhism and saw monks as repugnant. This time, with Zhu Qinglan standing nearby, Wang permitted the monk to speak. Tanxu explained the general principles of Buddhism, and emphasized that the path of the Buddha is connected not only to Buddhists, per se, but to all of society. The entire nation depended on the social welfare and individual enlightenment that Buddhism promoted. Constructing the temple would benefit not only Buddhism, but all Chinese.

Wang was unimpressed. "Master," he replied, "I have heard everything you are saying, but constructing a temple is for the benefit of those who practice that religion: it seems to me that building a City-God temple would be more useful than constructing a Buddhist temple!" A City-God Temple would be open to all Chinese: "Look inside the ordinary City-God temples. You see a mountain of swords and a forest of spears. Above the doorway are inscribed the characters 'You can enter!' This is understandable to the common people. Yet, what you say not even understandable to me! To use our money in this way is not effective."

This argument sheds light on the nature of religion and civil society in twentieth-century China. As a Christian, Wang rejected the idea of a Buddhist temple on both religious and secular grounds. Buddhism was a rival religion, not a secular cult that could be used to promote the nation-state. Further, Wang rejected the idea that the Chinese nation was, or should be, Buddhist: his idea of China was Christian. Christianity claimed millions of followers in China, and the idea of a Christian China was a real—if ambitious—goal for many of them.[5] This added yet another element that resisted the promotion of Buddhism: the traditional state cult, which had fallen in 1911, viewed Buddhism with suspicion, as a potentially heterodox and subversive rival; many modernizers rejected the idea of religion altogether (Protestant Christianity, as the accompaniment to Western imperialism, was a possible exception); and Chinese Christians, adhering to the first and second commandments, refused to countenance other gods or idols.

Wang continued to withhold the balance of the money promised from his office, but other members of the government pledged their support. By the end of the evening, 25,000 yuan had been raised, almost the full amount required. From this point on, General Zhu became one of Tanxu's most important patrons. In addition to his help developing the temple in Harbin, Zhu also wrote dozens of letters of introduction for help with the Surangama Temple in Yingkou.

In exchange for his support, Zhu Qinglan insisted that Tanxu take on the leadership of the Paradise Temple. Tanxu accepted. As soon as he had fulfilled his three years' commitment in Shenyang, he devoted himself to constructing the temple in Harbin and also to overseeing a school. Tanxu believed that Harbin, with its flourishing economy and rapidly growing population, presented great opportunities. However, the spiritual needs of the region's Chinese population were underserved, Tanxu believed, especially among the more conservative elements.

> At this time, throughout the country there was an interest in promoting things that were new, and promoting revolution: national revolution and revolution in the family. The common old-fashioned people did not approve. The people with money and food did not want to send their sons to these new schools. When they heard that Paradise Temple was offering an education in virtue, most of them were delighted to enroll.[6]

Together with Zhang Leting, a local educator, Tanxu founded a school that would provide a traditional education, based on the Confucian and secular classics as well as Buddhism. They quickly recruited twenty students. Zhang Leting lectured on Confucian classics and Chinese literature, while Tanxu lectured on the Surangama Sutra. Once the temple was complete, the school would move into the temple grounds.

Tanxu's experience in Harbin highlights a significant, yet often neglected, segment of the Chinese population during this era. Tanxu and his associates saw themselves as nationalists, whose goal was to promote and strengthen the country. China would be weaker and less competitive without the educational and moral foundation their school would provide. This was a common sentiment in China at this time. However, studies of this period typically focus on more radical groups, keen on revolution "in the nation and the family," as Tanxu put it. These included the two dominant political parties of twentieth-century China, the Nationalist (Guomindang) Party and the Communist Party. They diverged on many issues and became mortal enemies, but both of these parties wanted to modernize China and move it away from its traditional past. Neither was favorably disposed toward Buddhism: the Nationalists pushed hard to promote modern ideas, working to eliminate superstition and "backward" cults (and many of their top officials were Christians).[7] The Communists opposed religion of every kind, with a vehemence that ranged from disdain to violence (reaching a climax during the Cultural Revolution of the 1960s).

Opponents of these two groups are often characterized, casually, as reacting to the turmoil of the twentieth century by putting their heads in the sand, falling back on tradition and ignoring the impending crises. This was not the case for Tanxu: he had experienced the Boxers and felt that their violent anti-foreignism was dangerous and foolish. He respected the technical skill of the foreigners he had seen on the battlefields and in the shipyards of northeast China. However, he did not attribute Western success to technological innovations. Instead, he believed that foreigners had succeeded primarily because of a stable, united society and a strong spiritual foundation. A reassertion of China's traditional culture—for Tanxu, grounded in Buddhism—would enable the nation to succeed both at home and abroad.

Tanxu's reputation as a temple-builder led to more opportunities. Around the same time that he had started work in Harbin, the governor of Jilin Province, based in Changchun, invited Tanxu to that city to lecture on the sutras. The interplay of forces in Changchun echoed the situation in Harbin: Tanxu enjoyed official patronage, including support from the military leadership, but he again faced religious resistance to his program. In Changchun, the resistance came from Daoists. As in Jingxing County, local Daoists utilized Buddhist scriptures in their practice, but focused on supernatural powers that could be conjured by invoking various spirits, bodhisattvas, and Buddhas. Several of these Daoists attended Tanxu's lectures on the Surangama Sutra. Afterward they reported back to their master, who dismissed Tanxu as lacking insight into the true, deeper meaning of the sutra. It was in this deeper level that the sutra's magical properties were to be found, and only the Daoist practices could unlock these secrets.

A contest ensued between the two clerics. After Tanxu lectured, the Daoist master challenged his interpretations and spoke to the audience about how the Surangama Sutra was employed in Daoist practice. The result of the evening—according to Tanxu—was that a handful of important officials declared that they would be followers of the Buddha, and this led many in the audience to do likewise. Whatever the reasons, the civil administrator of the city and the governor-general of Jilin Province organized a campaign to found a Buddhist temple in Changchun.

Initially, as in Harbin and Shenyang, the funding for the temple, to be named (like the temple in Shenyang) Expansive Wisdom Temple (Boruosi), drew on both official and public support. Many of the most prominent men in Changchun, including the governor-general and local magistrate, as well as the head of the local chamber of commerce and other military and civilian officials, gave money, but most of them donated as private citizens, in some cases giving tremendous sums. The magistrate of the county gave more than 10,000 yuan. The government, per se, did not contribute, but most government officials did. Official bodies also made donations in kind to the temple—the provincial finance ministry provided trains to transport lumber harvested from the surrounding mountains for the construction. Because he was already committed to running Paradise Temple in Harbin, and because there was strong local leadership in Changchun, Tanxu did not feel the need to directly oversee most of the construction of the Expansive Wisdom Temple, though he visited often.

Back in Harbin, Tanxu faced growing opposition within the Buddhist community. Funding was a constant problem, and many members of the community advocated less-stringent enforcement of monastic regulations to enable other income streams, such as a tearoom at Paradise Temple, where Tanxu and other monks might give informal lectures on the sutras. Laymen and women might come and stay at the temple in order to educate themselves in some isolation from the outside world, without themselves becoming monks. This was unacceptable to Tanxu, who believed that the monastery was a place of meditation and practice for monks, who had taken vows to follow the Buddha's path. To compromise the standards or discipline within the monastery would dilute the power of the Buddha's teaching and encourage the government and society to see monasteries as refuges for the lazy and the fearful. Tanxu already knew that many people believed monks to be motivated by the desire to lead a comfortable life, free from the need to work or raise a family.

Alert to the perception that monks were lazy or dishonest, Tanxu took care to diligently oversee the construction of the temple. Applying his training as an accountant to audit the books, he found thousands of yuan worth of discrepancies. Tanxu pointed out the exact nature and extent of the mistakes, which suggested clearly who was benefiting from the errors. The subcontractors were accustomed to "gifts" or other forms of corruption to supplement their incomes. Tanxu alleged that one contractor was embezzling money from the temple to buy opium. Outraged at losing these payments and embarrassed at being called out by Tanxu, many of the managers involved in the construction began a campaign to discredit him and the dispute continued as the temple rose.

Despite conflicts and corruption, however, the temple was completed in the autumn of 1924. On the eve of the official opening on October 26, General Zhu came to the temple to see that all was in order. The arguing between the different factions continued, right to the end. Critics complained to the general that the temple's interior was plain and dull: guests would expect more statues and idols, and more impressive ornamentation. In fact, Tanxu had de-emphasized elaborate displays, and decoration had been kept to a minimum. In a compromise, dozens of bodhisattva statues were placed in the guest dormitory for the opening celebration.

The next morning, hundreds of men and women came to celebrate the temple's opening, including most of the important officials in the city government, eager to use the temple as a centerpiece of their program to promote Harbin's new, post-colonial identity. The three-story main pavilion glistened in the clear autumn air.

Among the worshippers and dignitaries offering incense, one man appeared exceptionally emotional. While others circulated, offering prayers and incense to various shrines and idols throughout the temple, this man—a laborer who had worked on the construction of the temple—remained focused on a statue of Sakyamuni, the historical Buddha, in the main pavilion. As the sun set, after most of the guests had left for the day, the man was heard sobbing. Agitated, Tanxu and another monk went to investigate. Struggling to speak through tears, the man explained that he was the Buddha's uncle, the father of Ananda. Tanxu was alarmed by the man's erratic behavior and eventually called the police. Unable to communicate with him, the police finally carried the man out of the temple.

Tanxu does not reflect further on this individual, whom he believed to be mad. But twenty years later he still remembered the incident well enough to include it his memoir. Why? This is interesting for several reasons. It speaks to Tanxu's fear of disorder that he would have such a person forcibly ejected from the temple. The episode may also have stuck in Tanxu's mind because the man had associated himself with the figure of Ananda, Sakyamuni's first cousin and one of the most complex figures in the early history of Buddhism.

Ananda was one of the Buddha's closest disciples and his personal attendant; he features in most of the sutras that record the Buddha's sermons, either as a main character in a dialogue or as the transmitter of the Buddha's words. He is notable for his humanity and his failings, which would have resonated with Tanxu, whose own life was dominated by strained attachments and complicated relationships. The scriptures record that the Buddha once observed to Ananda that a Buddha, if requested, could extend his life on earth by a thousand years. Three times (in one story as many as fifteen times) the Buddha repeated this statement, but Ananda was distracted and did not respond. Later, as the Buddha was approaching death, Ananda begged him not to go, but Sakyamuni replied that it was too late and scolded him for not asking him to stay when he had the opportunity. Ananda is thus held responsible for the end of the Buddha's ministry on earth, which might have gone on for another millennium.

Ananda always struggled to follow the Buddha's insistence that we detach ourselves from human relationships. One of the first lessons that any seeker must master on the path to enlightenment is to extinguish attachments. The decision to become a monk is not simply to separate physically from the comforts of friends and family, it is also to separate from the emotional support those attachments provide. As the monk struggles to separate from even his own sense of self, the attachment to others must be removed. It is perhaps the most fundamental and the most difficult task along the Buddha's path, for it is at war with the most basic of human instincts, present from the first moments of life: the instinct to bond emotionally and physically with others.

Even once Ananda achieved enlightenment, after the Buddha's death, he seems never to have truly embraced this separation. He mourned deeply at the death of his close friend Sariputra, another disciple of the Buddha. When the Buddha himself died, alone among his followers Ananda gave voice to his grief, inviting accusations that he had not achieved enlightenment and was not qualified to lead the Buddhist community (sangha) after Sakyamuni's death, despite being the closest thing to an heir that the Buddha had left behind. Dogged by such accusations, and by jealousy of his relationship with the Buddha, Ananda lived out the rest of his life a lonely man. He took up his position as the patriarch of the sangha and achieved nirvana, but his life on earth was shadowed by the loss of his friend, as he expressed in his poem "Ananda Alone":

> 1034. All the directions are obscure,
> The teachings are not clear to me;
> With our benevolent friend gone,
> It seems as if all is darkness.
>
> 1035. For one whose friend has passed away,
> One whose teacher is gone for good,
> There is no friend that can compare
> With mindfulness of the body.
>
> 1036. The old ones have all passed away;
> I do not fit in with the new.
> And so today I muse alone
> Like a bird who has gone to roost.[8]

Tanxu does not mention his emotional reaction to the troubled man or his story beyond his frustration that he prevented the temple from closing the front gate on time, but his inclusion of this incident demonstrates it stayed with Tanxu for many years. There are reasons to think that the evocation of the character and story of Ananda would have resonated with him, particularly at this time. Tanxu had insisted that another abbot be found for the Surangama Temple in Yingkou, because his own name there had been too damaged by the way he had abandoned his family. So evidently he was aware of the stigma attached to his choice. He was still traveling back and forth to Yingkou, where he could have seen his family regularly. Around this time, one of his sons came from Yingkou to Harbin, seeking to become a monk himself. For Tanxu, the attachments of family and the material world were never far away. Did he fear that, like Ananda, he was too human to completely free himself from these ties? Or, like the Buddha's other contemporaries, did he regard Ananda as weak, unable to expand his mind and continuing to see death as an end?

Whatever the case, Tanxu did not have a chance to contemplate these questions for long that evening, for as soon as the grounds had been cleared and the gate locked, shouts again disturbed the night. This time, fire had broken out, started by the electric lights strung for the celebration. The fire was quickly extinguished, but it brought out all of the principals of the temple construction to investigate. Some blamed Tanxu and the monks for negligence, while others felt it was supernatural punishment for malfeasance in building the temple. Tanxu noted that one of the workers—it was believed though not proven that it was the one who had been evicted earlier in the evening—had used electric lanterns to illuminate the idols and statues in his quarters, and that these had been left on and started the fire.

The damage was quickly repaired, but the fire had one lasting effect: General Zhu had apparently had enough of the project, and soon after the opening he resigned his position in Harbin and returned to Shenyang. Tanxu remained in Harbin another five years without his patron. Fundraising became even more important without the powerful general to ensure the temple's finances. The school continued to generate income, and, as for many Buddhist clergy, funeral services became an important means of making money. Tanxu remained worried about the temple's future, especially as he struggled to maintain the monastery according to traditional rules. Pressure mounted on Tanxu to pursue more entrepreneurial approaches. Although the temple had been built, most of the parties involved were unsatisfied: Tanxu was frustrated with the lack of monastic discipline; many members of the Buddhist Association were frustrated both by the temple's meager revenue and what they perceived to be an antipathy to laypeople.

Discouraged by the local situation, Tanxu spent most of the years from 1924 to 1928 away from Harbin. With General Zhu gone, he had no patrons to defend his position against laymen who had more personal and material ambitions for the temple. Still, Tanxu was the most prominent monk in the region, and his support for the project was essential. He could not easily be removed. So, with his position secure but uncomfortable, Tanxu traveled as much as possible, developing other projects and avoiding the stresses of Harbin.

Tanxu made two important journeys in 1925. The first was back to his home temple in Ningbo. He had not communicated with his former teacher Master Dixian since he had left—with permission for twenty days' leave—five years before. As monks traveled up and down the coast, Tanxu at first heard that Dixian was angry and disappointed at Tanxu's deception and desertion. With time, however, the news changed. Dixian's priority had always been the revival of Buddhism in North China. As he learned that Tanxu had successfully founded temples in Yingkou and then Harbin, his opinion of his former disciple improved. Dixian invited Tanxu back to Guanzong Temple so that he could formally ordain him as a master and forty-fourth-generation patriarch of the Tiantai sect, a lineage dating back to 575, when Zhiyi founded the sect at Tiantai Mountain in Zhejiang Province. Eager to receive Dixian's mantle, Tanxu hurried to Ningbo, where he accepted the transmission from his master. In just fifteen years, Tanxu had gone from a layman with no formal training to a master of one of China's most influential Buddhist sects.

Tanxu's other major journey in 1925 was to Japan. Befitting his influence in the northeast and also his new role within Tiantai, Tanxu was invited that summer to visit Japan as part of the first congress of the East Asian Buddhist Association. The meeting, to be held in Tokyo, was organized in part by Taixu, the most influential monk in China during this period. Taixu and Tanxu held quite different views about Buddhism in China. Taixu embraced reform, and the seminaries he founded had modern curricula, including foreign languages and Western mathematics. Those founded by Tanxu, on the other hand, focused narrowly on scriptural exegesis and Chinese literature. Their differences notwithstanding, Tanxu was one of twenty-one Chinese delegates invited to attend the congress in November 1925.[9]

Fearing seasickness, Tanxu did not set sail from Tianjin with the majority of the delegation. Instead, he and a companion went by train through Manchuria and then south down the Korean peninsula to Pusan. From there, a short sea voyage across the Straits of Shimonoseki took them to Japan. They joined the other Chinese monks at the Eastern Paradise Temple, in Kobe, for the train journey to Tokyo. Tanxu was eager to observe this new country, although the banalities of travel took their toll on the fifty-year-old monk:

> The Japanese railroad was very narrow, and the tracks were lined with rice paddies; there was not any unused land. I saw a few villages scattered among the fields, all very orderly, with wooden houses. On the whole route I did not see any horses or cattle—I don't know where they would raise them! From Kobe to Tokyo was an overnight train, and the train welcomed aboard some primary school students who kept us awake the whole night talking and singing—I did not sleep the whole way![10]

The monks were received elaborately in Tokyo. Limousines met them at the station and took them to the temple that was hosting them, and children and women (whom Tanxu believed to be the wives of Japanese monks) had made garlands of flowers for their guests. Tanxu was discomfited by this, but was persuaded to wear them so as not to give offense.

The conference fell short of its stated goals. Nearly all the members of the East Asian Buddhist Association were from China and Japan, undermining its claim to broad representation. Small delegations from Taiwan and Korea—both Japanese colonies at the time—also took part, but no one represented the vibrant Buddhist communities in Southeast Asia, including Vietnam, Thailand, and Burma. It was suggested that the name of the organization be changed to the Sino-Japanese Buddhist Association, but the organizers resisted: it was important for the congress to represent all of East Asia, and thereby demonstrate Japan's leadership role in the region.

Addressing the congress, however, Taixu criticized Japanese monks on several counts. They were, he said, too influenced by modern life—a telling accusation from a monk considered too modern many Buddhists in China. Unlike their counterparts in China, the Japanese were unable to withstand privation. They lacked the deep religious conviction and rigorous discipline of Chinese monks; as evidence of this he noted that many Japanese monks kept wives and ate meat. He criticized Japanese Buddhism for being too nationalistic (although Taixu himself was an aggressive Chinese patriot) and also too sectarian. Drawing on his observations on this trip, Taixu said that the Japanese sangha could not be a model for reviving Buddhism in China.[11] The criticism leveled at Japan was not limited to religious matters. One Chinese delegate excoriated the host country for professing to seek friendly ties with China, while at the same time acting belligerently toward the Chinese people, as exemplified by the 21 Demands.[12]

The conference ended with a resolution to hold the next meeting of the association in Beijing (this resolution was never enacted). The Chinese delegates were then taken on a three-week tour of Japan, where they were received as honored guests, and welcomed in Kyoto by a crowd of ten thousand. Tanxu, however, did not take part in the tour. He had contracted dysentery and returned home immediately after the conference concluded. He left complaining that the young children who had given them garlands on their arrival had subsequently taken on the role of spies, set to keep vigilant watch over the conference participants. Tanxu's parting comments foreshadowed the shape of Sino-Japanese relations for decades to come:

The Japanese had long cherished intentions toward China and if the Chinese government did not strengthen itself in the future,

China would certainly be controlled by Japan. Looking at the Chinese people, their spirit is in decline and dispersal, as though they are sick, while the Japanese people have risen up, like a great flood. These are both because of the policies of their governments, who teach individuals to fight with guns and swords, and are ignorant of educating the people; they have caused China to be paralyzed and spiritless, without any ability to organize. Still in [Manchuria] there are a few important men who have their own domains, and force people to perform for their pleasure. How can a nation like this survive?![13]

As if in fulfillment of his words, the China to which Tanxu returned was in the midst of a civil war. Guo Songling, one of Zhang Zuolin's lieutenants in the northeast, had risen up against his senior officer, and there was fighting throughout Manchuria. During this "warlord era," China was divided among dozens of major military leaders, and hundreds of minor ones, whose territories ranged in size from that of large European countries to just a county or two. Tanxu's experience with Japanese and Europeans had convinced him of the importance of national unity; now the lack of unity in China was preventing him from traveling in his own country. Unable to reach Beijing, where he was due to lecture, Tanxu instead returned directly to Harbin. Not long after this, Guo's rebellion collapsed after popular support and warlord allies failed to live up to expectations.

In Harbin, the situation remained unresolved. Torn between his own desire to enforce monastic discipline and pressure from laymen who wanted the temple to be more profitable, Tanxu sought support from his old master. He invited Dixian to Harbin in the spring of 1929 to perform the initiation rites at Paradise Temple. Qingchi, who had first assisted Tanxu when he left family life, was also invited. The presence of two eminent monks added great prestige to Tanxu's leadership at the temple. Emblematic of the chaos that dominated this era in Chinese politics and society, war now broke out between China and the Soviet Union over the management of the railroad that ran through Harbin. As Dixian chanted, artillery shells could be heard exploding in the distance. Many present wanted to evacuate the city, and to help Dixian flee from danger. Qingchi disagreed: the monks had already left behind their lives for the sake of the dharma, why should they worry what the cause of their deaths might be? Dixian did not reply, but smiled, and continued chanting. Tanxu claims that Dixian meditated for seventeen hours uninterrupted, undistracted by the sounds of gunfire in the distance or the political chaos they represented.

The initiation rites meant that the temple was now well established. It was time for Tanxu to turn his attention elsewhere. For the next several years, he would delegate daily administration of the temple to Qingchi and others while he traveled between Harbin and Beijing, giving lectures and cultivating contacts for the construction of more temples.

The conflict between China and the U.S.S.R. was short-lived. Within a few weeks, the Soviets had prevailed and forced China to abide by a 1924 agreement mandating joint management of the railway. Tanxu had lived through numerous military conflicts, and this one probably did not trouble him much. It had been twenty-five years since the last time war had forced him from his home; although banditry remained endemic in northeast China, Tanxu was not prevented from traveling among his many temples, in Harbin, Changchun, Shenyang, and Yingkou, as well as smaller temples with which he was associated throughout the region, including Haicheng and Suifenhe.

This changed with the Japanese invasion of Manchuria in September 1931. Tanxu was in Harbin, at Paradise Temple:

> Rumors were on the street that the Japanese army had already arrived. After lunch, we suddenly heard the sound of artillery. A [Chinese] garrison commanded by Li Du had begun to assemble soldiers behind the temple to organize resistance to the Japanese, hidden by the temple walls. Surrounded by soldiers, I saw that this was very dangerous, and had everyone go into the library pavilion and revere the Buddha. Outside, rifle-fire rained down, and we circumambulated the Buddha. Bombs outside exploded with a tremendous boom! The buildings and the ground shook.
>
> We dared not move. A moment later we saw a young child, a primary school student, wandering outside, and several men went out to investigate. Just then, an airplane flew overhead, and

I determined that the situation was too dangerous, and I called everyone back inside. I saw Master Nengcheng in the courtyard, and he opened the main gate to look and called that the soldiers had already gone and that there was nothing going on. Everyone then emerged from the library pavilion, and looked around the temple courtyard. Bombs had toppled trees onto the classroom buildings. All the glass had been completely shattered. There was an old hermit monk, Master Jingming, who was more than sixty years old. He was deaf, and knew nothing of what had been going on, and was not afraid. He didn't understand what we were so afraid of. We had seen that many cars and horses had been killed in the bombardment, took him to the front gate, and had him look out. Once the gates were opened, I saw that the front of the gate was blocked by dead horses and cars destroyed by artillery.

Soon afterward, Li Du and his army began to move toward Shuangcheng, some 100 *li* away. Initially, Li's troops had been behind the temple, and they had seen the planes that were dropping the bombs. Because the plane had been flying so low, the troops had been able to use rifles to shoot at the plane, and they managed to shoot one down. They followed the plane to the site where it had crashed, and found the fuselage. The pilot was attempting to set the plane alight, to destroy the aircraft. Many White Russians and Chinese came out to see what the commotion was. The Japanese pilot threatened to shoot them, but they refused to go. Suddenly, a series of bombs fell and there was a tremendous bang. Altogether it seemed that hundreds of people were killed. There was nothing for me to do. I began to recite the Lotus Sutra.[14]

The attack on Harbin marked the beginning of nearly two decades of war for Tanxu. He did not change his activities markedly after the Japanese invasion, which soon led to Manchuria being separated from the Republic of China as "Manchukuo," a Japanese-sponsored independent state. Tanxu continued to lecture at Paradise Temple and traveled frequently between Harbin and Changchun (soon renamed Xinjing, the "new capital" of Manchukuo). In Changchun, the Expansive Wisdom Temple, still under construction, was razed by the new administration (characterized by Tanxu as "Japanese") for the creation of a new boulevard, part of the grand architectural and urban planning scheme for the new capital. Rather than rail against the occupiers, though, Tanxu saw this as a blessing in disguise, noting that "[a]lmost the entire budget was funded by the [new government] in the end, and although it was unfortunate to have our site destroyed, the end result was still good!"[15]

Despite the eagerness with which he accepted their support, Tanxu was immediately suspected by the Japanese of involvement with the resistance. His patron, Zhu Qinglan, was active in the guerilla movement and led an army against the occupiers. The link between Zhu and Tanxu was well known to the Japanese, and starting in the fall of 1931 Tanxu was regularly followed by informants. The government even placed a spy—Imai Akirayoshi—in the temple, living as a monk, to assess not only Tanxu's political activities, but those of the entire temple, since it had been founded with General Zhu's support. Even in hindsight and with an obvious political incentive to claim otherwise, Tanxu insists in his memoir that he was *not* involved in the anti-Japanese resistance. He admits that his association with Zhu Qinglan and the activities of another monk—Ciyun—aroused suspicion, but that he himself was never directly involved.

The Japanese agent remained at the temple for about six months and questioned all of the monks. When Tanxu traveled to Changchun, Imai interrogated the monk left in charge, hoping to find proof of Tanxu's guilt. But the monks denied that he had any involvement in the resistance, according to Tanxu's account:

> "My teacher is an old monk, and he spends every day constructing temples and lecturing on the sutras. Right now he is constructing the Boruosi in Changchun. There may be monks in the resistance army, but Tanxu is certainly not one of them. If you investigate his words, I assure you that you will see what is in his mind!"

Imai understood Jueyi to be speaking very vehemently and candidly! There was not one bit of ambiguity. It was clear that Tanxu was not one of the anti-Japanese monks. After this, Imai returned to the secret police, and returned later to again investigate the situation. The actual agent working for General Zhu's staff was Ciyun, and Jueyi had done an excellent job staving off Imai and keeping him away from the real agent.[16]

Tanxu's attitude here is ambiguous. He is eager to show that he was not involved in the resistance, but he seems pleased that the monks who were actively involved were protected and not discovered by the Japanese.

After going out of his way to prove to the Japanese that he was not part of the anti-Japanese resistance, Tanxu accepted an invitation from General Zhu to join in him in Xi'an, the northwestern Chinese city that had become the base for many elements of the Chinese army, which the Republican Chinese government had ordered to abandon Manchuria to the invading Japanese. Within months of the Japanese invasion, just before the formal proclamation of Manchukuo, Tanxu left Manchuria, at the invitation of a general in the anti-Japanese resistance, to work in the Yellow River Valley, in the cradle of Chinese civilization.

CHAPTER 7

Famine and Flight

Once known as Chang'an, the City of Eternal Peace, Xi'an was different from most of the other stops on Tanxu's itinerary because it had a long history as a Chinese city. Harbin, Yingkou, and Dalian all owed their existence, or at least their importance, to foreigners. Chang'an had once bustled as a center of international trade, but it was indisputably central to China's history. It became the capital in 206 BCE, during the Han dynasty, which established Confucianism as the foundation of Chinese statecraft and created the institutions of government that would define ideals of Chinese governance for the next two thousand years. During four hundred years of Han rule, Chang'an was established as the Chinese terminus of the Silk Road, which for centuries carried goods, people, and ideas across Asia.

During the Tang era (618–907), Chang'an was probably the largest city in the world, with a population of one million. It was also among the most culturally and religiously diverse cities of any age. Most of the palaces and monuments of its former glory have vanished (recently some replicas have appeared in theme parks and reconstructions, like the garish "Tang Paradise"), but some survive, including the Great Wild Goose Pagoda, which housed the first Buddhist scriptures to be brought from India and translated into Chinese. Fueled by traders from across Eurasia, Chang'an's markets buzzed with dozens of languages. Buddhist, Daoist, and Confucian temples could be found, of course, but so too could Muslim, Christian, Jewish, Manichean, and Zoroastrian places of worship. Tang emperors invited clerics to the court to debate the virtues of their faiths. Fashion, music, and dance from across the continent filled the streets, which were arranged in an orderly grid, policed by a detailed self-surveillance system and protected by an immense city wall that encompassed some fifteen square miles.

In the eighth century, civil wars, rebellions, and invasions, particularly the rebellion led by the Turkic General An Lushan, signaled the beginning of the Tang's decline. When the dynasty finally fell two hundred years later, Chang'an's reign as China's capital ended, as did its political and economic importance, and its prosperity. Warfare, political instability, and climate change disrupted the overland trade routes. The caravans from Samarkand, Khotan, Kashgar, and other Central Asian cities that had connected Chang'an to the Mediterranean and to India disappeared. A thousand miles inland and without a commercially navigable river, its status as capital gone, Chang'an lacked the natural resources to distinguish itself. The surrounding region declined, and the monuments of its past eroded in the harsh climate, while the residents struggled to coax a living from poor soil and fickle weather. The region rebounded somewhat in the Ming dynasty (1368–1644), and Chang'an (renamed Xi'an) remained a large city, but by Tanxu's time it was provincial and poor. Gone were the trappings of wealth, power, and sophistication that had once marked it as the center of a powerful and cosmopolitan empire.

When Tanxu traveled there, late in the winter of 1932, Xi'an was not even reachable by railroad (a line would be extended there two years later). Tanxu's train terminated at Tongguan, a strategic pass between the Yellow River and the Qinling Mountains about seventy-five miles east of Xi'an. Traversing the pass, Tanxu followed in the footsteps of centuries of conquering armies, including those of An Lushan, who captured the capital in 755. The local Buddhist Association met Tanxu in Tongguan and hosted him for one night before driving him the next day across the arid plains of Shaanxi Province.

Xi'an had been a center of Buddhism since the arrival of the first Buddhist texts from India, and many of China's most important Buddhist monuments were there. But as Xi'an's fortunes deteriorated, the place of Buddhism also fell; most of the temples and

monasteries in the region were in disrepair. Tanxu saw a direct cor-
relation: Xi'an had prospered when Buddhism was important in
the city's life; when Buddhism declined, so did the city. This conviction strengthened Tanxu's commitment to revitalizing Buddhism
there.

Tanxu was also committed to famine relief: central Shaanxi Province had been in the grips of severe famine since a poor harvest in
1928. Crops failed again the next year, and the next, and yet again in
1931. On the drive to Xi'an, Tanxu observed "thin soil and poor people." The adjectives could just as easily be reversed. Historian Eduard Vermeer characterized this region in the twentieth century as
"one of China's worst places to live, frequently visited by drought
and famine, infested with bandits and forever poor."[1] In Shaanxi's
unpredictable climate there was often either too little rain or too
much. In either case, crops failed, and each successive failure accelerated a cycle of misery. Among people driven to desperation by the
lack of food, banditry and warlordism flourished, which in turn
exacerbated the famines.

A local newspaper account, detailing the range of misery that
afflicted Shaanxi's peasants, blamed the famine on "drought, locusts,
flood, pests, hail, soldiers, bandits, storm, frost," and "rats." Drought
gripped the Shaanxi plains for four years. By 1929, the China International Famine Relief Organization estimated that 80 percent of
the population was surviving on straw, dried leaves, and tree bark.
In Guanzhong, the region of central Shaanxi through which Tanxu
was traveling, two to three million people—one out of four—died
during the height of the famine. Some counties lost more than half
their population to starvation and relocation. Witnesses describe
corpses lining the roads, dead cattle rotting in their fields, and naked
beggars maimed by frostbite. Rumors—at least—of cannibalism
hounded survivors.[2]

In the famine, parents faced impossible dilemmas. Keeping a
family together might mean starvation for all of its members, or else
food might be withheld from some so that others—usually the
young adults—would have the strength to work or forage for food.
The best option was often to split up, with one or both parents mi-
grating to regions where food or work was more plentiful. Children
might be left, perhaps at a school, temple, church, or orphanage, or

in the worst cases simply abandoned. Some parents no doubt hoped that someone better able to care for the child might take it in and raise it; others perhaps felt that death was preferable to a short life filled with hunger and suffering. Children could also be sold: girls as wives; boys as laborers or, to families without male offspring of their own, as heirs. These heart-rending practices were tacitly permitted by China's imperial governments, if the sellers could demonstrate the extent of their desperation.[3]

For centuries, China's sophisticated famine-relief system had provided help in times of need. The Qing dynasty maintained an elaborate network of granaries throughout the empire, accumulating grain during times of surplus and distributing it when needed. Properly administered, the granary system improved distribution and stabilized prices, as well as providing direct relief in times of famine, but the system was enormously complex and expensive to maintain and was in widespread disrepair by the middle of the nineteenth century. The fall of the Qing dynasty in 1911 left China without a stable or effective central government, worsening prospects for famine relief.[4]

As the country devolved into warlordism, Shaanxi Province became the domain of Feng Yuxiang, the so-called "Christian General" famous among Westerners for baptizing his troops en masse with a fire hose. Feng's defeat had facilitated Tanxu's arrival in Shaanxi, but it also exposed the devastation wrought by warlord rivalries. Feng's armies had emptied what remained of the central government granaries during the 1920s, and after Feng's "retirement" the provincial budget had done little either to restock the granaries or relieve the famine: 50 percent of the budget went to defense and 30 percent to administrative costs. The entire budget was only $20 million, and none of it was spent on direct famine relief.[5]

A normal grain harvest could sustain the province for eighteen to twenty-four months, sufficient protection—assuming rational and sympathetic government policies—for this climatically vulnerable region. However, successive years of drought and Feng's predatory taxes to support his army spelled catastrophe. Other factors compounded the agony: many peasants converted croplands into poppy fields, hoping to benefit from the high prices driven by opium addiction. The result was that even less food was produced, while the number of opium addicts increased. This reduction in the food supply might have been offset by grain shipped in from other regions, but military exigency led Feng's troops to blockade road and river transport in the region. This prevented news of the famine from spreading and made it impossible to import grain. Feng's army also commandeered horses, carts, and trucks, further diminishing the possibility of relocating or importing food. Grain that did flow into the region had to evade bandits seeking food or profit.[6]

Tanxu reached Xi'an in the winter of 1932, traveling along a road built by the China International Famine Relief Association. He was familiar with famine from his experience in Jingxing County ten years earlier. In Shaanxi, he again worked to alleviate the material misery of the people, while his sermons had the long-term aim of releasing them from suffering altogether through dedication to the Buddha's path and eventual enlightenment. His hosts in the Buddhist Association, led by a layman, Cui Xianshu, took him to visit some of the areas hardest hit by famine. In the disaster areas, Tanxu moved among the refugees, investigating their situation, determining how relief funds might best be used, and offering guidance and hope in the form of the Buddha's teachings.

The question of charity was complex. In Buddhist philosophy, any material comfort or attachment can be seen as a distraction from the work necessary to attain enlightenment. Followed to a harshly logical conclusion, this belief makes the provision of material aid an impediment to the search for enlightenment, although withholding it intensifies physical agony in the moment. Many religious traditions promise that suffering in this world will lead to greater reward after death. Poverty might even enhance one's chances of eternal reward: the Christian tradition, for instance, contends that "[i]t is easier for a camel to pass through the eye of a needle, than for a rich man to enter into the kingdom of heaven" (Matthew 19:24). Yet few religious people would call it merciful to ignore the hungry and the poor so as to hasten their entry into the next world and their promised inheritance. Tanxu himself insisted on the importance of compassion, including feeding the hungry. It would be cold comfort to tell the starving that the sooner they succumb the sooner they will be rewarded, whether in heaven or in rebirth. Yet, was it really compassionate to help people without addressing the conditions that had led to their suffering in the first place?

Cui Xianshu shared with Tanxu an episode that illustrated the dilemma. On an earlier visit to the region, Cui had come upon an abandoned temple, where refugees had sought shelter from the cold. They had built a fire in the temple to keep warm and gathered closely around it. Their clothes in tatters, their faces sallow and drawn, these were the poor and suffering common people. After a few days, Cui prepared to leave, but comforted the refugees with news that in a few days a man from Shanghai would arrive with charity. Cui expected this news would be greeted with joy, but no one responded. One man in particular regarded him contemptuously. Not understanding, Cui asked the man—who turned out to be a local relief worker himself—why no one was rejoicing at this news. He replied:

> It would be just as well if you do not come here to hand out money; if you come here once, it only harms us. The last time you prepared to distribute handouts, the men at the garrison told us that people were coming to give us help. We were overjoyed, and thanked them profusely. They came and distributed money to us, and we used it to get things we needed, but after it was all distributed, we were still hungry, it was still cold, and we still had no work. Within in a few weeks, most of the people who had gotten money had starved to death! So I say, do not give us alms, for it will not avert the calamity.[7]

If he could not mitigate the effects of famine, other aspects of Tanxu's mission in Xi'an were difficult as well. General Zhu had invited Tanxu to help revive temples and establish schools in the city. His ambition was to renovate the Maternal Grace Temple (Da Ci'ensi). First built during the Sui dynasty (589–618), the Maternal Grace Temple became famous in the Tang era when it housed the Buddhist scriptures (sutras) brought back from India by the pioneering monk Xuanzang (whose career had been fictionalized in the *Journey to the West*). Xuanzang served as abbot of the temple, which grew to encompass nearly 70 acres, with more than 10 separate compounds and 1,900 rooms within its walls. The sutras themselves were housed in the Great Wild Goose Pagoda at the center of the complex, at nearly 300 feet high, one of the tallest structures in the world at that time.

Except for the pagoda, the temple did not survive the fall of the Tang dynasty, and it lay dormant for five hundred years until the 1450s, when it was reestablished on a much smaller scale. The pagoda was rebuilt numerous times and reduced in height by three stories following damage from a major earthquake in 1556; the current layout dates from a 1604 renovation. The temple was again destroyed during the Muslim uprising of the 1860s and rebuilt a few decades later. The temple continued to be active, though on a modest scale, until Zhu Qinglan, Tanxu's patron, undertook to restore it in 1930. (Today, the Big Wild Goose Pagoda—leaning to one side as a result of the 1556 earthquake—is one of the oldest stone structures in China and among Xi'an's premier tourist attractions.)

Involving such a valuable landmark and many acres of grounds, the renovation would be an expensive project. This was easily the most historically significant temple with which Tanxu had been associated. Tanxu had been invited in part because of his success finding donors for similar projects in Manchuria. However, Xi'an was economically stagnant, not a vibrant entrepôt like Harbin or Yingkou. In other cities, Tanxu had relied on businessmen to support his projects, but in Xi'an there were few people wealthy enough to patronize a new temple. General Zhu himself sponsored the school and financially supported most of the students. The head of the provincial government had donated to the school, and other outside donors came forward as well, but their contributions amounted to only a fraction of what was needed.

Tanxu struggled with the school for about half a year, from February to September 1932. He lectured on sutras, participated in famine relief, and tried to raise money for the projects, but with little success. He traveled throughout the region, visiting many of the most important Buddhist shrines in Xi'an and the surrounding area. Zhu Qinglan was often away, fighting against the Japanese, and Tanxu had few friends or supporters in Xi'an. He was already frustrated with the situation when he received news that his teacher, Master Dixian, had passed away.

Tanxu does not detail his reaction to the news, but then he rarely discusses personal relationships in his memoir. Perhaps he was unwilling to revisit the pain associated with such memories, or maybe his monastic discipline enabled him to keep such emotions at arm's length. Whatever his state of mind, as soon as he received the news Tanxu made preparations to travel to Ningbo for the memorial service. The letter had taken some time to reach him in Xi'an: Master Dixian had died in early August and he needed to hurry if he was to arrive in time for the memorial service and dedication of the master's shrine. Over the protests of the local Buddhist community, Tanxu got ready to return to Zhejiang Province. The most direct route would be to retrace the path by which he had come—going by car to Tongguan, where he could catch a train for Shanghai. However, the road was now considered impassable because of landmines and bandits. The alternative was to travel by boat down the Wei River. This was risky, too—bandits and warlords still controlled many parts of the river and attack from the riverbank was a constant danger. Nevertheless, this appeared the best option.

Far inland, away from the moderating influences of the ocean, seasons in Xi'an can change suddenly, and a cold wind was already blowing as Tanxu boarded his vessel for the journey downstream. Two boats—little more than rafts, really—would travel together. For this first stage of the voyage they had neither rudders nor sails: the crew relied on poles and ropes held from shore to navigate the shallow and meandering channel. The five passengers sat on the open deck, shivering in the October wind. Besides Tanxu, there was another Buddhist monk, a young man named Citong, who had listened to Tanxu's lectures in Xi'an and was bound for Shanghai to continue his studies. Also on board was a tax official returning to Beijing, accompanied by his brother, wife, son, and a great deal of luggage.

They boarded early in the afternoon, but a series of delays prevented them from casting off until nearly sundown. The river was too treacherous to navigate in the dark, so departure was postponed until the following morning. The group slept on the deck, struggling to find shelter from the unrelenting wind. The soil in this part of China is particularly fine, and the wind picked up dust and deposited it everywhere. After a fitful night's sleep, the travelers awoke having made no progress toward their destination and covered in a fine layer of dust that had found its way into every exposed opening, filling their eyes, ears, and noses. The noodles to be shared for breakfast were black, coated with dust.[8]

With the dawn, the boat set out downriver. To navigate the shallows on this stretch of river, two men walked alongside the boat on shore, holding lines to guide it away from the shifting shoals and to help free it when it ran aground, which happened frequently. Travel was uneventful, but painfully slow: after six days on the river, they had progressed only twelve miles downstream, finally reaching the next town, Lintong. (Some fifty years later, the Qin emperor's "terracotta army" would be discovered in Lintong, making it one of China's greatest centers of tourism.) Although progress had been slow, at least the only serious hazard they had encountered had been boredom.

At Lintong, the river became deeper and more navigable, and sails were unfurled to move more quickly. Risk, however, increased along with speed: bandits controlled much of the river below Lintong, and it was reported that eight or nine out of every ten boats venturing beyond this point had encountered problems. Shaanxi was rife with bandits. The province was home to tens of thousands of them during the 1920s, and many others made incursions from neighboring provinces. One historian described Shaanxi as a "bandit world."[9]

Sailing into this dangerous stretch of river, the boat traveled only at night, silently and showing no lights. The passengers hid in the cargo hold below the deck, crammed among the luggage belonging to the tax collector and his family as well as the hundreds of volumes of Buddhist sutras that the Xi'an Buddhist Association was sending as a gift in honor of Master Dixian. Citong, the young monk, was very frightened. He had spent most of his life in a monastery; bandits and warfare were common throughout China at this time, but for him until now they had been only terrifying rumors. Tanxu, of course, had experienced banditry and worse. He did his best to comfort his young companion, but also made preparations in case bandits should intercept their ship. The Buddhist Association in Xi'an had given him 50 yuan for his journey. He took 40 from his satchel, and hid it under some cloth in a wicker basket. He had Citong also place 10 yuan in the satchel, and hid the rest of his money. Silently chanting the name of Amitabha Buddha, they huddled together.

One of the hands on the boat, an old man, broke the silence, announcing that their fears had been realized. "No good!" he said. "Bandits have stopped the boats, and demanded 1,000 yuan for us to pass. Mr. Zhu, on the first boat, has given 500 yuan, it is up to you all to provide the rest."

Tanxu replied quickly. "And if we have no money? What then?"

"I am only the messenger. I don't want to see disaster befall all of us." He opened his shirt, revealing a large scar running down his chest. "This is what happened last year when we were stopped but had no money. It is from a steel blade, a constant reminder of that night."

A few moments later two of the pirates came below, demanding to speak to the Tanxu.

"I am right here. Come here, friend."

The two men drew pistols. "Everyone has to pay in order to pass through here. No exceptions!" They held their guns to the monk's head, but Tanxu replied calmly: "You and I are all people who have chosen to live outside ordinary society. People in difficulty can come to us for help. Does this not make us friends? Today, although times are difficult, certainly we can help one another." As he spoke he produced a leather satchel that contained the 20 yuan, 10 each from himself and Citong.

"Gentlemen! Today I am very embarrassed. I do not carry much money, but the two of us have 20 yuan. Would this pay for our passage?"

One bandit shouted, "That is not nearly enough! Give us 500 yuan!"

At this point, Citong and the laymen were too scared to speak or move. Tanxu muttered the name of Guanyin under his breath, and then continued. "Please understand. We have sat on this boat for more than two weeks, enduring many hardships. All the money we have is to buy a train ticket, for ¥6.50, and some food for the journey. Even this money was given to us by the laymen from our temple. If we had more money we certainly would help you!"

The two bandits again rejected Tanxu's offer, "It's not enough! Even if we wanted to, we couldn't let you pass for 20 yuan. Only the boss can decide if we should let you go. We will go get him—tell him your story and see what he says."

When the two men left, Tanxu tied a rope to the basket containing their money and lowered it slowly outside the window of the boat. Dangling low, near the water, the basket could not easily be seen in the dark of night.

A few moments later, the bandits returned, accompanied by their leader and repeating their earlier threats. Tanxu insisted that this was all the money they had, and assured him that if they searched the boat they would find nothing else. For a few tense minutes the three men searched the boat, but found only Buddhist scriptures. Angry at finding nothing, the pirates seemed more threatening than before, and Tanxu's plan seemed destined for failure.

Instead, the bandit leader surprised them.

"Forget it," he said. "Damn monks never have much money!" And just like that they left. They stole whatever they could carry, including many of the Buddhist scriptures and the relief supplies that had been sent by the Buddhist Association, leaving the boat with little more than a lamp, but everyone was alive and unhurt.

Citong sat shaking, stunned by what had happened and how close they had all come to death. Tanxu was trying to calm him when they heard cries from outside. They ran out and found the tax collector, sobbing. The bandits had taken all of his money and clothing, and they knew no one in Tongguan to help them get home to Beijing. He was threatening to throw himself in the river. Tanxu, who had stayed the night at the Buddhist temple in Tongguan on his way to Xi'an, wrote a letter of introduction for him, explaining what had happened and asking that any possible help be given to the family.

The next morning at dawn the boat resumed its journey. Within a few miles, they encountered a boat heading upriver, and heard that bandits were active just downstream. Tanxu was unwilling to press their luck further. After discussing their options with the other passengers, he went ashore to seek help from the magistrate of Lintong County, which they guessed to be the nearest jurisdiction. Taking 30 yuan, he set off on foot. It should not have been far to Lintong City, but Tanxu walked further and further along the road with no sign of a city or even a village at all.

Finally, as the sun began to sink lower in the sky, he reached the edge of Lintong City. He was anxious because he would clearly have to spend the night there, but had no contacts or arrangements in the city. He was overjoyed to meet an old Daoist monk near the edge of the city and asked him where he might find help. The monk directed him to the local Buddhist Association, not far away. There, he could pass the night. The head of the Buddhist Association had come regularly to Xi'an to hear Tanxu's lectures. He immediately recognized the eminent monk, and was eager to help, particularly when he heard that he was transporting sutras (what few the pirates had left). He wrote out a letter of introduction to the magistrate, asking for his assistance.

The next morning, the letter was sent, and the magistrate responded with an offer of two soldiers to guard the passengers and their cargo on their journey downstream. But Tanxu decided against continuing the river journey. Instead, he hired a cart to take him back to Xi'an. Even though they had been on the river for more than two weeks, they had traveled only a short distance, and the cart was able to bring Tanxu back to Xi'an in just a day (today, buses carry tourists from Xi'an to Lintong in about an hour).

The temple staff and Buddhist Association were overjoyed at Tanxu's safe return, for they had heard about the bandits on the river. After a few days to recover and collect new supplies for the journey, he left by car for Tongguan. In contrast to the abortive river journey, it was an uneventful trip, and took only half a day.[10] In Tongguan, Tanxu boarded a train for Shanghai.

It was necessary to change trains in Luoyang. Luoyang was another of China's ancient imperial capitals, and like Xi'an it was full of monuments, including some important Buddhist temples. Hoping to visit these sites, Tanxu disembarked, first stopping at a small restaurant to fortify himself. The restaurant was most unwelcoming. The staff refused to serve him, and all the customers in the crowded restaurant treated him rudely. Eventually, he persuaded a waiter to bring him some noodles, but the waiter was clearly reluctant to do so.

Tanxu asked one of the laymen who had accompanied him from Xi'an if he understood why he was receiving this treatment. He was told that it was a local superstition: it was considered bad luck to see a monk in the morning. The entire restaurant felt that Tanxu's presence was cursing them, or at least setting them up for a bad day. Tanxu found this impossible to believe—but when he returned to the same restaurant later in the day, they welcomed him quite warmly.

Tanxu hoped to visit the White Horse Temple, considered the first Buddhist temple in China. According to the sixth-century historian Yang Xuanzhi, the monastery was founded by Emperor Mingdi of the Han dynasty, who reigned from 58–75 CE from his capital at Luoyang. In a dream, Mingdi saw a "golden god," standing more than ten feet tall and with the light of the sun radiating from his head. This god was called Buddha, he learned in his dream, and he inhabited the Western lands. Inspired, the emperor sent men in search of this god. The search parties returned with sacred Buddhist texts, which they carried back on white horses. A monastery was established at the capital to house these texts, and it was given the name White Horse Temple in honor of the animals that had brought such valuable cargo to China.[11]

White Horse Temple is several miles outside of the city center, far from the train station. Tanxu tried for several hours to find the famous temple, but without success, perhaps because the temple, like so many in China, had fallen into disrepair. (A renovation project began just a few years later, in 1934.) Disappointed, Tanxu stayed the night in Luoyang and then, eager to pay his respects to Dixian, continued on to Shanghai.

In Shanghai, Tanxu visited the Buddhist press on whose behalf he had been working. The men involved with this press, including Ye Gongchuo and Chen Feiqing, supported Tanxu's other projects throughout China. They were pleased to see him, having already received word from Xi'an that the shipment of books had been hijacked by bandits, but that Tanxu was safe. They talked about a number of new temple projects for which they wanted Tanxu's support. One was in Qingdao, another in Xuzhou. Several possibilities had arisen in Manchuria, but Tanxu could not go there at the time because it was controlled by the Japanese, who suspected him of working for General Zhu's resistance army. After a few days discussing different options, he returned by ferry to Ningbo to visit Master Dixian's shrine. Because he had been delayed by the river pirates in Shaanxi, Tanxu had missed the public ceremony dedicating the memorial, but went to offer his respects on his own.

Dixian's remains were placed at Wu Lei Mountain, and Tanxu stayed the night at this temple. Once again—predictably by this point?—he does not record his feelings on visiting the grave of his old master. We cannot know if his silence reflects his success in removing emotional attachments, his reluctance to share those attachments, or simply oversight. Perhaps he felt pride at having succeeded in becoming a monk—becoming patriarch of an entire sect. Or he may have felt humbled by the memory of his old master, and rededicated himself to Dixian's goal of reviving Buddhism in the north. Tanxu was by this time nearly sixty years old, and Dixian's passing surely reminded him of his own mortality.

All that is recorded is that Tanxu went to the shrine and prayed there, by himself. The next day he returned to Ningbo, where he lectured at the King Ashoka Temple, one of China's most important temples and home to several relics of the Buddha. King Ashoka, who united most of India and adopted Buddhism, ordered temples built across Asia to house relics of Sakyamuni, the historical Buddha. Legends say that some 84,000 of these temples were built, starting in the third century BCE, including nineteen in China. All of them were named King Ashoka Temple, after their patron. The temple in Ningbo was constructed in 282 CE during the Western Jin dynasty and rebuilt numerous times over the centuries: the buildings Tanxu lectured in dated from the Qing dynasty.

After lecturing on the Diamond Sutra for several days, he returned to Guanzong Temple for what would be the last time. He stayed only one night, in the dormitory where he had studied to become a monk twenty years earlier. While there, he might have reflected that his career sat at a crossroads. His short time in Shaanxi had not been successful. He had not renovated the temple in Xi'an to the extent he wished, and famine continued unabated. His time there had been cut short by the death of Dixian, and bandits and other problems had frustrated his return to Ningbo. Even earlier, his last years in Harbin had been marked by bitter partisanship and ended with the Japanese invasion. Tanxu must have wondered what awaited him as he returned by ferry to Shanghai, alone once more and with uncertain prospects, retracing the route he had followed after leaving Guanzong Temple for the first time.

Arriving in Shanghai, Tanxu found that Chen Feiqing had booked him passage by boat to Qingdao, where he hoped Tanxu would help him found a new temple. Though Tanxu had never visited Qingdao itself, it was in coastal northern China, where he had lived most of his life. He might have welcomed the chance to return to his home region after the struggles he had encountered inland, and he agreed to make the voyage.

CHAPTER 8

Qingdao

Qingdao, a busy port on the Shandong Peninsula, begins the twenty-first century as one of China's most progressive and livable cities. Hosting the 2008 Olympic sailing competition was intended to raise its profile internationally, but Qingdao remains best known—especially outside China—for its namesake brewery, which retains the British postal spelling, "Tsingtao." There is more than beer to recommend the city. Its rocky coastline resembles northern New England; a miles-long footpath winds along the shoreline, past picturesque wharves and broad beaches, punctuated by oceanfront restaurants, hotels, and villas. Brides from across the region come here for wedding portraits, arriving by the busload to be photographed in front of the crashing surf.

It is not coincidence that China's most famous beer originated in its only significant German colony. Germans started brewing beer there when they arrived in the 1890s, using hops brought from Europe. Today, guides lead tourists through the century-old brewery, depositing them in a beer garden and taproom to sample the product and patronize the well-stocked gift shop.

The other most visible legacy of German colonialism in Qingdao is the architecture of the "old city" clustered around the harbor and the railway station. Wood-frame houses with red tile roofs dominate, along with Protestant and Catholic churches. These buildings—more evocative of Franconia than Shandong—stand in contrast to traditional Chinese architecture, but also to the luxury condominiums and hotels that line the newer sections of the city. There, the newly wealthy embrace Deng Xiaoping's proclamation that "to get rich is glorious!"

as they walk their dogs and park their sport-utility vehicles in gated seaside communities. Qingdao's thriving industrial sector, including the consumer-appliance giant Haier, helps support a standard of living that is among the highest in China.

Tanxu's first impressions of Qingdao when he arrived in 1932 echoed his reaction to Harbin. He saw it as a place where Chinese and foreign influences competed, and where a Buddhist temple might promote a sense of Chinese identity:

> Qingdao in the past had absolutely no Buddhism. It was originally a fishing village, and then a seaport where merchants gathered. Its history is less than 100 years. Particularly after it was colonized by the Germans, construction in the city flourished! The mountains and landscape were very beautiful, and within the city the architecture was filled with a foreign color, unlike any other city.[1]

As Tanxu observed, Qingdao's history was short. Despite being one of North China's most attractive natural harbors, Jiaozhou Bay was little developed until the second wave of European colonialism in the late nineteenth century. Germany, a latecomer to the European competition for territories in Africa and Asia, designated Jiaozhou Bay as the site for a Chinese colony. In addition to the promising harbor, it was close to Shandong's coalfields, which the Germans hoped to develop to support a coaling station for their shipping in the Pacific.

In 1897, the murder of two missionaries gave Germany a pretext to intervene, and that November its naval forces took the harbor, unopposed. The treaty signed March 6, 1898, leased the peninsula on the eastern side of Jiaozhou Bay to Germany for ninety-nine years, just as the New Territories had recently been added to Britain's colony in Hong Kong. Though formally a leasehold, from the start Germany regarded the territory as a colony: the treaty gave German troops free passage in a fifty-kilometer zone surrounding the leased territory and forbade the Chinese government from acting within that zone "without the previous consent of the German government." The treaty further granted Germany economic and commercial privileges throughout Shandong Province, making the entire region a German sphere of influence, with the nascent city of Qingdao as its hub.[2]

Qingdao grew explosively. A small fishing village of perhaps 700 inhabitants in the 1890s, by the time of the first colonial-era census, in 1901, its population had grown to 15,500, of whom 600 were foreigners. The population reached 35,000 in 1908, 56,000 in 1914, and by the 1920s approached 300,000. While the city's architecture may have been German, its population continued to be overwhelmingly Chinese. In 1914, 53,000 of the inhabitants were Chinese and 1,855 were German.[3]

At the start of World War I, Japanese and British forces overran the city's German defenders after a six-week siege.[4] China, like Japan, entered the war on the side of the Allies, and the Chinese government expected to recover Qingdao after Germany's defeat. But Japan, which had demonstrated its world-class military power by defeating Russia in 1905, aspired to political and economic domination of China and sought to assume Germany's role as the colonial power in Qingdao. The Japanese successfully lobbied their position at the Paris Peace Conference. It was the Versailles Treaty's recognition of Japanese dominion over Qingdao that had inspired the May Fourth Movement, in which students led nationalist protests against the imperialism of foreign governments and the weakness of their own. Amid international pressure, Japan had returned administration of the city to China in 1922; when Tanxu arrived, Qingdao was a directly administered municipality of the Republic of China.

When Tanxu arrived, nearly twenty years after the end of German rule, Qingdao retained a European flavor. Its population was an international mix, familiar to Tanxu from his time in Harbin, Yingkou, Dalian, and other ports. Nearly 450,000 people lived in Qingdao in 1932, including 13,000 foreigners representing 17 nations. Holiday-makers swelled the population in summer; the mild climate, European architecture, and dramatic scenery made Qingdao one of the most attractive vacation spots in China for both foreign expatriates and well-off Chinese. One British expatriate labeled Qingdao the "Brighton of the Far East."[5] An American sent to Qingdao to represent Texaco was unrestrained in his enthusiasm for his new assignment:

[Qingdao] is, according to everyone I have spoken to, just about the best place to live in China. It is far and away the healthiest, with mountains, woods (rare in this country), seashore with fine bathing and also good mountain water, fresh milk, etc. The most popular summer resort in the far east, [Qingdao] is crowded with visitors during the warm season.[6]

Tanxu was equally impressed:

Amid the lush vegetation can be seen red roofs and jade green eaves, set off by the light reflected off the water, it was truly a city of artistic natural beauty. Because the winters here are not too cold, nor the summers too hot, many wealthy people, including foreigners, choose to spend their holidays here. Foreign immigrants, from every country, settled here, and the place was truly a place where the Chinese and the foreign mixed together.[7]

It was Qingdao's status as a vacation spot, not its commercial or strategic importance, that sparked the campaign to erect a Buddhist temple there. Ye Gongchuo and Chen Feiqing visited the city in the summer of 1931 and found it a beautiful and pleasant place, but lacking a legitimate Buddhist temple. There was a small sutra library and reading room, itself only a few years old, but no proper temple and certainly no monks.

The only Chinese temple in Qingdao was the Tianhou Temple. Tianhou, the "Heavenly Empress," is seen as the protector of mariners. She was—and remains—popular in seaports, where at least one temple dedicated to her can usually be found, often located at a place where shipwreck survivors came ashore. The origin myth of her cult dates to a woman named Lin, who lived in Fujian Province from 960–87. She told of a dream in which she helped her brothers return safely to port in a storm. When the brothers arrived home, they described a female spirit that had helped them survive. The story spread throughout the coast, and "Aunt Lin" became a local deity. In anthropologist James Watson's analysis, state intervention transformed this local deity into a nationally prominent goddess, the "Empress of Heaven," centuries later.[8]

Other religious traditions had roots near Qingdao as well. Not far from the city, the mountains of Laoshan harbored hundreds of ancient Daoist, and some Buddhist, temples, many perched near waterfalls or sheltered among dense pine groves. The oldest temples on Laoshan date back more than a thousand years, and these sites are among the most important to the early history of Daoism in China.

Upset by the neglect of Buddhism in Qingdao, Ye Gongchuo and Chen Feiqing organized a series of meetings to promote their vision of a Buddhist temple. At one of these, convened at the communications ministry, Chen and Ye urged that such a temple would be important not only for practicing Buddhists, but for all Chinese in the city, and for the city's Chinese identity.

> Qingdao is an important port and commercial center. Foreign religious organizations are numerous. However, it is a Chinese place with no Chinese Buddhist Temples, just a Tianhou Daoist Temple. This is not only a blight on the city's appearance, it is an extreme embarrassment to the manners and morals of the time!"[9]

At the meeting the mayor of Qingdao was persuaded to lease at half-price a plot of land for the building of the temple, and donations of 10,000 yuan were solicited from several important officials, including Ge Guangting, the head of the Jiao–Ji Railway. The Jiao–Ji Railway (short for Jiaozhou–Jinan) had been one of Germany's first projects in Shandong, predating the treaty that established Qingdao. In the fall of 1897, construction began on the line linking the provincial capital at Jinan, Jiaozhou Bay, and the coalfields and mines of central Shandong. As in Harbin, the railway was an important instrument of colonial power, and the manager of the railway held political and economic influence far beyond what the title might suggest.

With the movement to build a temple underway, a monk was sought to lead the project; Tanxu's reputation for founding temples brought his name to the top of the list, but at first he had been unavailable because of the Japanese invasion of Manchuria and his flight to Xi'an. Tanxu's arrival in Shanghai was the opportunity the Qingdao Buddhists had waited for. Letters of introduction were written, tickets were bought, and arrangements were made: soon, Tanxu was on a boat for Qingdao, where he arrived in the fall of 1932. He met the local officials, including the mayor, Shen Honglie, who remembered Tanxu from an earlier meeting in Shenyang, at the Temple of Expansive Wisdom there. (Tanxu also founded a much larger temple of the same name in Changchun.) Shen had important government connections: he was active in the KMT government and commanded troops in the resistance to the Japanese. For several weeks, Tanxu lectured on the Diamond Sutra at the education ministry, meeting potential donors and persuading them of the importance of the new Qingdao temple for both China and Buddhism. He went to Beijing, where he sought assistance from General Zhu in raising money, and together they visited prominent temples in the capital that might serve as models or inspirations for the Qingdao project. Mayor Shen subsidized most of these trips.

Tanxu drew on his now-extensive experience to bring to fruition the ambitions in Qingdao. He drew on the idea of "expedient means," using different messages to appeal to different donors. To some he emphasized the centrality of Buddhism in Chinese culture and the need for Chinese cities to have Buddhist temples. This was an especially powerful argument in cities like Qingdao and Harbin, with European colonial legacies. He persuaded others to give money so that they would have a place to further their study of the Buddha. For still others, giving money to a temple was a way to accumulate merit. It is difficult to assess his true motivation—if this is even a useful way of thinking. He said as much himself:

> When a monk becomes a master he does not talk of Buddhist matters at all, but discusses worldly events: culture, economics, military affairs, etc. . . . all of this as a means to understand people's thoughts and feelings, and to make connections with them.[10]

His memoir is addressed to students of Buddhism: he recited it to novices and other monks as they prepared for their initiation ceremony. It is hardly surprising that he emphasizes the religious motivations for his activity, although the political element is also present. Both are evident in the fundraising and construction of Tranquil Mountain Temple (Zhanshansi) in Qingdao.

The case of Wang Jinyu, an important official during the Republican era who had retired to Qingdao, illustrates how Tanxu appealed to officials' religious motivations, and also the challenges posed by recruiting government officials to the cause of temple construction.

For centuries, officials had tended to mistrust monks because they rejected the mainstream society for which they were responsible. Likewise, the monks' teaching that the rewards and punishments of civil society were only pale—and ultimately insignificant—reflections of the true reality were perceived as challenges to authority. Officials often saw the hierarchies within Buddhism, including the loyalty of student to master, as being in conflict with secular obligations to the state. Periodically, the Chinese state dissolved Buddhist monasteries and seized their property, in the manner of Henry VIII's dissolution of the monasteries in Tudor England. At other times, the state patronized Buddhist temples, hoping to ensure their loyalty through generous subsidies. Today, the Chinese government manifests a similar concern about Roman Catholicism, creating a parallel "Catholic Patriotic Association," which follows the formal structure and liturgical practice of the Catholic church, but recognizes the Chinese central government—not the Vatican—as the ultimate earthly authority over church affairs.[11]

This long history of mistrust between political and clerical elites posed a challenge. Wang Jinyu was a devout Buddhist, but his experience as a politician had made him suspicious of monks. Monks had criticized his actions as slighting the truth in favor of political expediency, while Wang, for his part, believed that monks lived in isolation from the real world and did not appreciate political exigencies. So, although he attended Tanxu's lectures and services in Qingdao, he did not introduce himself, but relied on his own study and reflections in deciding how to apply what Tanxu taught.

Many in Qingdao were urging Tanxu to enlist Wang Jinyu to support the temple. Tanxu refused to have a meeting arranged, waiting for time and circumstance to bring the men together. When they did, Tanxu engaged Wang in discussion of important religious questions. Wang asked what Tanxu had learned from his study of Buddhism. Tanxu replied humbly that, "you could say that I have learned nothing at all from my studies. However, I have come up with six characters that express my opinions: 'Kan po! Fang xia! Zi zai!' "[12]

These six characters resist translation into English. Lok To—Tanxu's dharma heir—explained them as "See through to the true essence; let go of desires; be at peace." These principles enabled Tanxu to work in a wide variety of physical and political circumstances, for they were all predicated on the understanding that the work you are doing in the physical world is not the ultimate work that needs to be done. They do not deny the importance of the physical world, but they underline that things in themselves are not finally important.

Wang Jinyu apparently was pleased by this response: he smiled and invited Tanxu to dinner at his home the next day, along with several other important members of the temple project. Wang Jinyu, his wife, and their four-year-old daughter worshipped at an altar in their home, impressing Tanxu with their devotion and knowledge of the rites. After the service and a meal, talk turned to the temple: Wang committed to support it enthusiastically, and his example inspired others to increase their support. By the summer of 1933, enough money had been raised and only a site was needed for construction to begin. (The government had promised a plot of land, but a specific location had yet to be chosen.) As in Harbin, Tanxu advocated a symbolically powerful location near the old town, to emphasize that Qingdao had transcended its colonial past and was now a Chinese city where Buddhism played an important role. However, among the narrow streets and crowded houses of the old city there was no space for a large temple complex. Tanxu rejected several proposed sites in the mountains surrounding the city, feeling that in such a location, the temple would be neither politically significant nor convenient for worshippers. A compromise was found in a city park on the edge of the city. The temple would stand above Qingdao on the mountains rising inland from the shore, but not so high up as to be isolated. Construction of Tranquil Mountain Temple began in October of 1933, on a site of about five acres. The following year, an additional grant more than doubled the temple's area.[13]

Over the next five years, the main pavilion rose above the city. In front of the pavilion the main gate proclaimed, in large yellow characters, "Tranquil Mountain Temple," The characters reflected in a large pond, constructed for the ceremonial release of sea creatures. This common ritual—still performed today—is often sponsored by laymen who purchase fish, frogs, and other animals from restaurant tanks in order to free them as a means of accumulating merit. The main pavilion opened in the spring of 1934, as construction continued on the other parts of the temple.

Once it had opened, Tanxu was not satisfied with the location of the temple. The site had been pronounced very favorable by fengshui consultants, and it combined the social, political, and religious roles that the temple needed to serve. It was, however, a compromise: the surroundings were peaceful and ideal for meditation and study, but it was too far from the center to make a powerful political statement, and it was inconvenient for many laypeople to visit. With this in mind, construction began in 1934 on a new building in the center of the city.

Along with Tanxu, Wang Jinyu and Shen Honglie (the mayor) were the driving forces behind this new structure, a stupa. Tranquil Mountain Temple, in the hills, was a place for the monks, but the stupa would be a convenient place for the laity to hear the sutras inside the city. The Memorial Stupa was located at 11 Yushan Road on a small plot of public land, about one acre in size. There were many white pines on the site, and from a distance it was very imposing. Atop a hill, with a commanding view of the entire city, it had been a German artillery platform. In building a shrine there, Tanxu and Wang Jinyu said that they were working for peace, transforming a military installation into a religious edifice. Wang Jinyu personally financed most of its construction.

The first structure there was a flat-roof, foreign design. This reflected the wishes of Mayor Shen, whose house was also in a foreign style. As in Harbin, many local officials, eager to proclaim themselves progressive and cosmopolitan, lived in houses of European style and sometimes of European construction. For a stupa, though, the symbolism was ambiguous. A modern, Western-style structure was appealing because it suggested that Buddhism was a living religion and not a fossilized relic. However, eschewing traditional Chinese architecture might suggest that Chinese tradition might not play a prominent role in the new China. Tanxu, who was conservative in most matters, favored a more traditional style, with "a simple elegance of design that would inspire faith in people's hearts."

It was decided to erect another building in front of the first one, this time of traditional design. Once it was completed, the effect was just what Tanxu had hoped. It recalled the Paradise Temple in Harbin which, in addition to overlooking the procession route between the Christian churches and cemetery, stood on a bluff over-looking the Chinese district and was a beacon on the city's skyline. In Qingdao, Tanxu wrote, "the buildings are entirely Western in design, all red and green scattered throughout a dense and gloomy forest; only the Tranquil Mountain Temple Memorial Stupa stood out on the top of the mountain, showing people a Chinese-style building, and enabling people to have the hope and knowledge that there was a temple."[14]

In addition to the Memorial Stupa, in that same year a primary school was established at the main temple. This was the initiative of Mayor Shen, and funding for the school came from the city depart-ment of education and also from the railway administration. The curriculum was not focused exclusively on Buddhism: the mayor insisted on a strong science component. With the temple success-fully opened, Tanxu retired as abbot on September 19, 1934, appointing a monk named Boshan in his place. He remained ac-tive, lecturing at the temple, the school, and at the Memorial Stupa in the city.

The most active phase of Tanxu's career had ended. Tranquil Mountain was among the largest and most important temples founded during the revival of Buddhism in early twentieth—century China, and its success established Tanxu as one of the key figures in this movement. It is not clear whether Tanxu's efforts to give Qingdao a Chinese face made an impression on the numerous foreigners living in the city. Some foreigners mention a Chinese temple in Qingdao, but they usually refer to the Tianhou Temple, which was on the waterfront within sight of the city's colonial center. While Tanxu and city officials emphasized the importance to Chinese national pride of buildings like Tranquil Mountain Temple, foreigners were more likely to comment on the initiation fee at the International Club ($100 in 1936), the fate of the *Hindenburg*, or the coronation of King George VI. Gould Thomas, the American representative of Texaco in Qingdao, took the occasion of the Coronation Ball—hosting more than six hundred people from all of Qingdao society—to reflect on the expatriate experience:

> From this side, the U.S. is not looking so good: high taxes, labor troubles, dust storms and endless political bickering that will probably amount to nothing. Here, on the other hand, . . . for-eigners have more individual freedom than any group of people on earth. They pay no taxes and are practically lords in their own right. They enjoy extraterritoriality, which means that the folks at the U.S. Consulate are the only officials . . . who can bring me to justice.[15]

Tanxu's Qingdao was very different from Gould Thomas's. Of course the men themselves, and their experiences, were very different: while Tanxu was fleeing the Japanese invasion and confronting famine in Shaanxi, Thomas was attending Yale. Neither man was typical of Qingdao in the 1930s, but each represented an important element: a Chinese elite seeking to give the city a new identity, and a Euro-American community enjoying the waning days of colonial-ism. Both these groups, along with all the rest of Qingdao, were soon overwhelmed, as Japanese forces launched their invasion in the summer of 1937, inaugurating the most controversial, and hard-est to decipher, period of Tanxu's career.

CHAPTER 9

Life During Wartime

Tanxu's memoir confirmed for me that wartime categories—collaboration or resistance; agent or victim; hero or traitor—obscure more than they enlighten: in contrast to the moral complexity of the time, these labels are simplistic. For much of his career, Tanxu lived in territory occupied by the Japanese, and his memoir says little about his relations with the occupier. Making sense of the silence is more challenging for a historian than interpreting his words.

After the Japanese invaded Manchuria in September 1931 and established Manchukuo as a proxy state, China was under constant pressure from Japan. A stream of concessions followed—including demilitarizing the region around Beijing and permitting Japanese troops to be based in China. The Chinese government was required to take responsibility for controlling anti-Japanese sentiments, which the Japanese blamed for poor relations between the two countries. There were a series of "incidents"—confrontations between Japanese and Chinese. On the night of July 7, 1937, Japanese forces on maneuvers skirmished with Chinese government troops. Details about the "Marco Polo Bridge Incident" (as it came to be known in the West) remain unclear, and it is not certain which side fired first. Neither China nor Japan wanted to escalate this incident into open war, but that is just what happened. Japanese reinforcements were sent to the area. Three divisions landed—like so many invading armies before them—at Tanggu, just a few miles from Tanxu's birthplace, on July 25. Within a week, the Japanese captured Tianjin, and soon afterward took Beiping (the renamed

Beijing).[1] On August 7, Chiang Kai-shek and the Guomindang leadership mobilized all Chinese armies, and the war between China and Japan began in earnest. As summer turned to fall, Japanese troops extended their control across eastern China.[2]

Qingdao immediately went on alert. It was only three hundred miles from the fighting, and many Japanese resided in the city. The Japanese assault focused on Shanghai and Nanjing—the largest port and capital, respectively—however, and fighting bypassed Qingdao as the Japanese moved south. Chinese forces employed a strategy of attrition, rarely resisting the Japanese advance directly. Although there was no fighting in Qingdao, anticipation of war led to chaos. "What a situation," wrote Gould Thomas in late August,

> over three-quarters of the Chinese population have left, practically all the stores are closed, everything is on a cash basis, and no one has any money. The food problem is getting tough as the farmers won't bring anything. . . . People are begging for space on ships to leave but practically no ships are available.[3]

Throughout the fall and into the winter, rumors of a Japanese attack swirled around Qingdao. The city's Japanese residents evacuated in September, and looting of abandoned Japanese property was rife. Curfews failed to stop the looting. Looters captured by the police were shot, the bodies left on the sidewalks as warning to others. Thomas's description of the scene evokes Lu Xun's classic short story, "The True Story of Ah Q," in which the unwitting "revolutionary" is captured and shot by the soldiers he had tried to join. Gould Thomas writes,

> Every once in a while the police or marines capture a whole group and throw them into the back of an open truck with their arms bound. The officials then stage a parade, with bugles playing to attract attention. When the truck comes to a likely corner, one of the poor devils is dumped out, made to stand up . . . and then shot in the head. He sprawls bleeding on the pavement and the horrible procession drives to another location where the job is repeated.

In the last week of 1937, the Chinese authorities in Qingdao suddenly evacuated, turning the city over to several days of even more intense looting (Europeans and Americans in the city organized a militia to protect their property). Order was only restored when Japanese marines landed at Qingdao on January 10, 1938; within two weeks an occupation government was established.[4]

Tanxu had operated in conflict zones and political gray areas for most of his life. He had spent almost his entire career in treaty ports, colonies, or semi-colonies, where the lines dividing ruler and ruled, and Chinese and foreign, were convoluted and frequently in question. Except for a few months in Harbin in 1932, though, he had not lived under Japanese occupation. It was significantly different from living under European colonialism, or in its shadow. No longer did a stupa or a half-hipped, half-gabled roof present an obvious contrast to the culture of the occupying power. Furthermore, because Japan sought to use Buddhism to unify Asia within its Greater East Asia Co-Prosperity Sphere, Buddhism's power as a marker of Chinese identity was eliminated.

Buddhism also featured as part of Japan's New People's Principles (*xinmin zhuyi*), which stood in contrast to Sun Yat-sen's Three People's Principles of Nationalism, Democracy, and "the People's Livelihood" (sometimes translated as Socialism). The New People's Principles marked an attempt to provide an ideological foundation for the unification of China and Japan (along with the Japanese-installed regime in Manchukuo) under Japanese leadership. In Manchukuo, the Japanese built their rule on the Kingly Way (*wang dao*), a Confucian concept that determined the righteousness and legitimacy of a ruler. In North China, Japanese Major General Kita Seiichi proclaimed—in the same month that Japanese marines captured Qingdao—that "it was necessary to go back to Confucian times to find a really satisfactory system for the rule of the Chinese people."[5]

Kita was given control of all Chinese government organs under Japanese occupation in North China. Responding to the concern that Japan was "Manchurianizing" China, and also worried that a stress on traditional Confucian concepts would alienate young Chinese, Kita developed the New People's Principles as a more modern alternative to the Kingly Way for justifying Japanese rule in China. The New People's Society (*xinmin hui*), which he established to spread the Principles, was so successful that according to historian John Boyle it "all but replaced the Provisional Government as the governing body of North China."[6]

Like the Kingly Way, the New People's Principles were rooted in Confucianism, but other East Asian belief systems contributed as well. Bushido, the Japanese warrior code, justified Japan's domination of China. Buddhism, too, played an important role in the New Principles' syncretic ideology: historically Mahayana Buddhism united Chinese and Japanese culture, while the Theravada tradition flourished in Southeast Asia and Buddhism's roots were in India. Buddhism could thus unite the entire continent under the slogan "Asia for the Asiatics." The Japanese made plans for a Buddhist university to help deepen and spread the message of pan-Asianism.[7]

Tanxu's account of the Japanese occupation of Qingdao is all but silent about his own interactions with the Japanese. He seems to have maintained the same pattern of activities as before, traveling throughout North China, lecturing on sutras, and taking part in various ceremonies and rituals. If collaboration is not the right word, perhaps acquiescence does apply. There is certainly no evidence that Tanxu actively resisted the Japanese. Historian Xue Yu's research found that Tanxu took part in a ceremony for Japanese soldiers organized by the Japan-China Buddhist Study Society, and that he later served as chair of the Common Buddhist Purpose Society branch in Qingdao. Perhaps significantly, these events are not mentioned in his memoir.[8] Tanxu describes his visits to various temples and organizations, including the Red Swastika Society (a quasi-Buddhist relief agency, modeled on the Red Cross), during the war, but little can be gleaned about his political life, other than that he was apparently able to travel without great difficulty.

As soon as the word "collaboration" is used, blame and judgment displace understanding or analysis. Timothy Brook defined collaboration as "the continuing exercise of power under the pressure produced by the presence of an occupying power."[9] Under this definition, Tanxu clearly was a collaborator; he was no longer abbot of Tranquil Mountain Temple, but he continued to perform ceremonies and rituals, and otherwise exercised influence over Buddhist clergy and laity throughout the war. However, by this definition nearly everyone who lived through foreign occupation can be labeled as a collaborator. Larry Shyu and David Barrett's edited book on this topic is subtitled: "the limits of accommodation."[10] "Accommodation" seems a more useful way to understand the actions of individuals under totalitarian regimes. As even Brook notes, in his review of another work on collaboration during the Sino-Japanese War, collaboration is not a single response, but a complex range of reactions. It is morally more complex than "resistance":

> [R]esistance simplifies the range of moral choices available to the occupied, and is complex only insofar as the resister manages to find ways to stay alive. Collaboration on the other hand is a matter of shifting definitions and inconsistent responses. To collaborate is to involve oneself in constant renegotiation with the enemy, with one's associates, and with oneself.[11]

Václav Havel, the Czech dissident, playwright, and president, strikes a similar note in his essays about life under totalitarianism. For Havel, the important thing is not to assign guilt, but to recognize that everyone living under the regime is culpable: "We are all—though naturally to different extents—responsible for the operation of totalitarian machinery. None of us is just its victim: we are also its co-creators." Havel denies that a bright line divides resistance from collaboration. Instead, he sees an important "line of conflict" that "did not run between the rulers and the ruled, but rather through the middle of each individual, for everyone in his or her own way is both a victim and a supporter of the system."[12]

This is certainly the position in which Tanxu found himself after 1938. The most morally transparent position would have been to refuse to live under the Japanese. Some monks did take up arms against the occupiers; Tanxu did not, and in fact worked hard to convince the Japanese—who suspected him of belonging to the resistance—that he had not. His memoir neither justifies nor defends his actions. Rather, he describes matter-of-factly his work spreading the dharma, which continued much as it had for decades.

As one of the most prominent monks in occupied China, Tanxu would have been very useful to the Japanese plan to build a religious or ideological bridge between the two nations. He was invited to go to Japan during the war, but refused, saying that he was not interested in politics. Two of Tanxu's students, Ruguang and Shanguo, were clearly collaborators by any definition. Shanguo, who succeeded Tanxu as abbot of the Expansive Wisdom Temple in Changchun, actively cooperated with the Japanese, visiting Japan in 1938 and then becoming a branch chairman of the General Buddhist Association of Manchukuo. Ruguang became abbot of Paradise Temple in Harbin and also held a leadership position in the General Buddhist Association of Manchukuo.[13]

That two of his students worked actively with the Japanese authorities in Manchukuo might be taken as evidence that Tanxu, too, was willing to accommodate the occupying forces, who tolerated, if they did not patronize, Tanxu's temple in Qingdao. After the war's end, Tanxu traveled to Changchun at Shanguo's invitation, possibly a sign that he did not disapprove of his former student's actions during the occupation. On the other hand, Tanxu himself declined invitations to Japan and refused to take leadership positions in the Manchukuo or collaborationist Buddhist bureaucracy. These refusals suggest that, unlike Shanguo and Ruguang, he was not willing to work closely with the Japanese, though for what reasons we cannot know.

We are left, then, with few tools for evaluating Tanxu's claim to be apolitical. Throughout his career he was inspired by the desire to revive Buddhism in North China, but he also worked to promote Chinese culture in the face of foreign colonialism, especially by building temples in Yingkou, Harbin, and Qingdao. This "cultural nationalism" was often supported by authorities who saw that Tanxu's temple construction was useful in their own efforts to promote Chinese nationalism. From 1922 on, Tanxu cooperated with secular authorities in ways that helped him promote Buddhism, but the balance between political and religious motivations is unclear.

Tanxu also cooperated—at least passively—with Japanese authorities in Harbin, Changchun, and Qingdao. His cooperation enabled him to help sustain thriving Buddhist temples and monasteries in areas under Japanese control. Although it may seem credulous to accept Tanxu at his word that he was motivated by religion and eschewed politics, ultimately this seems the most plausible resolution of the conflicting claims about his work during the war. At the same time, it must be noted that he was willing to overlook or dismiss pressing political and even moral concerns in the name of promoting Buddhism.

Japanese sources are silent on the role of Tranquil Mountain Temple during the occupation. This is hardly surprising; the occupiers had more important concerns. One of Qingdao's primary functions for the Japanese was as a recruiting ground for labor. The occupation of Manchuria was largely motivated by the need for natural resources, including agricultural products, and extracting these resources required labor. The migration of workers to Manchuria had been disrupted by Japan's war with China. Now the New Policies Association began recruiting laborers with promises of a better life, subsidized by the Japanese, in Manchukuo.[14] As the war dragged on, however, voluntary migration was inadequate to meet the need, and the Japanese began to compel immigration to Manchuria. Qingdao became a processing center for laborers brought there from throughout Shandong Province and the surrounding region. Several thousand laborers were quartered in camps in and around Qingdao at any given time during the 1940s.

The requisitioning of labor was familiar to Chinese peasants, who for centuries had been subjected to corvée-labor commitments. Registering as a monk was a means of avoiding obligations to the state, including the corvée. It seems likely that some Chinese would have entered the temple in Qingdao in order to avoid being sent to Manchuria as laborers. If so—and there is no direct evidence to support this theory—the temple would have functioned as an instrument of passive resistance to the Japanese regime.

Scraps of information about the war years in Qingdao can be gleaned from the autobiography of Master Lok To, who enrolled as a student in Tanxu's seminary in 1941. Lok To reports that the seminary operated as usual, serving the monastic community and the local Chinese population: there were other temples set aside expressly for the Japanese. Conditions at the monastery remained good until the last few years of the war, when food became scarce.[15] With most provisions being redirected to the military and to the labor camps, the monks of Tranquil Mountain relied on what they could grow at the monastery. The deteriorating conditions in the city suggested that Japan was losing the war, but no one could have predicted the speed with which the end came after atomic bombings of Hiroshima and Nagasaki.

The suddenness of the Japanese capitulation added to the chaos that accompanies the end of any war and laid bare the internal political divisions in China. Within weeks of the surrender, five uniformed armies were fielding weapons in and around Qingdao. Chinese Nationalist and Communist forces competed for the early advantage in the civil war that was now at hand. Japanese troops remained armed and in control of material assets, including the railroad that ran to Qingdao, while they awaited formal surrender and repatriation. (This was in accordance with the instructions of the Allies, who wanted to ensure that Japanese resources were transferred as efficiently as possible to the Nationalists.) The fourth army, belonging to the Japanese–allied Chinese regime, had surrendered, and most of its members were recognized and redeployed by the Nationalist government. The fifth force was the American marines.

The Americans planned to use Qingdao as a base for repatriating Japanese troops. More than half of the Japanese armies in North China were to board ships for Japan at Qingdao, and the marines arrived in Qingdao in early October to facilitate their surrender. The situation was delicate. Communist forces controlled most of Shandong Province. Qingdao itself was in Nationalist hands, as was the airfield, about ten miles outside of the city. According to American military records, the Communists approached the U.S. commander and asked if his troops would stand aside and permit them to enter Qingdao and "destroy" the other Chinese forces (i.e., the Nationalist and former collaborationist armies) as well as the Japanese who were awaiting surrender. The Americans refused, citing orders to maintain the status quo.[16]

The Americans were the third foreign power to occupy Qingdao in fifty years. For a marine, Qingdao was good duty to draw: a coastal city with broad beaches, a mild climate, and European colonial roots. At first, most residents saw the American troops as a great improvement over the occupying Japanese and their harsh regime, but relations quickly soured. Complaints about the Americans' behavior began almost immediately. Charges of rape were common. In one case, an American marine was alleged to have raped a Chinese waitress in a taxicab. Chinese police interviewed the cabdriver and the plaintiff. Both insisted that the sex had been forced, and asked the American forces to try the marine in a court-martial. The Americans, however, found "no evidence to support that allegation that force had been used on the girl," and concluded that the driver and the girl were engaged in prostitution (which was legal). No charges were filed.[17]

In another case, on March 30, 1947, an American sailor named Pedro Arraba stabbed a rickshaw puller in front of a nightclub after a dispute over the fare. The victim, Su Mingcheng, chased Arraba into the club, and there collapsed and died. Many other rickshaw pullers were gathered outside the club, seeking fares. They pursued Arraba, cornering him before he was apprehended by Chinese police. The U.S. Military Police were quickly informed, and they arrived to take Arraba in for questioning.

There was strong pressure to try Arraba for murder in Chinese courts; Su Mingcheng, just twenty-two years old, was a sympathetic figure, and the case was being pressed by Qingdao's powerful rick-shaw pullers' union, already frustrated by the extralegal status of the Americans. (Traffic accidents involving pedestrians and American jeeps—often fatal—were a constant source of tension.) However, the American investigators decided on a charge of involuntary manslaughter, and the trial was conducted by court-martial on the USS *Jason*, offshore. Arraba (who pleaded not guilty) was convicted and sentenced to ten years' confinement, as well as loss of rank and a dishonorable discharge. The sentence was later reduced to five years by U.S. naval authorities, on grounds of improper admission of evidence.[18]

The U.S. Marines and representatives of Chiang Kai-shek's government took the formal surrender of the Japanese Qingdao garrison—some ten thousand men—on October 25, at Qingdao's horseracing track, an evocative relic of an era that had ended. The Japanese surrender did not end the conflict. Armed encounters between the U.S. forces and the Communist People's Liberation Army—though rarely involving casualties—would be common during the civil war. The American commanders described Qingdao as "a Nationalist island in a Communist sea" and called in air support to maintain their perimeter around the city and to protect the Jiao–Ji Railway that connected Qingdao to inland areas.[19]

Like the Japanese occupation, the civil war had little effect on Tanxu's work. He moved freely between Tianjin and Qingdao, raising money for the completion temples in both cities. In 1947, he returned to Changchun, where he again officiated at an ordination ceremony. On the previous occasions, in 1936 and again in 1941, the city had been "Xinjing," the capital of Manchukuo. Now, its old name restored, it was no longer politically important but it was still threatened by conflict. The Communist forces had established a base in Manchuria, with some assistance from the Soviet troops who had taken the Japanese surrender in the region. The United States had airlifted Nationalist troops into southern Manchuria, but Communists remained powerful in the north. Harbin, where Tanxu had founded Paradise Temple, was the only city in China that the Communists controlled for most of the civil war. Changchun was near the front lines between Communist- and Nationalist-controlled territory, and it was difficult to get supplies into the city. Tanxu observed that everyone in Changchun—Buddhist or not—was a vegetarian because meat was scarce. The rail lines to Changchun were cut soon after he arrived, and Tanxu had to remain there for the winter.

Letters came regularly from Tianjin and Qingdao, begging Tanxu to return and help with the temple construction, but he remained in Changchun, lecturing and preaching. Early in the spring of 1948, he dreamed that a group of small children pointed him south, saying this was the way home. The dream motivated Tanxu to leave Changchun, even with the railroad still blocked. He hired a horse cart and together with five others left for Tianjin. The trip was nearly brought to a halt almost before it began: in just ten days, bandits stopped Tanxu's party seven times, eventually making off with all their provisions, money, and horses. Tanxu must have been reminded of earlier trips through southern Manchuria. Much had changed in the fifty years since he had fled Shenyang ahead of the Sino-Japanese War, but China was still divided among competing armies and occupied by foreign armies.

Although in ten days he had traveled less than two hundred miles, it was an education for Tanxu. He had seen firsthand China's condition after decades of war. Americans and Europeans tend to think of World War II as lasting from 1939, or 1941, to 1945. The Japanese had invaded Manchuria, however, more than ten years before Pearl Harbor; they had invaded the rest of China in 1937. Even before the Japanese came, warlordism and banditry were common in many parts of the country, and after the Japanese surrender the war continued, now between Communists and Nationalists. For the villages of Manchuria, warfare had been a part of daily life for nearly half a century. Most people had no memory of a time free from the threat of armed men. In just a few days of travel through this landscape Tanxu gained new insights:

> I had received an education about how difficult many people's lives were. There was much suffering, and yet I observed that the people always adapted. I thought about this constantly. No matter what time it was, I was always reflecting on this. During the 10 or more days of my journey, some days I ate three times; some days twice, other days just once; sometimes we had plenty of fresh water to drink, other days we did not.[20]

During the trip, the group relied on charity for accommodations, sometimes at local temples, but usually finding shelter in barns or farmhouses. Occasionally, according to Tanxu, supernatural forces interceded: stopping near a village called Taiyang Gou (Sun Creek), a pigsty was the only shelter the travelers could see. Exhausted, they asked the farmer's wife for permission to spend the night there. The household included three toddlers and was filled with activity, verging on chaos. Nevertheless, an old woman insisted that the men come inside and have tea. After tea, she found room for the oldest member of their group, who was nearly eighty, to sleep inside, while the rest were accommodated in the barn. During the night a rainstorm came up, and they all exclaimed at their good fortune in finding such a warm and comfortable place to shelter from the storm.

The next morning, as they prepared to continue their journey, the men wished to thank the woman who had taken pity on them the night before, but she was nowhere to be found. The farmer's wife told them that she was the only woman who lived there. Tanxu and his companions declared that it had been Guanyin—the

Bodhisattva of Compassion—who had appeared to them in the night and found them a place to stay. As they walked on, another cloudburst descended. This time they called upon Guanyin for help and were answered with an end to the rain and the sudden appearance of the sun through clouds Tanxu described as "raven-black."

The next night, they lodged in the village of Tieling, at a Buddhist temple dedicated to the Medicine King Bodhisattva. The men discussed their recent experiences with the monks of the temple. The aid that Guanyin provided had made their travels much more bearable. Without her intercession, the journey might not have been possible. On one hand, Tanxu saw the intervention of the bodhisattva as a suitable reward, justifying their faith in Buddhism. On the other, however, he saw a risk.

For many Chinese, the effectiveness of prayers to Guanyin and other bodhisattvas was a matter of superstition rather than religion. As Tanxu talked with the monks, they agreed that many people came to Buddhist temples seeking help with their problems, with no intention of following the Buddha's path. When their prayers were answered, people continued to patronize the temples, but they did not adopt the practices or intentions that would lead them to a more virtuous life or escape from samsara—the cycle of death and rebirth. They agreed that most people considered Buddhism in strictly pragmatic terms: was it effective in bringing them what they needed? While pragmatism could be a virtue, helping people to survive amid adversity, Tanxu felt that it discouraged the harder steps that would lead toward enlightenment.[21] For the rest of Tanxu's career, he focused on establishing libraries and preserving texts, in part as an antidote to this kind of superstitious belief.

The clear line that Tanxu draws between religion and superstition fits into discussions surrounding modernity and religions that had been ongoing around the world for several decades. Most notably, the 1893 Parliament of World Religions in Chicago had sought to locate global religious traditions in the context of modernizing Western Protestantism. The Nationalist government's campaigns to eliminate superstition and place China on the path toward modernization followed this same agenda. Tanxu's own life and career surely featured elements that could be seen as "superstitious," including his work with alchemy, his time as a fortune-teller, and his visions of the afterlife. It is noteworthy that Tanxu, a religious man and an advocate of tradition rather than reform, felt so strongly that the distinction between religion and superstition needed to be clearly drawn. It suggests the extent to which the dichotomy pervaded Chinese culture and society. (The separation of the two would also have been important to the young monks to whom Tanxu was delivering the lecture, which would become his memoir, as Tanxu sought to illustrate proper behavior for the next generation of monks.)[22]

Tieling was controlled by the Nationalist army, and the travelers were able to buy railway tickets for the short journey to Shenyang. Tanxu remained there for two weeks, evaluating the temples he had helped found and restore in that city, before continuing his journey south and west to Tianjin and then on to Qingdao. Nationalist troops and American marines defended the railroad from Tianjin to Qingdao, but as the Communists made inroads in the region, this became more and more difficult. In March 1948, the Communists captured several villages along the railroad line and severed the link between Qingdao and Tianjin—two of the most important ports along the northern coast. As Communist victory grew more likely, Tanxu increased his commitment to collecting and preserving Buddhist texts.

With the link to Tianjin cut, that path of escape from Qingdao was closed. The Communist Party was hostile to religion of every kind, suppressing it much more effectively, and sometimes violently, than had the Guomindang. Soon, reports of the humiliation of Buddhist monks and nuns—and even torture and executions—began to reach Qingdao. These reports could not be substantiated, but they cast doubt on the temple's survival under a Communist regime. If the monks could not stay in Qingdao, or perhaps anywhere at all in China, a new home would have to be found. The leaders of the temple turned to the young student, Lok To, for help.

Lok To had come to Tranquil Mountain Temple during the Japanese occupation, in 1941, at the age of eighteen. He had already been living in Buddhist temples for more than ten years. As a boy he had fallen gravely ill. His mother had gone to a local Buddhist temple to pray for his recovery, promising that her son would become a monk if he lived. When the boy regained his health, it was agreed that he would live at home until the temple called for him. For a few years he lived a normal boyhood, but when he was ten, the temple called for him to come live as a monk.

The transition from family life to a monastery was heart-wrenching:

> When I first left my family, in the temple I learned how to kow-tow, and how to make obeisance, and other simple rituals, but because I was so young, and had just left home, I missed my family very much, and every day I wanted to return home.
>
> I had an older brother and three younger sisters. I wanted very much to return home to play with them. Because of this, I went often to the masters, and cried, and said that I was going to get my things together and return home. Because of what had happened when I was younger, my mother and the master knew that I needed to become a monk, but because I was so young and missed my family so much the master often let me return home to visit my family.[23]

Because Lok To had come to the temple at such a young age and under unusual circumstances, instead of waiting to the normal age of eighteen, he was able to take the precepts early, which he did at Xinghua Temple in Xuzhou. Ordained as an itinerant monk, he went to Qingdao to study at Tanxu's seminary. He does not comment on the war years, other than to observe that food became scarce as the war dragged on, and that the position of the Japanese occupiers became more precarious.

When Japan surrendered, the Nationalist government sponsored the creation of a nationwide Buddhist Association. The association, headed by Taixu, was intended to help rehabilitate the sangha and to repair and renovate Buddhist temples. A branch of the association was to be established in every major city. In the fall of 1945, a meeting was held in Qingdao; Lok To attended. At the meeting, an American expressed the view that the United States was a fertile field for spreading the message of Buddhism. Lok To decided that from that time on he would work to spread the dharma in North America, and he began studying English, along with two or three other monks. A few months later, a friend wrote him from Hong Kong, describing the British colony as a good place to visit and, furthermore, an excellent place to study English. Lok To and his fellow English students made arrangements and sailed from Qing-dao to Shanghai in May of 1946, hoping there to find a ship bound for Hong Kong.

This was a time of hyper-inflation in China; prices could rise dra-matically from morning to afternoon. By the time Lok To and his companions arrived in Shanghai, their money was only enough for two tickets to Hong Kong, rather than the three they needed. They stayed several days at a local temple, trying to raise money for the third ticket. After selling what few articles they had, they were able to buy the third ticket—for 40 million yuan!—and sailed to Hong Kong.

When they arrived, the three monks looked for a place to stay. They had only the name of their classmate who had written to them and knew of no particular temple at which they could seek accom-modation. They were first brought to the Tung Lin Kok Yuen nun-nery, one of the most prominent Buddhist institutions in the colony that had been serving as the home of the newly founded Hong Kong Buddhist Association. Founded in the 1930s, Tung Lin Kok Yuen occupied a new campus of buildings in the Yau Ma Tei section of Kowloon. This nunnery operated the only seminary for girls in Hong Kong, with an eight-year curriculum that included history, Chinese, English, and mathematics, in addition to Buddhist sutras and other religious instruction.[24] This was a Pure Land temple, and very well organized, but men could not stay there and so the group moved on. Next, they went to a smaller temple located in Tsuen Wan in the New Territories. This monastery, called Tung Pu Tor, had also been established in the 1930s and was one of the few mon-asteries in Hong Kong that accepted refugees from the mainland. Even more unusual, it extended that welcome to northerners. Although they were welcome, Lok To and his companions found the southern monastic regimen very unfamiliar, just as Tanxu had done so many years before in Ningbo. After just a few days they decided to leave. Also during this time they learned that the class-mate who had urged them to come to Hong Kong had passed away. They now had no connections in the colony.

The three finally took lodging at Mt. Daofeng Monastery, which Lok To had heard was a center for religious studies. This was a unique institution in China. Founded in the 1930s by Scandinavian missionaries and researchers, Mt. Daofeng taught Christianity in a traditional Chinese setting. In its art and architecture the center resembled a Buddhist or Daoist temple, but the doctrine and sermons were entirely Christian. Lok To intended to stay there only a few days and perhaps to learn some points of comparison between Buddhism and Christianity. He stayed for some weeks, however, and as time went on he became convinced that the Mt. Daofeng center was deceptively designed to attract Daoist or Buddhist monks with the familiar setting of a temple and then convert them to Christianity. Lok To felt it was a threat to Buddhism. He began sharing his opinion with the abbot of a nearby Buddhist temple.

Frustrated by the unfamiliar language and customs and unsettled by his experience at Mt. Daofeng, Lok To was disappointed with his time in Hong Kong and solicited help from local Buddhists to return to Qingdao. Early in 1948, he boarded a ship bound for Shanghai.

On his way out, Lok To had passed quickly through Shanghai—his teacher at his first temple had told him it was a place to be avoided, that for a monk to go to Shanghai—literally "on the sea"—would be to go *xiahai*, "beneath the sea": to die. On his return journey, though, he stayed in the city for several days. Shanghai was always frenetic, but in the years of the civil war it was chaos. It had been a stronghold of the Nationalist government, but it was also a beacon for refugees and opportunists. Lok To found the city disturbing, and to him it represented Buddhism's precarious position in China:

> Seeing Shanghai made me very sad: many people were suffering. The ways of Buddhism were nearly absent, and the truth of the situation I am reluctant to speak of. Suffice it to say that there was much evil, and I felt that the Buddhist world of Shanghai, which needed to be rebuilt, had instead been beaten down, and a way needed to be found to revive it. Instead, after the Communist Party came, Buddhism was again beaten down.[25]

Lok To arrived back in Qingdao in March 1948, around the same time Tanxu returned from Manchuria and just as the leadership of the temple was seeking an escape plan for Tanxu and the other senior monks.

Shanbo, the abbot, now called on Lok To for help. "The situation in the country is very grave," he said. "We must evacuate. It is easy for the young ones to leave and find lodging, but I am not sure if the monks, particularly the monks of high standing, will be able to do so. Moreover, the Nationalist government has a few high officials who were monks, and when the Communists captured them they would not release them. Monks have been martyred in this way. We are northern monks and have no connections with southern monasteries, but you have just returned from the south and seen what is possible and what is not, so you must make a plan."[26]

They all agreed that Tanxu and other senior monks must leave, and that Hong Kong was the best destination. Lok To's contacts in Hong Kong were their only lead. Although he had not enjoyed his time in Hong Kong and had just made a difficult journey back to Qingdao, Lok To agreed to return to the colony to try to find a suitable place for his master.

The news that Lok To was preparing to return so quickly to Hong Kong aroused suspicions about the progress of the civil war. His classmates besieged Lok To to allow them to accompany him: they had only three tickets for the ship, but twenty-seven monks wanted to go! Deciding to take advantage of their common dress and hairstyle—brown robes and shaven heads—and also the mystique of the clergy, the monks boarded the ship in groups of three. Once on board, two from the group would hide in the cargo hold while the third took the tickets and returned to shore to get two more monks. Even given the confusion that might have been present at the docks and the monks' similar dress, it seems unlikely that no one on board ship would have noticed the deception. More probably, someone turned a blind eye to the ruse, but in any case Lok To reported that they repeated the process until all twenty-seven monks were on board—twenty-four of them below deck in the hold—and sailed to Shanghai.

Arriving in Shanghai, the monks split up into several groups and dispersed among local temples. By this time—mid-1948—it was evident that the Communists were winning the civil war, and travel out of China was becoming more difficult. The victorious Communists were moving from north to south, pushing a wave of refugees ahead of them. Shanghai, always a transportation hub, was mobbed with people seeking passage to the south or attempting to flee China altogether.

Lok To and his fellow monks sought passage to Hong Kong. Boats and trains were crammed beyond capacity, and ticket prices were pushed beyond reach by hyper-inflation, profiteering, and demand. Among the monks traveling with Lok To were Xing Kong, Sheng Hua, Zhi Kai (Chee Kai), and Da Cheng, some of whom would later become leaders in Hong Kong Buddhism. The group pursued every lead, eventually traveling to Hangzhou, a few hours south of Shanghai. From there, the journey became even slower and more difficult. It took nearly a year for the group to reach Guangzhou (Canton), one hundred miles from Hong Kong.

Lok To found accommodation at the Liurong Temple, one of the oldest temples in Guangzhou, dating back to the sixth century CE. The monks there had read an article by Lok To in the Buddhist press, warning about the Mt. Daofeng Christian center, and they agreed to help him cross the border into Hong Kong via the Kowloon–Canton Railroad (KCR). The KCR, opened in the second decade of the twentieth century, linked the waterfront at Tsimshatsui—in Kowloon, opposite Hong Kong Island—with Canton. With the assistance of the monks in Guangzhou, Lok To managed to reach Hong Kong, and returned to Xilin Monastery, in Shateen District, where he had been on his previous visit to the colony. He attended classes at the temple seminary to justify his presence, but was constantly working to find a way to bring Tanxu to Hong Kong.

The best hope to sponsor Tanxu was Ye Gongchuo, one of Tanxu's oldest acquaintances. Ye had been the minister of transportation in 1925 when Tanxu first went to Beijing, accompanying Dixian on his lecture trip to the north. The men had met intermittently in the twenty years since then, mainly in the early 1930s when Ye was one of the moving forces behind the founding of the Tranquil Mountain Temple. Ye had an active career in government, education, and the arts: he was instrumental in founding Shanghai Jiaotong University and served as director of classics at Peking University. He also acquired a reputation as a fine painter. His calligraphy was especially admired: Ye's characters adorned the entryway to the famous Tung Lin Kok Yuen nunnery where Lok To had first come in 1947.

Ye Gongchuo was not easy to find. Rumors circulated that he was in Canton, in Hong Kong, elsewhere on the mainland, or even in Taiwan. Lok To spent more than three months in Hong Kong following leads, all the while receiving increasingly alarming messages from Qingdao about the deteriorating military and political situation there. Desperate, Lok To turned to Guanyin for help, as he and so many others had done before. On a trip to Taipo village, far from Hong Kong Island in the New Territories, Lok To fell asleep in a temple and began to dream:

> I was on a small path in a forest, wandering toward a clearing, moving toward the light ... I walked on and found myself facing an old Buddhist temple, and on the entrance was written "Guanyin Tomb*," but I did not understand at all why this particular character "admire (mu慕)" would be used, rather than the right character, "tomb (mu墓)." I went closer to examine the character, and noticed that behind the stele was an old woman, dressed in black, resembling a peasant. I walked closer to her, and asked her to explain to me where I was. She replied to me, "This is not just the tomb of Guanyin." I asked her if anyone lived inside. She just told her to come with me. Together, we entered the main gate, and within we saw that there were four gates, and the old lady entered one of them on the right. I did not follow her, for I feared it was her private quarters, and waited outside.
>
> After I waited a while, I still had not seen her emerge, and so I resumed walking along the path, and I discovered that nearby was a large pavilion, its roof completely collapsed. Inside was a shrine to Guanyin. We monks, whenever we see a statute or shrine of a Buddha or a bodhisattva, will certainly offer obeisance, and so I went in and knelt before the shrine, touching my head to the floor. I made the first obeisance and nothing out of the ordinary took place, but when I bowed the second time, the bodhisattva stepped down from her platform, and touched my head. . . . [27]

Lok To interpreted the dream as a message about the importance of calligraphy, and so he decided to pursue Ye Gongchuo through his art. Lok To asked around, seeking to discover where the famous calligrapher's works could be purchased. He learned that a small gallery in Kowloon was the only supplier. Lok To went to the gallery and asked the proprietor to put him in touch with Ye Gongchuo. Wary of introducing a stranger to his important client, the owner refused, but agreed to pass on a letter. In the letter, Lok To explained the situation and his desire to bring Tanxu to Hong Kong.

A few days later, an associate of Ye Gongchuo found Lok To at the Xilin Monastery and arranged for him to meet Ye (at the Bank of East Asia on Queen's Road). The meeting was frustrating for Lok To because many people were present, making it difficult for him to plead the seriousness of Tanxu's situation. However, Ye gave Lok To a letter for Tanxu, unsealed, and Lok To sent it on by airmail to Qingdao.

After a few days, Lok To met with Ye Gongchuo alone and explained in more detail:

> I told him of the situation on the mainland and of Master Tan's plans to come south to Hong Kong to spread the dharma and to assist in education here. Although I never spoke the words "refugee" or "escape," he understood that this was my meaning, and then we talked about other things. He told me that he would need a few days to look into the possibility of a Buddhist Study institute, and that I should wait. He then said that he would see if he could find a place for him to "borrow" that would be large and peaceful enough to suit Master Tanxu, and would not cost any money at all. He would buy a small place and make Master Tan the abbot.[28]

With funds supplied by Ye Gongchuo and Wang Xueren, an old Buddhist hermitage was purchased. It was located in the New Territories, in a ravine not far from Kowloon. It was isolated and peaceful enough for Tanxu, it was felt, but it had not been well maintained. The monks set about restoring it in preparation for Tanxu's arrival. As the work progressed, Tanxu was invited to come south.

CHAPTER 10

Forward to the Past

Flights from Qingdao left Cankou airfield, an American military base ten miles outside the city. On the morning of April 1, 1949—one month before the last American marines would abandon the city to the People's Liberation Army—Tanxu boarded a Civil Air Transport flight to Shanghai. Communist forces, advancing steadily and occasionally firing on the American occupiers and their Nationalist allies from the surrounding hills, threatened the airfield's security as Tanxu prepared to leave. Civil Air Transport (CAT) was founded by William Willauer and General Claire Lee Chennault who, after the end of World War II, saw an opportunity in the devastated transportation infrastructure. Acquiring government surplus C-46 and C-47 transports, the two started CAT as a private commercial concern, which was soon transporting cargo around the country. As the civil war intensified, so did the need for air transport. The company was soon "deeply involved in the Chinese civil war . . . and often served as an adjunct to the Nationalist air force."[1] (CAT later became Air America, the Central Intelligence Agency's proxy air force in Southeast Asia during the 1950s and 60s.)

At age seventy-four, Tanxu was boarding an airplane for the first time in his life. He had good reason to be anxious. Three American flights had crashed at Qingdao in the previous two years, killing more than fifty people.[2] Two CAT planes and a U.S. Navy plane had crashed into the surrounding mountains trying to land. The two pilots of the Navy flight were still being held captive, and would remain in Communist custody for nineteen months, until June

1950.[3] Tanxu's flight, however, was uneventful: his plane flew the several hours to Shanghai without incident. He stayed there for a few days before resuming his journey, again by plane.

Tanxu's flight to Hong Kong took him out of China for the last time: Shanghai was—for a few more months—part of the Republic of China; Hong Kong was a British Crown Colony. The landing at Hong Kong's notorious Kai Tak airport would have been frightening, even for a veteran flier: the approach required the pilot to clear the mountains surrounding the airport and then dive steeply to the airfield, executing a sharp turn just before touchdown. (The necessity for this white-knuckle approach ended with Kai Tak's closure in 1998, but postcards for sale in the city still celebrate Boeing 747s descending at full-throttle just above the rooftops of surrounding apartment blocks.)

Tanxu arrived at Kai Tak on April 4, 1949, and was met by Lok To and a handful of others, who took him immediately to Happy Valley and the Tung Lin Kok Yuen nunnery. Like all of China, Hong Kong was in flux. Change was nothing new for Hong Kong. For more than a century, it had been perched at the edges of empires. In 1842, at the end of the First Opium War, the Qing Empire ceded Hong Kong Island, famously described as a "barren rock," in perpetuity to Great Britain. Britain won a further concession in 1860, adding to their new colony Kowloon, the mainland peninsula opposite Hong Kong—again "in perpetuity." In 1898, the New Territories, comprising a much larger chunk of the mainland as well as surrounding islands, were leased to Britain for ninety-nine years, creating the territory's current borders.

This territory had initially been sparsely populated but flourished under the British. In 1941, the Japanese attacked Hong Kong as part of the coordinated campaign that also targeted Pearl Harbor, Singapore, Manila, and other Asian ports. On December 8, hours after the attack on Pearl Harbor, fifty thousand Japanese troops (outnumbering the defenders by more than three to one) invaded the territory. Three weeks later, on Christmas Day, the British administration surrendered, marking the first time that a British colonial government had surrendered to an invading army. During the three years and eight months of occupation, the population of the territory fell markedly because of the stresses of war and pressures on public health and the medical infrastructure. Trade—the foundation of the economy—ground to a halt.

When Japan surrendered to the Allies, the future of Hong Kong was uncertain. Many, including American President Franklin Roosevelt, thought the colony should be returned to their wartime ally, the Nationalist government of China, but Britain quickly reasserted control over the territory. Newly released from prison camps, British officers and officials declared an interim government, and the Japanese occupiers promised to maintain order until they could formally surrender to British forces. On August 30, warships of the British Pacific Fleet steamed into the harbor and accepted the Japanese surrender. British rule was restored with remarkable speed, although some of the institutions of pre-war colonialism broke down. For example, bans on Chinese ownership of property on Victoria Peak and on certain beaches were rescinded or left unenforced. The restoration of British rule made Hong Kong even more attractive for refugees fleeing the civil war on the mainland. The population quickly returned to, and then exceeded, pre-war levels. Squatter towns sprang up in the New Territories and Kowloon.

Immigration from the mainland brought an increased Buddhist presence to Hong Kong and the New Territories. The refugees would find important temples there, some of them many centuries old, but there were few monasteries or seminaries. Coupled with the effects of the Japanese occupation, this meant that by 1949 there were virtually no monks or nuns in Hong Kong.[4] Within a few years of the end of the civil war, as many as one thousand monks had arrived, fleeing the anti-Buddhist policies of the Communist regime. Most were just passing through. Many continued on to Taiwan, which was eager to promote itself as a protector of traditional Chinese culture, including Buddhism. Others dispersed to Chinese communities in Australia, Southeast Asia, North America, and Europe.

Tanxu, however, would stay in Hong Kong. He spent his first night in the colony with the abbot of a temple in Happy Valley, and the next day met with Ye Gongchuo. It was agreed that Tanxu would preside over a new seminary, to be called the South China Buddhist Studies Center (Zhongnan Fojiao Xuehui), based in a restored monastery in the New Territories and funded by a board of trustees, mainly mainland refugees. In the meantime, Tanxu's reputation began to attract a steady stream of students, primarily from Canton and Shanghai, and he began lecturing novice monks on how to follow the path of the Buddha.

As Tanxu prepared for his new posting, events in China moved toward resolution. In October 1949, Mao Zedong proclaimed the founding of the new People's Republic of China, under Communist Party rule. The endgame of the civil war played out, as Chiang Kai-shek's Nationalists continued their retreat to the island of Taiwan, and even this refuge was not expected to last long: most observers anticipated that the Communists would attack the island imminently, and even the United States—the Nationalists' ally—appeared ready to stand aside should the Communists invade the island. Then in June, North Korea invaded South Korea. East Asia had become the main theater of the Cold War, with Chinese and American troops playing dominant roles in the Korean conflict. American vessels now moved into position to protect Taiwan as a bulwark against the threat of Communist expansion. Hong Kong found itself on the front lines of a Cold War that was heating up.

In February 1950, Hong Kong celebrated the first Lunar New Year since the end of the civil war. Much had changed since the last Nationalist troops had surrendered, a few weeks earlier. The easy connections between Hong Kong and Canton were severed. The railway between the two now stopped at Lo Wu, and so-called through trains would not resume for nearly fifty years. A barbed-wire and concrete barricade went up at the border. Hong Kong was now appended to a hostile neighbor, becoming even more strategically and symbolically important and also more vulnerable: the territory had (and continues to have) little fresh water, relying almost entirely on water piped in from Guangdong Province.

As the territory prepared to face an uncertain new year ahead, Tanxu delivered his first lectures at the South China Buddhist Academy. All of his students had experienced great unrest: the world in which they had been raised was changed, dramatically and apparently forever. There was little prospect of returning to the mainland. War, which had plagued China for most of the century, continued with new uniforms and new weapons. Not surprisingly, Tanxu's message focused on transcending this world. His first lecture of the new year was titled "On Amidism," and the topic was Pure Land practice.

According to Pure Land belief, the message of the Buddha has been diluted and obscured by the centuries since Sakyamuni's death. In the presence of the historical Buddha, two thousand years ago, one could receive his message so clearly and powerfully that enlightenment in one lifetime was a realistic goal. In the first generations after his death, the teaching remained pure and clear enough to lead seekers on the path toward enlightenment. As time passed, however, the message weakened, and the world's distractions multiplied, leaving believers with little hope of following the Buddha's teachings to enlightenment.

To overcome this, the Pure Land school developed, teaching reliance on the overriding compassion of the Amitabha Buddha for all sentient beings. Amitabha is committed to helping everyone attain enlightenment, and as early as the first century BCE, texts appeared suggesting that by invoking his name, seekers could achieve rebirth in a Pure Land. These Pure Lands, limitless in number, are the domains of Buddhas and bodhisattvas who preach the path of enlightenment with few distractions and overwhelming clarity. In this setting, the Buddha's message becomes clear, and enlightenment is attainable.

Pure Land practice is extremely accessible (for some critics, simplistic): anyone who recites the name accrues merit toward rebirth in the Pure Land. It is also compatible with almost all forms of Buddhism, requiring adherents only to repeat the name, "Amitabha" as often, and with as much sincerity, as possible. For this reason, Buddhist temples across the world echo with the sound of "Amitabha" (in various languages) throughout the day. Much of the theory and exegesis on Pure Land practice was developed by Zhiyi, the founder of the Tiantai school of which Tanxu was a patriarch; Tanxu was thus well-equipped to teach on the subject. Armed with a doctrine that was simple, accessible, and promised deliverance from a turbulent world, Tanxu began the new year.

If one keeps repeating the invocation "Namo Amitabha Buddha" until single-minded attention is reached, one may finally be led by Buddha to rebirth in the Western Paradise, where there is access to the Buddha's knowledge and insight and so recover the essence of Enlightenment. . . . Who does not wish to be enlightened? Who does not wish understanding?[5]

The greatest obstacle to enlightenment, Tanxu went on, is our attachment to our bodies and the physical world our bodies inhabit. The delusion that this body is our "self" binds us to the illusions of the material world. "The body," he writes, "is nothing but a container made of skin, filled with impurities, rotten and foul-smelling.

Now, if in the course of the present lecture someone should suddenly send in a skin container filled with excrement, even though tightly sealed, we would all consider it filthy and would hold our noses to avoid the smell. In fact, however, each one of us is an odorous container covered by skin and equipped with openings at both ends that emit unpleasant odors. Nevertheless, everyone considers this skin container to be the self, and so precious that it is adorned with cosmetics and nourished with food to enhance its beauty. In Buddha's view, this is the most dangerous of confused illusions. We must all be aware that this body of ours is really not the self but an object or instrument intended to serve—rather than rule—our lives. It is not the ego. It is not "I" or "we." It is rather "mine" or "ours," because this body is only part of what belongs to us. If we cannot put it aside, we are encumbered by that object.

For instance, when hungry, one cannot do without eating. When thirsty, one cannot do without drinking. At the end of one's life span, there is nothing to do but die. Facing something beautiful, one cannot resist casting a few more glances. Under conditions where there is indulgence of the five desires—for wealth, sex, food, fame, and sleep—one cannot resist experiencing enjoyment. Thus, a person is deprived of all mastery of the "self."

We should be aware that such things as eating, drinking, and enjoyment all pertain to material life. There is a beginning and an end to material existence. In addition to material life, each human being has a spiritual life, which has neither beginning nor end. This is the essence of enlightenment inherent in each of us. It is found everywhere. To practice Amidism one is to cultivate the spiritual life, and relying on Buddha's power and his own strength, he aims to be reborn in the Western Paradise.[6]

The practice of repeating "Namo Amitabha" can be taken to extremes: monks and laymen greet one another with the phrase and soon "Namo Amitabha" replaces many of the staples of ordinary conversation—"thank you," "goodbye," "you're welcome," and so on. In many temples today, battery-powered "chanting machines" are available, so that the invocation can play as a soundtrack for the entire day. Tanxu, though, emphasized that the phrase was not a magic spell. It was important because it called upon Amitabha for help, but it was also a method of quieting one's mind: the repetition enables the seeker to overcome the distractions of the surrounding world and focus on meditation and the goals of enlightenment. It is just as essential to be determined and focused as it is to repeat the invocation. An immoral life could not be redeemed simply by repeating the phrase, but combined with devotion to the Buddha's path, it is a powerful tool: "One invocation to Buddha Amitabha, if uttered properly, will immediately cause the six sense organs to become clean and clear."[7]

The appeal of this message would have been powerful for men seeking a way through, or out of, China's seemingly endless waves of violence and upheaval. Tanxu himself—seventy-five years old by the time of these lectures—had rarely seen the country at peace. The students, most of them younger than forty, had known nothing but war. In the face of this history, Tanxu encouraged his students to hope for more. "Ordinary people," he said, "usually consider it difficult to become a Buddha.

In fact, it is not so difficult. Both Buddha and ordinary sentient beings are invariably molded out of perception and contemplations. . . . Each person in the world has his own ideas. Scholars, farmers, workmen, businessmen, soldiers, public officials, etc., all have come to their present condition because of previous ideas. One becomes the embodiment of any fixed idea that is held in the mind.

Every day he looks at the Buddha, repeats the Buddha's name, bows and worships Buddha, mentally contemplates Buddha, and also hears Buddha's name proclaimed. At all times, his thoughts are on rebirth in the Western Paradise. In this way, he will surely be reborn in the Western Paradise, and will surely be able to realize Buddhahood.[8]

Tanxu finished the lecture with examples of Pure Land practitioners who were reborn in the Western Paradise. These examples, drawn from his experiences in Yingkou, Harbin, and Qingdao, all involved ordinary people who, through determined observance of Buddhist precepts and regular invocation of the Amitabha Buddha, were able to achieve rebirth there.

Tanxu was the most senior monk in Hong Kong, and thanks to the influx of refugees fleeing the mainland, students continued to flock to the seminary. Money, however, was scarce. Lok To was haunted by the deprivations that his master had to endure: he wrote of one occasion waiting for Tanxu to disembark the Star Ferry, which crossed Victoria Harbor between Hong Kong and Kowloon. The upper deck was much more comfortable, but it cost 20 Hong Kong cents, twice as much as the lower deck. When Lok To glimpsed Tanxu, an old man standing among the crowds on the crowded deck, adjacent to the engines and breathing their exhaust fumes, he wept: "I waited on the dock, and when I saw this 76-year-old master standing on the boat, I was filled with bitterness, and prostrated myself before him three times, performing the kowtow."[9] Lok To and Tanxu tried to obtain additional funding so that the seminary could accommodate more of the eager students arriving from the mainland. The move backfired—the board agreed to permit more students, but refused to increase the budget, squeezing the seminary more tightly than ever. Twenty-one students were now expected to get by on the resources that had barely supported ten. A year later, the board again felt that the budget was overweight, and proposed that the students spend half their time working to support the seminary.

Tanxu protested that this was unacceptable: students could not learn if they had to spend so much time working. Again, the board was unmoved; rather than increase the seminary's budget, the board proposed to turn it into a part-time textiles factory, producing undershirts and socks. After meeting with the board, Tanxu returned to the seminary and told Lok To that the board of directors had instructed him to buy sewing machines and begin knitting socks.

The proposal to turn the monks into textile workers illustrates a convergence of factors at work in 1950s Hong Kong. After the Nationalist defeat, refugees from the mainland flooded into the colony, primarily from Canton and Shanghai. After falling to 600,000 by the end of the war, by March 1950 Hong Kong's population reached an estimated 2.4 million. This 400 percent increase included many practicing Buddhists, whose arrival fueled the rebirth of Buddhism in Hong Kong, including Tanxu's South China Buddhist Studies Association. More significant to Hong Kong's future, the immigration of the late 1940s brought financial, artistic, and industrial expertise from Shanghai, laying the foundation for Hong Kong's modern economic boom. Soon Hong Kong was a leading exporter of cheap textiles due to a combination of modern machinery installed after the war, lax or nonexistent labor laws, new immigrants eager for work, and free-trade government policies. By 1955, British manufacturers were protesting the low cost of Hong Kong textiles, upset at being undercut by their own colonial workers.[10]

Despite their misgivings, the monks attempted to merge these two immigration-fueled trends: Buddhism and industrialization. Lok To and the others purchased six sewing machines and thread. The seminary's students received sewing instruction from Tung Lin Kok Yuen nuns, but the work was too slow to be profitable: after a week, they had produced just ten socks! By offering a laundry service—washing, dyeing, and ironing—the monks managed to earn enough to pay their expenses, but this had left them with no time to study. Clearly, they needed another option.

The solution came from Buddhist ritual: the *shuilu fahui*, or Rite for Deliverance of Creatures of Water and Land (sometimes abbreviated as the Land and Water Rite). This elaborate ceremony, thought to have been first performed in 505 CE and in wide practice by the tenth century, combines Chinese, Indian, and Tibetan Buddhism, as well as Daoism and elements of Chinese popular religion. Daniel Stephenson has called it "arguably the most spectacular ritual in the Chinese Buddhist liturgy"; this ceremony requires tremendous resources, including "a seemingly endless stream of clerical officiants, acolytes, and subsidiary staff . . . three to four thousand handcrafted paper placards, writs and petitions, papier-mâché effigies, and other paraphernalia." The inner sanctuary of the temple must be decorated with specific scrolls or wall paintings, and the temple also must provide special foods for the deities encountered in the ceremony, as well as the participants.[11]

The main purpose of the rite is to assist sentient beings to attain enlightenment; it is a rite of universal salvation. Participants (both real and symbolic representations) are led from the temple's lower hall, through a cleansing bath, and into the upper hall, where they are given ritual food and symbols of the Buddha's teaching before being sent out to the Pure Land, where they can achieve nirvana. The "participants" in the ritual are highly unusual: based on the inhabitants of the six traditional Buddhist realms (gods, demigods, humans, animals, Hungry Ghosts, and demons), they are modified to represent different elements of Chinese bureaucracy, Daoism, and folk religion, including Daoist immortals, emperors, Confucian worthies, and government officials. This syncretism made the ritual appealing to a broad cross-section of Chinese society, not just to Buddhists, and it was performed in a variety of contexts and for many purposes ranging from "protection of the nation and timely rain, to the New Year, Cold Food and Mid-autumn Festivals, and even annual celebrations at local shrines."[12]

It was precisely the ceremony's broad appeal that worried Tanxu, who was reluctant to perform this rite, feeling it was too superstitious and encouraged folk beliefs in spirits and ghosts rather than dedication to the path of the Buddha. Others argued that the ceremony would be popular in Hong Kong, attracting money and donors to the temple.[13]

Eventually Tanxu relented, but the necessary ritual elements were not to be found in the colony. All of the things they needed, however, were easily had at temples on the mainland. Baodeng and Yongxing—two monks who would themselves become leaders in the Hong Kong Buddhist community—were sent to Qingdao to obtain the required implements.

Traveling from Hong Kong to Qingdao and back in 1952 might seem no simple matter. It defies the image of an "Iron Curtain," as in Eastern Europe, descending on the mainland with the founding of the People's Republic in 1949. The success of the two monks' trip demonstrates the new regime's imperfect control of its porous borders and reflects the more moderate policies that would give way to the extremism of the later 1950s and 1960s, during the Great Leap Forward and Cultural Revolution. At this time, by contrast, the People's Republic was actively recruiting Chinese living abroad to return and help build "New China," a call that was heeded by many overseas Chinese. Capitalists were permitted to own property and operate businesses in many coastal cities during these first years of the PRC. It's not clear exactly how the two monks made their way back to Qingdao, but it seems to have gone smoothly, and they obtained the needed implements. When they returned, the ritual was performed, probably according to instructions laid out in a manual published around 1600. It raised HK $30,000 (around US $3,000), which was more than enough to finance the operation of the seminary. This ritual became an annual feature of the Hong Kong Buddhist landscape The financial worries of Tanxu and his patrons faded, along with the need to knit socks or take in laundry.

During this last phase of Tanxu's career, he worked to improve the material state of Buddhism in Hong Kong and especially to preserve important Buddhist texts. His work with texts had begun in Ningbo, when he had left the temple, against the wishes of his master, to help with the publication of sutras. It was his desire to gather and publish texts, as well as founding temples, that had brought Tanxu to Manchuria, and then to Xi'an, Shanghai, and Qingdao.

Ye Gongchuo had also been collecting texts long before his arrival in Hong Kong. In the 1930s he had worked in Shanghai gathering Master Dixian's works for publication. In the process, he decided that a full reprinting was called for, which would require a Buddhist master to review the texts and correct mistakes. He went to Qingdao's Tranquil Mountain Temple to seek Tanxu's help; Jiang Weiqiao, a lay Buddhist based in Hong Kong, agreed to finance the undertaking. Little came of the project initially, but when Tanxu and Ye met in Hong Kong, they restarted the endeavor with Jiang's assistance. The project took on the additional goal of rescuing and preserving texts that were in jeopardy from the Communist revolution on the mainland. The monks in Tanxu's seminary began collecting books and texts, forming the Chinese Book Center (*zhonghua shuju*). The students learned to print and publish, and worked on the project constantly when they were not in class or meditation. Within eighteen months they had printed the entire collection, more than a thousand volumes.

To preserve these texts and to make them available to the public, Tanxu oversaw the creation of the Buddhist Library of South China, on Boundary Street, which divided Kowloon from the New Territories. Tanxu raised money by lecturing regularly at the site, where he also lived. By the time the library opened in 1958, Tanxu was perhaps the most eminent monk in Hong Kong—venerable enough to be given pride of place at the Tung Wah Hospital's Prayer Meetings, which called together many of the colony's monks and nuns.[14] It was a major event when the Buddhist Library opened, with two hundred thousand volumes, including seven copies each of all the major sutras, dictionaries, reference texts, and commentaries. To celebrate the occasion, Tanxu gave a series of lectures on the Heart Sutra, one of the shortest and most widely read of all Buddhist texts.

Tanxu delivered the lectures over nine days in April 1958. He spoke in Mandarin, and his words were simultaneously translated into the local Cantonese by one of his students, Wang Kai.

The Heart Sutra's brevity belies its complexity. Its most famous phrase—usually translated as "form is emptiness; emptiness is form"—is among the most cryptic. In Lok To's translation of Tanxu's 1958 lectures, this phrase is rendered "Form does not differ from voidness, and voidness does not differ from form. Form is voidness, and voidness is form; the same is true for feeling, conception, volition, and consciousness."[15] Tanxu says that this is perhaps the most essential of the Buddha's teachings, and one of the most complex. He tries to explain the concept by analogy to our senses: sight, for instance, cannot be attributed to our eyes alone. A dead body has eyes, but no sight. Sight derives from what he calls our "seeing nature," and this seeing nature has no substance: it cannot be located, physically, in the body. Not existing physically, it can be said to be void. Yet despite this absence—this voidness—the seeing nature exists, for it is responsible for our vision. In this way, Tanxu establishes that the void is real. And for vision to take place, both eyes and the "seeing nature" are necessary. He then goes on to ask, when understanding sight, how we distinguish between the eyes and the seeing nature. His answer is that we cannot: they are aspects of the same phenomenon, and because one is void, or emptiness, and the other is substance, or form, we come to realize that the two cannot be differentiated: form is emptiness, and emptiness is form.[16]

The concept Tanxu elucidates here is among the most fundamental paradoxes of Buddhism, or of any philosophical tradition. The claim "form is emptiness and emptiness is form" is often taken as nihilistic: nothing truly exists (or at least we cannot know whether anything truly exists). However, the importance of the concept lies in the relationship between form and function: in Tanxu's example, the eye and the seeing nature. Lok To explained this concept to me using the example of a table (many teachers use the same lesson). He said the table was a product of conditioned arising, that is, that it did not have any independent existence. I asked if this meant that the table did not really exist. Laughing, he said we could say that the table did not exist, but we would still trip over it if we tried to walk through the center of the room. Likewise, we could say our chairs did not exist, but that would not cause us to fall to the floor.

The Heart Sutra is not saying that nothing truly exists—"form is emptiness" does not mean that our perceptions deceive us into thinking that objects exist when they do not—rather, it suggests that form and emptiness are all the results of conditioned arising. All depend for their existence on an infinite series of connections among form, function, and perception. Because they both derive their existence in the same way, they are equivalent: form is emptiness, and emptiness is form.

Offering what may be an unintended lesson in assessing what is real, some scholars have questioned the authenticity of the Heart Sutra. They cite inconsistencies in different versions and sections of the text, and argue that it was originally written in Chinese in the sixth century, then from there traveled to India and was translated into Sanskrit.[17] Others disagree, and attribute the inconsistencies to the ordinary processes of translation and transmission. In either case, the Heart Sutra has been a canonical text for more than a thousand years and its influence is undeniable, but the controversy is both fitting and ironic, for the text itself calls into doubt the very idea of authenticity.

Each Sunday, Tanxu lectured at the library, attracting large crowds to the small room on Boundary Street. His lectures focused on the sutras that had been most important to his own life and career, beginning with the Surangama Sutra—the first text he had studied in Yingkou, some fifty years before—and then the Lotus Sutra, the central text of Tiantai. These lectures were the culmination of Tanxu's career as a Buddhist master, the distillation of the knowledge and insights he had accumulated over decades of study. The doctrine of no-self, the parables of the Burning House and the Phantom City, the principle of conditioned causation and dependent arising—he was able to explicate and develop all of these.

In Hong Kong, Tanxu was also able to carry on the mission entrusted to him by Dixian, though not exactly as Dixian had envisioned. Dixian had wanted Tanxu to revive Buddhism in North China and Manchuria. He accomplished this by founding important monasteries throughout this region. Today, the most prominent Buddhist temples in the north are those founded by Tanxu. His dedication to Buddhism and his skill at forging alliances with officials, and advancing their agendas along with his own, had contributed to his success. But perhaps the most important factor was his familiarity with the region's customs and language. In Hong Kong, Tanxu was an outsider: the language and habits were foreign to him, and the government was not Chinese. Yet, like Harbin, Qingdao, Yingkou, and others, Hong Kong was a mix of Chinese and foreign cultures. Tanxu did not have the political influence or mandate to establish a significant Chinese cultural presence there. But as the most prominent of the monks who remained in Hong Kong after the immigration of the 1940s, Tanxu devoted his energies to reinvigorating and developing Buddhism in the Sino-British realm of Hong Kong.

Tanxu had never been content to stay in one place, seeing it as his duty to travel and spread the dharma. Now, Tanxu's student Lok To followed his example. Lok To had first come to Hong Kong to improve his English, as a step towards fulfilling his dream of spreading the dharma to America. For ten years, during which he helped evacuate Tanxu from Qingdao and find him a refuge in Hong Kong, he had postponed his desire to go abroad. Tanxu had urged him to go, but Lok To refused, unwilling to leave while the monastery in

Hong Kong was short of money. With the library opened, and the Land and Water Rite now providing a yearly income, his teacher was finally safe and secure. Lok To again raised the topic of going abroad.

In the fall of 1962, Lok To met with Tanxu to discuss his proposed departure. Tanxu was now eighty-seven years old and increasingly frail, and Lok To hesitated to leave. Tanxu, though, insisted:

> Spreading the dharma abroad is not easy. There will be much bitterness and many obstacles. But always remember the principles that led you to become a monk in the first place. Today you must go, and spread the dharma in the West. Do not worry about me. We will see each other when you return![18]

With his teacher's blessing, that December Lok To flew from Hong Kong to San Francisco. Working with Master Shao Yin (later the head of an important Buddhist university in Taiwan), Lok To traveled east, going from San Francisco to Toronto and finally to New York. Continuing in the tradition of Tanxu, he was engaged in establishing a temple to serve the Chinese émigré community in New York when he received a letter from Hong Kong that Tanxu had taken ill, but that the doctors expected a full recovery. A few days later, however, a phone call came with the news that Tanxu had passed away while meditating. Lok To hurried back to Hong Kong to take part in his teacher's funeral.

Tanxu died on August 11, 1963, at age eighty-eight. In many ways, he had lived two lives. The first was typical of many men of his generation. He endured war, poverty, and family crises. He worked, married, and raised a family. He saw eight children born, and two daughters married. But this life ended in 1917 when he left to become a monk. His second life began when he was forty-two, and lasted even longer than the first. In his life as Tanxu he became one of the most prominent monks of his generation, traveling many thousands of miles and talking to many thousands of people. His funeral was held in the town of Tsuen Wan, at the Wan Faat Tsing She, the temple where he had spent his first night in Hong Kong, fourteen years before.

Wang Kai, who translated many of Tanxu's last lectures from Mandarin into Cantonese, wrote a memorial for his master. He remembered Tanxu's human face, a face that can be glimpsed in photographs that show him smiling and laughing with friends:

> One day, I brought my younger son K'o Hsin with me to the Library; but the boy, being so young, was very disrespectful. Not only did he not bow, he practically ignored the master and amused himself as he wished. But the master only smiled and said, "This is innocence, the original face of all people." He gave the boy some treats and then said to him, "I am going to save some more candy for you, so come to see me again; when you grow up, remember to be generous when a monk asks for a donation. Be generous so you will receive blessings in return!"

From reminiscing about Tanxu's life, Wang Kai then went on to mourn his passing, his grief echoing the sadness of Ananda at the death of his master, centuries ago:

> Now that he is gone, I realize how lucky I was to have received the wonderful Dharma and, even more so, how privileged I was to have been so closely associated with such a great teacher. . . . Without my Master I am a man without blessings. Shall I ever meet a True Master again? When am I going to hear once more the radiant Dharma. I do not know.[19]

Tanxu's students, colleagues, friends, and followers shared this deep sense of loss. In Hong Kong, he had not only helped preserve and spread Buddhism, he had been an anchor for the refugee community, many of whom shared and treasured his northern manners and language. Hundreds of people came to Tsuen Wan for the funeral of "the Master of Chamshan." Condolences and outpourings of grief came from across China and from as far away as Switzerland. Photographs of the memorial service show many different segments of Hong Kong society gathering to honor his memory.

In one poignant image, a monk—whom I have not been able to identify—wipes away a tear as the crowd honoring Tanxu begins to move out of the hall. This simple gesture shows the power of human friendship and also the challenges that test all Buddhist monks. Separation from loved ones is one of the eight great sufferings named by the Buddha. The goal of Buddhist practice is to overcome the attachments of the world that lead to such suffering, but as the photograph reveals, this is not accomplished easily. Much like Ananda on the death of the Buddha, the monk's tears reveal that even the act of teaching about freeing oneself from worldly attachments itself creates powerful relationships, and thus further obstacles to enlightenment.

And this may be the central contradiction of Tanxu's career. He constantly preached the illusion and cruelty of the material world we live in, yet dedicated himself to strengthening the institutions and facilities of this world. He spoke of the need to overcome personal attachments, yet he created powerful attachments among his followers. He taught that all humanity shared a common destiny that transcended nation or politics, yet worked to strengthen his nation's cultural identity and ultimately fled his native land to escape political persecution.

Tanxu's earthly remains were placed in a memorial stupa in Hong Kong's New Territories. The temple, which Tanxu had begun but did not see completed, had the same name as the temple he had founded in Qingdao, romanized from Cantonese as "Chamshan." This final resting place, on a terrace above Clearwater Bay, is a setting of arresting beauty. Caressed by warm, moist breezes, it is a place that challenges the first noble truth that "all existence is suffering."

Epilogue: The Past in the Present

As I researched and wrote about Tanxu, I presented my work in progress in various forums. On one occasion, the college hosting my lecture produced a beautiful publicity poster, superimposing an image of Tanxu in his monk's robes over the tropical mountain scenery of Chamshan Monastery. I sent a copy of the poster to my contacts at the Young Men's Buddhist Association, eager to show them some tangible evidence that their invaluable help was producing results. I had subtitled the talk "Looking for China in Architecture, Religion, and Politics."

Several weeks later, Hoi, who had been my guide and host through much of Tanxu's world, phoned me at my office. Our conversations were infrequent, though regular, as I turned to him for answers to my questions about Tanxu, his memoir, Lok To, or Buddhism generally. It was the first time we had talked in more than a month, and I was eager for news about Lok To's health. Physically strong, Lok To—eighty-two years old—was having trouble with his memory. He was aware that he was not remembering as much as he once did, and situations that called for him to summon his recollections caused him a great deal of stress. His doctors had advised that such situations were to be avoided. Hoi suggested that we cancel my scheduled meeting with Lok To. He did not propose another date.

As the conversation neared an end, Hoi brought up the poster. I had thought it would be reassuring and exciting, but it had raised questions among some of Tanxu's spiritual heirs—mainly monks at temples in North America. They were concerned that it mentioned "religion and politics." They wanted to correct my misimpression: Master Tanxu was not at all political. Everything he did was to promote the dharma.

Hoi conveyed this message without a hint of criticism. He told me he had explained to the other monks that I was a historian and needed to look at "the whole picture." I assured Hoi that although I wanted to develop the most complete understanding of Tanxu I could, my goal was not to politicize his career or life, or to make Tanxu look either better or worse than he was, but to present a plausible narrative and explanation of his life and work. I understood the source of the concern. The topic of religion is sensitive in the People's Republic of China. Many Buddhist temples are being re-opened, renovated, and promoted, often with support and funding from overseas Chinese. Tanxu's heirs were reestablishing contact with monasteries in the mainland. This was politically delicate, especially in the context of protests in Tibet and the run-up to the Olympic Games, which were going on at the time. The words "religion and politics" superimposed on a picture of Tanxu were seen as an alarming indication of what I might say about their master. I was unable to reschedule my meeting with Lok To.

My first reaction was disappointment and hurt. I had invested myself in the lives of these men. When I reflected on these events, however, they made clear some of the tensions that had driven the project from the beginning.

It was the interaction of religion and politics that had brought me to this story in the first place. Before encountering Tanxu, I had understood that Buddhism was not generally a political religion. The idea that Buddhism denied the material world and was therefore incompatible with political activism may have been overstated, but scholars of Chinese Buddhism had in fact found few Buddhists with political ambitions. The reformist monk Taixu was an important exception; indeed, he was considered controversial in part because of his political activism. In his seminal work on the topic, Holmes Welch stated clearly that nationalism did not play a driving role in the Buddhist revival in China.

The placement of Tanxu's temples made me question that generalization. It seemed more than coincidence that Tanxu's major projects were undertaken in cities with large foreign communities, often colonies or former colonies. Digging deeper, I found that Tanxu and his government patrons established and supported Buddhist temples for the explicit purpose of promoting a Chinese cultural, religious, and political presence in places where foreigners had dominated. I was interested in understanding how Buddhism could co-exist with Chinese nationalism. Tanxu's memoir provided insights into the motivations and circumstances of a monk who had been an advocate for both. Buddhism could be a component of Chinese nationalism: both categories were adaptive and flexible.

Tanxu's story highlighted the importance of questioning nationalist narratives. There was not just one vision of what the Chinese nation was or should be. Tanxu's mission to rebuild China with a Buddhist religious foundation complemented and sometimes competed with other ideas about the state, ranging from radical revolutionaries who rejected all forms of Chinese culture to modernizers who wanted to reform Chinese society, sometimes along Western lines, and traditionalists who sought stability in Confucianism. Although Tanxu's autobiography was written to display the design that he saw governing his life, the details reflect the contestation that characterized his times.

Tanxu's story mapped neatly onto a century of Chinese history, from the late Qing to the cusp of the Cultural Revolution. Major themes—dynastic decline, imperialism, nationalism, cultural crisis—appeared with first-person immediacy in his autobiography. I had studied and taught the Boxer Uprising, the Sino-Japanese War, and the Russo-Japanese War, and I had led discussions of how these events shaped the psyche of a generation of Chinese. But Tanxu helped me see how these events shaped the life of one man. His experiences illustrated the manner in which the lives of individuals produce and reflect broad social processes. People do not simply tap into pre-existing social contexts. Or rather, they do, but those contexts are themselves the creations of the experiences and actions of individuals and groups. Tanxu's story is important neither because he is "typical," nor because he was a powerful individual who single-handedly shaped history (if either category of person even exists). Reading Tanxu's memoir and writing his story, I didn't find a man buffeted by outside forces beyond his control; instead, he represented millions of Chinese who responded to events as they could. The interaction of these individual responses shaped China's history—in many ways, it *was* China's history. As the author Lu Xun observed—in the same year that Tanxu left Ningbo to begin his career founding temples—"the earth had no roads to begin with, but when many people pass one way, a road is made."[1]

Tanxu's story also highlighted for me the interaction of the present and the past. My unlikely discovery of Lok To and his connection to Tanxu made the story more personal by putting me in touch with men who had worked closely with Tanxu, but also because it enabled me to visit the places that were crucial to Tanxu's personal and professional journey. Tanxu's story didn't exist only in the pages of his memoir or in China's past. It lives on in people and places that exist to this day. Writing this story, I was reminded that all historians write about the past, but they can only write from the perspective of the present, applying standards and methods perhaps unknown to their subjects. Furthermore, readers bring their own standards to bear on both the historian and the subject. Although the past cannot be changed, *history* changes constantly.

Encountering Tanxu's story through his friends, students, and works brought home the close connection between historian and subject. My "travels with Tanxu," as I call them, are not unique. Many historians (and even more often anthropologists and sociologists) participate in the stories they tell. I did not become a monk or take up Buddhism, but I took steps into Tanxu's world, and those steps—in Hong Kong monasteries, New York brownstones, and a temples across East China—changed me as well as the story I was writing. This happens to all historians: writing history is mutually transformative for author and subject. The myth of the objective narrator is just that. By becoming more conscious of that process, I believe I gained a better understanding not just of Tanxu's history, but of the historian's craft.

In this spirit, I traveled to Tiantai Mountain. Zhiyi, the founder of Tiantai Buddhism, established Guoqing Temple there some 1,400 years ago. There is no evidence that Tanxu himself ever set foot in these mountains, but they were the source of his tradition. Spending time there, I thought, might help me better understand Tanxu's life. At Guoqing Temple, I encountered many evocative scenes. Some were grand, like thirty-foot-tall Buddha statues, carved and gilded five hundred years ago, or the six-foot-high "snake" bell, so-called because anyone who hears its chime and does not rise to stand is deemed too lazy to need feet or legs and will thus be reborn as a snake. Others were embodied in small gestures, like the sequence in which a monk touches hands and knees to the ground when kneeling for prayer.

The guesthouse I stayed in rose up above the temple grounds where the land began to climb toward the nearby peaks; the elevation afforded exceptional views. Despite the 90-degree heat of the day, the air was clear. Across the small river valley a stupa, erected 1,100 years ago during the Sui dynasty, stood watch over the temple, rice paddies, and tourist hotels that flanked the entrance to the national park. I sat in the courtyard, beneath a camphor tree which, according to the sign at its base, had been there nearly as long as the stupa. As my laundry dried alongside that of pilgrims from Korea, Japan, and other parts of China, I passed a few hours writing in my journal and talking with the other residents.

A young monk who was in charge of hosting me came to discuss the next day's itinerary—we would drive up into the mountains and visit several temples, including the place where Zhiyi had preached the first Tiantai sermons, in the sixth century CE. The monk seemed happy to have an outsider in the temple, one with whom he could share his knowledge of Buddhism and the region. He was unclear just *why* I had come to Guoqing Temple, which was hardly surprising since I was unsure myself: I wanted to "follow in Tanxu's footsteps," but Tanxu had never been here, as far as I knew. There were no documents here that would help in my research. My goal was vague and unsystematic: to learn about a place by simply being there and experiencing it. My guide seemed happy to oblige; he mapped out an itinerary for me to visit a handful of temples, including some historically important ones, but also some of the small huts used by hermit monks. He handed me a few books about Tiantai thought and history and arranged for me to meet the abbot of the temple and some other important monks. He looked amused when I asked how he dealt with mosquitoes, given the Buddhist precept against killing. "Killing mosquitoes does not mean one is not a Buddhist," he had said. "Mosquitoes spread lots of diseases. They are not good."

But most evenings I reflected alone, writing in my journal, considering Tanxu's place in the history that had radiated from this mountain and in turn my own place in his story. This place seemed completely separate from the temple in Harbin where I had first heard the name Tanxu and the Bronx apartment where I had met his colleagues and students. But in the temple museum I found a statue given by Lok To in honor of his teacher, Tanxu. I found the figure—an emaciated Buddha on the verge on enlightenment—particularly powerful. I thought about this image as I sat on the terrace, trying to understand my role in Tanxu's history, while still deeply suspicious of the idea that I was somehow part of the story I was writing. Twilight began to fall, and the mosquitoes claimed the courtyard. I retreated to my room as the sun set over the mountains.

Glossary of Selected Names and Places

NAMES

An Lushan 安祿山

Ba Jin 巴金
Bai Chenghuang 白城隍
Baoyi 宝一

Chanding 禪定
Chen Feiqing 陳飛青
Chiang Kai-shek 蔣介石
Chunkui 純魁
Ci Yun 茲云

Da Cheng 達成
Ding Ling 丁零
Dixian 諦閑

Ge Guangting 葛光庭
Guangxu 光緒
Guanyin 觀音
Guo Songling 郭松齡

He Yutang 何玉堂

Imai Akirayoshi 今井昭慶

Jiang Yi'an 姜軼庵
Jin Desheng 金德胜
Jingming 靜明

Jue Yi 覺一

Kang Youwei 康有為

Li Du 李杜
Liu Wenhua 劉文化
Lok To 樂都
Longxian 隆銜
Lu Bingnan 陸炳南
Lü Fuchen 呂輔臣
Lu Xun 魯迅

Ma Jiping 馬冀平
Mao Zedong 毛澤東

Nengcheng 能成

Pang Mutang 龐睦堂

Qingchi 清池

Renshan 仁山
Ruguang 如光

Shanbo 善波
Shanguo 善果
Shen Honglie 沈鴻烈
Sheng Huai 聖懷
Song Jiaoren 宋教仁

197

Song Xiaolian 宋小廉

Taixu 太虛

Wang Deqing 王德清
Wang Futing 王福庭
Wang Jingchun 王景春
Wang Jinyu 王金鈺
Wang Langchuan 王郎川
Wang Shouchun 王壽椿
Wang Zhiyi 王志一
Wu Yong 伍雍

Xing Kong 性空

Yan Fu 嚴復
Ye Gongchuo 葉恭綽
Yinkui 印魁
Yuan Shikai 元世凱

Zhang Leting 張樂亭
Zhang Zuolin 張作霖
Zhao Zhenhou 趙鎮候
Zhi Kai (Chee Kai) 智開
Zhu Qinglan 朱慶瀾

PLACES

Beijing 北京
Beiping 北平
Beitang 北糖
Bohai Gulf 渤海

Cankou 沧口
Changchun 長春

Dagu 大沽
Dalian 大連

Gaoming Temple 高冥寺
Guanzhong 關中
Guanzong Temple 觀宗寺

Hai River 海河
Harbin 哈爾濱
Hong Kong 香港
Huai River 淮河

Jiaozhou Bay 膠州灣
Jingxing County (Hebei) 井陘縣
Jiyun River 積雲

Laishui County (Hebei) 涞水县
Laoshan 崂山
Liaodong 遼東
Lintong 臨潼
Liurong Temple 六榕寺
Longevity Temple (Wanshousi) 萬壽寺
Luoyang 洛陽
Lüshun 旅順

Manchukuo 滿洲國
Mt. Daofeng Monastery 道風山

Nanjing 南京
Ningbo 寧波
Ninghe 寧河

Paradise Temple (Jilesi) 極樂寺

Qingdao 青島

Red Snail Mountain 紅螺山

Shanghai 上海

Shanhaiguan 山海關
Shenyang 瀋陽
Shuangcheng 雙城
Suihua 綏化
Surangama Temple
  (Lengyansi) 楞嚴寺

Taiyang gou 太陽溝
Tanggu 塘沽
Temple of Expansive Wisdom
  (Banruosi) 般若寺
Tianjin 天津
Tieling 鐵嶺

Tongguan 潼關
Tranquil Peak Temple
  (Zhanshansi) 湛山寺
Tung Lin Kok Yuen 東蓮
  覺苑

Xi'an 西安
Xinjing 新京

Yangzhou 揚州
Yantai 煙台
Yingkou 營口

Zifu Temple 資福寺

OTHER TERMS

Chu jia 出家

Huiguan 會館

Kan po! Fang xia! Zi zai!
  看破！放下！自在！
kang 炕

ling 靈

shuilu fahui 水陸法會

Tianhou 天后

Wangdao 王道

Xinmin zhuyi 新民注意

Notes

Prologue

1. Jill Lepore, "Historians Who Love Too Much: Reflections on Microhistory and Biography," *The Journal of American History* (June 2001): 129–44.

Chapter 1

1. By Johannes Nieuhoff, Steward to the Ambassadors; this 1st [French] edition printed in 1668. http://wason.library.cornell.edu/Tianjin/history.html.

2. Kwan Man Bun, *The Salt Merchants of Tianjin* (Honolulu: University of Hawaii Press, 2001), 26.

3. David Harris, *Of Battle and Beauty: Felice Beato's Photographs of China* (Santa Barbara, Calif.: Santa Barbara Museum of Art, 1999), 58.

4. Kwan, *Salt Merchants of Tianjin*, 22–25.

5. Tanxu, *Yingchen huiyilu* (Recollections of the Material World) (Reprint Shanghai: Shanghai xinwen chubanju, 1993) I, 1. (Subsequently abbreviated YCHYL I. There are multiple printings and editions of this memoir, first published in Hong Kong in 1954. Widely circulated editions include Hong Kong: Chamshan Temple, 1974; Shanghai: Shanghai xinwen chubanju, 1993; Taibei: Longwen chubanshe, 1993; Hong Kong: Qianhua lianshe, 1994; Taizhong: Taizhong lianshe, 2000.)

6. Prasenjit Duara, "Superscribing Symbols: The Myth of Guandi, Chinese God of War," *The Journal of Asian Studies* 47, no. 4. (Nov. 1988): 778–95.

7. *Ninghe xianzhi yi zhu* (Annals of Ninghe County) (Tangshan: Gai Hui, 1987), 971.

8. This boy was known by at least four names during his life: Wang Shouchun, Wang Futing, Longxian, and Tanxu. I have tried to be consistent and use the name appropriate to each time of his life.

9. Previous 2 paragraphs: YCHYL I, 4–5

10. YCHYL I, 6.

11. YCHYL I, 7–8.

12. YCHYL I, 8.

13. YCHYL I, 10.

14. YCHYL I, 11–15.

15. A. Charles Muller, trans. *The Diamond Sutra*, ch. 32. www.acmuller.net/bud-canon/diamond_sutra.html (accessed May 9, 2010).

16. A. F. Price, trans. *The Diamond Sutra*, ch. 32. http://community.palouse.net/lotus/diamondsutra.htm (accessed May 9, 2010).

17. YCHYL I, 16.

18. O. D.Rasmussen, *Tientsin: An Illustrated History* (Tianjin: The Tientsin Press, 1925), 36–49.

19. Nathan Sivin, *Chinese Alchemy* (Cambridge, Mass.: Harvard University Press, 1968), 11–12.

20. Sivin, *Chinese Alchemy*, 155–57.

21. YCHYL I, 17.

22. YCHYL I, 18–19.

23. S. C. M. Paine, *The Sino-Japanese War of 1894–1895* (Cambridge: Cambridge University Press, 2003), esp. 132–35.

24. According to the traditional Chinese reckoning system, all children are one year, or *sui*, at birth, and are considered one *sui* older at each New Year, rather than each birthday. An infant turning two *sui* could be anywhere from two days old to a day less than two years old, by the Western dating system.

25. YCHYL I, 19–21.

26. Joseph Esherick, *The Origins of the Boxer Uprising* (Berkeley and Los Angeles: University of California Press, 1986), xiii.

27. Esherick, *Origins*, 218.

28. Boxer verse quoted in Esherick, *Origins*, 299.

29. YCHYL I, 22.

30. During the earlier conflict, British troops had attacked a fort at Beitang itself, but that fort had not been rebuilt after that war, and so the landing parties did not pass through Beitang as they had a few decades earlier.

31. William Duiker, *Cultures in Collision: The Boxer Rebellion* (San Rafael, Calif.: Presidio Press, 1978), 70–81.

32. YCHYL I, 23.

33. James Hevia, *English Lessons: The Pedagogy of Imperialism in Nineteenth-Century China* (Durham, N.C.: Duke University Press, 2003), 195–96.

34. Duiker, *Cultures in Collision*, 158–59.

35. YCHYL I, 24.

36. YCHYL I, 26.

37. YCHYL I, 29.

Chapter 2

1. Tess Johnston and Deke Erh, *Far From Home: Western Architecture in China's Northern Treaty Ports* (Hong Kong: Old China Hand Press, 1997), 39.

2. Richard Connaughton, *The War of the Rising Sun and the Tumbling Bear* (New York: Routledge, 1988), 78.

3. *Yingkou shizhi* (Annals of Yingkou City) (Beijing: Zhongguo shucang chubanshe, 1992), vol. I: 36–37. (Hereafter abbreviated YKSZ.)

4. E. T. Williams, "The Open Ports of China," *Geographical Review* 9, no. 4 (April–June 1920): 331.

5. YKSZ, 44.

6. Consulate-General of the United States, Newchwang, China, August 16, 1904, to the Department of State, Item 265, "Report General Conditions during the Evacuation of Russia and incoming of Japanese" (National Archives Microfilm Publication M-115, roll 5), U.S. Department of State, Dispatches from the United States Consuls in Newchwang, 1865–1906, General Records of the Department of State, Record Group 59, pp. 2–3.

7. YCHYL I, 37.

8. Discussion of fortune-telling based on Richard J. Smith, *Fortune-Tellers and Philosophers* (Boulder, Colo.: Westview Press, 1991), esp. 172 ff.

9. YCHYL I, 33–39.

10. YCHYL I, 40–41.

11. Jonathan Spence, *The Search for Modern China* (New York: W.W. Norton, 1990) 300–303.

12. Ernest P. Young, *The Presidency of Yuan Shih-kai* (Ann Arbor: University of Michigan Press, 1977), ch. 5, esp. 116–19.

13. Based on Marie-Claire Bergère, *The Golden Age of the Chinese Bourgeoisie, 1911–1937*, trans. Janet Lloyd (Cambridge: Cambridge University Press, 1986).

14. Holmes Welch, *The Buddhist Revival in China* (Cambridge, Mass.: Harvard University Press, 1968), 288–89.

15. YCHYL I, 42.

16. Kathryn Bernhardt, "Divorce in the Republican Period," in *Civil Law in Qing and Republican China*, ed. Kathryn Bernhardt and Philip C.C. Huang, 187–214 (Stanford, Calif.: Stanford University Press, 1994), 189–91.

17. YCHYL I, 42.

18. Donald S. Lopez, Jr., *The Story of Buddhism* (San Francisco: HarperSanFrancisco, 2002), 43.

19. YCHYL I, 44.

20. YCHYL I, 44–46.

21. YCHYL I, 46–47.

22. YCHYL I, 49.

23. YCHYL I, 50.

24. YCHYL I, 51.

25. Welch, *Buddhist Revival*, 9.

26. Welch, *Buddhist Revival*, 19.

27. Welch, *Buddhist Revival*, 39.

28. Welch, *Buddhist Revival*, 71.

29. Welch, *Buddhist Revival*, 97.

30. YCHYL I, 53.

Chapter 3

1. YCHYL I, 58.

2. YCHYL I, 79–85.

3. Judith A Berling, "Death and Afterlife in Chinese Religions," in *Death and Afterlife: Perspectives of World Religions*, ed. Obayashi Hiroshi (New York: Greenwood Press, 1992), 188–89.

4. Burton Watson, trans., *The Lotus Sutra* (New York: Columbia University Press, 1993), ix–x.

5. A compelling case involving suspicions surrounding monks is the subject of Philip Kuhn's *Soulstealers: The Chinese Sorcery Scare of 1768* (Cambridge, Mass.: Harvard University Press, 1990).

6. YCHYL I, 90–91.

7. Valerie Hansen, *Changing Gods in Medieval China* (Princeton, N.J.: Princeton University Press, 1990), 75.

8. YCHYL I, 139.

Chapter 4

1. YCHYL I, 146.

2. Frank Dikötter, *Things Modern: Material Culture and Everyday Life in China* (London: Hurst & Company, 2007), 214.

3. YCHYL I, 178–79.

Chapter 5

1. Karl Marx, *The Eighteenth Brumaire of Louis Bonaparte* (Reprint, Rockville, Maryland: Wildside Press, 2008), 15.

2. The anti-temple edict in particular, and the question of religion's place in a modern China more generally, is addressed by Vincent Goosaert, "1898: The Beginning of the End of Chinese Religion," *Journal of Asian Studies* 65, no. 2 (May 2006): 307–36.

3. YCHYL I, 188–90.

4. YCHYL I, 187–93.

5. YCHYL I, 196–99.

Chapter 6

1. YCHYL I, 208.

2. James Carter, *Creating a Chinese Harbin* (Ithaca, N.Y.: Cornell University Press, 2002).

3. Rebecca Nedostup has documented and analyzed the Guomindang's struggles with temple festivals and other aspects of religion as it tried to project a modern image in "Ritual Competition and the Modernizing Nation-State," ch. 3 in *Chinese Religiosities: Afflictions of Modernity and State Formation*, ed. Mayfair Meihui Yang (Berkeley and Los Angeles: University of California Press, 2008), 87–112.

4. YCHYL II, 23–25.

5. Ryan Dunch, among others, discusses Chinese Protestants' vision of a Christian China in *Fuzhou Protestants and the Making of a Modern China, 1857–1927* (New Haven, Conn.: Yale University Press, 2001).

6. YCHYL I, 220.

7. See Nedostup, *Superstitious Regimes: Religion and the Politics of Chinese Modernity* (Cambridge, Mass.: Harvard East Asian Monographs, 2010) and "Ritual Competition."

8. "Ananda Thera (Ananda Alone)," trans. Andrew Olendzki, www.accesstoinsight.org/tripitaka/kn/thag/thag.17.03.olen.html.

9. For details on Taixu's life and career see Don Pittman, *Toward a Modern Chinese Buddhism: Taixu's Reforms* (Honolulu: University of Hawaii Press, 2001).

10. YCHYL II, 40.

11. Welch, *Buddhist Revival in China*, 168.
12. YCHYL II, 43.
13. YCHYL II, 44.
14. YCHYL I, 242–44.
15. YCHYL II, 5.
16. YCHYL I, 243.

Chapter 7

1. Eduard Vermeer, *Economic Development in Provincial China* (Cambridge: Cambridge University Press, 1988), 28.
2. Vermeer, *Economic Development*, 32–35.
3. Kathryn Edgerton-Tarpley, *Tears From Iron* (Berkeley and Los Angeles: University of California Press, 2008), 192–93.
4. On the history and operation of the Qing granary system, see Pierre-Étienne Will, *Bureaucracy and Famine* (Stanford, Calif.: Stanford University Press, 1990).
5. Vermeer, *Economic Development*, 35.
6. Vermeer, *Economic Development*, 35–39. This section draws on Vermeer's thorough study as well as four important scholarly works on famine and famine relief in China: Edgerton-Tarpley, *Tears From Iron*; Lillian M. Li, *Fighting Famine in North China* (Stanford: Stanford University Press, 2007); Pierre-Étienne Will and R. Bin Wong, *Nourish the People* (Ann Arbor: Michigan University Press, 1991), and Will, *Bureaucracy and Famine*.
7. YCHYL II, 66–67.
8. YCHYL II, 78.
9. Phil Billingsley, *Bandits in Republican China* (Stanford, Calif.: Stanford University Press, 1988), 30.
10. YCHYL II, 80–83.
11. Yang Hsüan-chih. *A Record of Buddhist Monasteries in Lo-yang*, trans. Yi-t'ung Wang (Princeton, N.J.: Princeton University Press, 1984), 232.

Chapter 8

1. YCHYL II, 115–16.
2. John Schrecker, *Imperialism and Chinese Nationalism: Germany in Shantung* (Cambridge, Mass.: Harvard University Press, 1971), 33–42.
3. Population figures are compiled from *Qingdao shizhi: renkou zhi* [Local History of Qingdao: Population] (Beijing: Wuzhou zhuanbo chubanshe, 2001), 35–37 and 45–46; George Steinmetz, *The*

Devil's Handwriting: Precoloniality and the German Colonial State in Qingdao, Samoa, and Southwest Africa (Chicago: University of Chicago Press, 2007), 435–36.

4. An account of the siege can be found in Edwin P. Hoyt, *The Fall of Tsingtao* (London: Arthur Baker, Ltd, 1975).

5. Schrecker, *Imperialism*, 217.

6. Gould Thomas, *An American in China, 1936–1939* (New York: Greatrix Press, 2004), 72–73.

7. YCHYL II, 115–16.

8. James L. Watson, "Standardizing the Gods: The Promotion of T'ian Hou ('Empress of Heaven') Along the South China Coast, 960–1960," in *Popular Culture in Late Imperial China*, ed. David Johnson, Andrew Nathan, and Evelyn Rawski (Berkeley and Los Angeles: University of California Press, 1985), 292–324.

9. YCHYL II, 120.

10. YCHYL II, 123.

11. As discussed in chapter 3, suspicion of monks increased during the Qing dynasty, which required its male subjects to adopt the "queue," the Manchu hairstyle that included the familiar ponytail down men's backs. Because the shaved head worn by monks precluded wearing the queue, Manchu rulers were frequently suspicious that "monks" were in fact political dissidents masquerading as monks so that they could shave their heads to avoid physically demonstrating their loyalty through the queue.

12. YCHYL II, 125.

13. YCHYL II, 126–27. The text states here that construction began in October of 1931, but this seems to be a mistake, given the other dates and Tanxu's whereabouts.

14. YCHYL II, 168–70.

15. Thomas, *American in China*, 120–21.

Chapter 9

1. Chiang Kai-shek relocated the capital of the Republic of China to Nanjing, which literally means "southern capital," in 1927. Nanjing had last been capital of China during the early Ming dynasty, which moved the capital to Beijing ("northern capital") in 1403. Beijing was formally named Beiping ("northern peace") until 1949, when Mao Zedong reestablished it as the capital, this time of the People's Republic.

2. Based primarily on Edwin Hoyt, *Japan's War* (New York: McGraw-Hill, 1986), 148–50.

3. Thomas, *American in China*, 138.

4. Thomas, *American in China*, 159–65.

5. *China Weekly Review*, January 1938, quoted in John Hunter Boyle, *China and Japan at War, 1937–1945: The Politics of Collaboration* (Stanford, Calif.: Stanford University Press, 1972), 85. I have based this discussion of Kita on Boyle's work.

6. Boyle, *China and Japan at War*, 93.

7. F. Hilary Conroy, "Japan's War in China: An Ideological Somersault," *The Pacific Historical Review* 21, no. 4 (Nov. 1952): 372.

8. Xue Yu, *Buddhism, War, and Nationalism* (New York: Routledge, 2005), 166.

9. Timothy Brook, *Collaboration: Japanese Agents and Local Elites in Wartime China* (Cambridge, Mass.: Harvard University Press, 2005), 2.

10. David P. Barrett and Larry N. Shyu, eds., *Chinese Collaboration with Japan, 1932–1945: The Limits of Accommodation* (Stanford, Calif.: Stanford University Press, 2001).

11. Timothy Brook, review of Poshek Fu, *Passivity, Resistance, and Collaboration: Intellectual Choices in Occupied China 1937–1945* (Stanford, Calif.: Stanford University Press, 1993), *Journal of the Economic and Social History of the Orient* 39, no. 1 (1996): 80–82, esp. 80.

12. Václav Havel, *The Art of the Impossible: Politics as Morality in Practice*, trans. Paul Wilson (New York: Knopf, 1997), 4, and Havel, *The Power of the Powerless: Citizens Against the State in Central-Eastern Europe* (Armonk, N.Y.: M.E. Sharpe, 1985).

13. Xue Yu, *Buddhism, War, and Nationalism*, 169.

14. Zhang Jianping, "Japan's Exploitative Labor System in Qingdao," ch. 11 in *China at War: Regions of China, 1937–45*, ed. Stephen R. MacKinnon, et al., 227–44 (Stanford, Calif.: Stanford University Press, 2007), 234.

15. Lok To, "Autobiography," transcript of lecture in Chinese, January 7, 2001, Zhanshan Temple, Toronto.

16. Henry I. Shaw, Jr., "The United States Marines in North China, 1945–1949," Washington, D.C.: Historical Branch, G-3 Division Headquarters, U. S. Marine Corps, rev. 1963.

17. Zhiguo Yang, "U.S. Marines in Qingdao: History, Public Memory, and Chinese Nationalism," in *Exploring Nationalisms of China: Themes and Conflicts*, ed. C. X. George Wei and Xiaoyuan Liu, 57–75 (Westport, Conn.: Greenwood Press, 2002), 64.

18. Yang, "U.S. Marines in Qingdao," 67–68.

19. Shaw, "U.S. Marines in North China," section 7.

20. YCHYL II, 18.
21. YCHYL II, 19–21.
22. For more on this topic, see Richard Hughes Seager, *The World's Parliament of Religions: The East/West Encounter, Chicago, 1893* (Bloomington: Indiana University Press, 2009).
23. Lok To, "Autobiography," 2–3.
24. Holmes Welch, "Buddhist Organizations in China," *Journal of the Hong Kong Branch of the Royal Asiatic Society* 1 (1960–61): 98–114, esp. 107.
25. Lok To, "Autobiography," 10.
26. Lok To, "Autobiography," 10.
27. Lok To, "Autobiography," 13.
28. Lok To, "Autobiography," 14.

Chapter 10

1. William M. Leary, Jr., "Aircraft and Anti-Communists: CAT in Action, 1949–52," *The China Quarterly* 52 (Oct.–Dec. 1972): 654–69, quotation p. 654.
2. Richard Kebabjian, "Crash Details," planecrashinfo.com. http://www.planecrashinfo.com/1948/1948-43.htm; http://www.planecrashinfo.com/1947/1947-2.htm. (accessed May 9, 2010)
3. Tom Cooper, "China and Taiwan Since 1945, Part I," Air Combat Information Group. www.acig.org/artman/publish/article_145.shtml. (accessed May 9, 2010)
4. Welch, "Buddhist Organizations in Hong Kong," 99.
5. Tanxu, *On Amidism* (Hong Kong: Buddhist Book Distributors, 1973), 5–6.
6. Tanxu, *On Amidism*, 9–11.
7. Tanxu, *On Amidism*, 11.
8. Tanxu, *On Amidism*, 24–25.
9. Lok To, "Founding the South China Buddhist Studies Institute," 64.
10. Frank Welsh, *A History of Hong Kong*, rev. ed. (London: HarperCollins, 1997), 452–59.
11. Daniel B. Stephenson, "Text, Image, and Transformation in the History of the *Shuilu fahui*, the Buddhist Rite for Deliverance of Creatures of Water and Land," ch. 2 in *Cultural Intersections in Later Chinese Buddhism*, ed. Marsha Smith Weidner, 30–72 (Honolulu: University of Hawaii Press, 2001), 30–31. My description of the rite is based on Stephenson.

12. Stephenson, "Text, Image, and Transformation in the History of the *Shuilu fahui*," 32.

13. The ceremony remained rarely performed until the 1980s, because of the expense and size of the ritual. It retains cultural, political, and religious importance in Hong Kong today, according to Yiu Kwan Chen, "Popular Buddhist Ritual in Contemporary Hong Kong: Shuilu Fahui, a Buddhist Rite for Saving All Sentient Beings of Water and Land," *Buddhist Studies Review* 25, no. 1 (2008): 90–105.

14. Welch, "Buddhist Organizations in Hong Kong," 99.

15. Tanxu (as Grand Master T'an Hsu), *The Prajna Paramita Heart Sutra*, 2nd ed., trans. Ven. Dharma Master Lok To (New York: Sutra Translation Committee of the United States and Canada, 2000), 71.

16. Tanxu (T'an Hsu), *Prajna Paramita Heart Sutra*, 75–77.

17. Jan Nattier, "The Heart Sutra: Chinese Apocryphal Text?" *Journal of the International Association of Buddhist Studies* 15, no. 2 (1992): 153–223.

18. Lok To, "*Zhuisi enshi lüexu zhuangban huanan xuefoyuan zhi jingguo* "Founding the South China Buddhist Studies Institute," in *Tanxu dashi zhuisilu* (Remembrances of Master Tanxu) (Toronto: Buddhist Association of Canada, 2001), 70.

19. Wang Kai, "Memorial for My Master" in *Prajna Paramita Heart Sutra*, 50.

Epilogue

1. Lu Xun, "My Old Home." Jonathan Spence quotes the same passage in *The Search for Modern China*.

Index

Note: Page numbers in *italics* refer to maps.

Judaism, 75
Jurchens, 108

Kang Youwei, 96
karma, 72–75, 96
King Ashoka Temple, 11, 141
Kingly Way (*wang dao*), 156
King of Hell, 23–26, 34, 38, 85
Kita Seiichi, 156
Korea
    and East Asian Buddhist
        Association, 122
    Korean conflict, 177
    Sino-Japanese War (1894–95), 4,
        32–34, 36
    and travels of Tanxu, *14, 82, 97*
Kowloon, 173, 175
Kowloon–Canton Railroad (KCR), 171

Laishui County, Hebei, 64
Land and Water Rite, 182–83, 210n13
language, regional differences in,
    68–69
Lecture Hall
    and blended religious traditions,
        48–50, 76
    return of Tanxu to, 88
    and Surangama Temple, 99,
        100–102, 105
lecturing career of Tanxu, 98, 103, 105,
    178–81
legal system, 37
Lepore, Jill, 2
Liang Qichao, 52
Liaodong Peninsula, 36, 44–45
libraries established by Tanxu, 165, 185,
    187
Li Du, 124–25
Lin, 146
Lintong City, 136, 138, 139
Liurong Temple, 171
Liu Wenhua, 49–51
Lok To
    arrival in the Bronx, 6
    author's relationship with, 1, 191,
        192, 194
    as Dharma heir of Tanxu, 6
    health of, 191
    on Heart Sutra, 185
    move to the United States, 187–88

and retreat of Tanxu to Hong Kong,
    166–73, 175
seminary experience of, 160–61
on suffering of Tanxu, 181
loneliness, 9–10
Longevity Temple, 98, 103, 105
Longxian, 64–67
Lopez, Donald, 57
Lotus Sutra, 50, 76, 187
Lo Wu, 177
Lu Bin, 7
Lu Bingnan, 99–101
Lü Fuchen, 103–4, 105
Luo Tan, 34
Luoyang, 139–40
Lushan, An, 128, 129
Lu Xun, 53, 155, 194
lying
    parable on, 77
    of Tanxu, 60, 84–85, 86, 104

Mahayana Buddhism, 94, 157
Ma Jiping, 109
Manchukuo, 156, 160
Manchuria
    Communist forces in, 163
    as cultural crossroads, 107–9, 110
    and Dixian, 187
    Japan's invasion of, 124–25, 154
    and lecturing career of Tanxu, 105
    natural resources of, 160
    struggle for control of, 44–46
Manchus, 80, 207n11
Mandate of Heaven, 97
Manhattan, Hong Kong compared to,
    10
Mao Zedong, 177, 207n1
"Marco Polo Bridge Incident," 154
marriage of Wang Futing, 21. *See also*
    wife of Wang
Marx, Karl, 96
Maternal Grace Temple, 133
May Fourth Movement, 83, 145
Meiji Restoration (1868), 32
memoirs of Tanxu, 2–3
Memorial Stupa, 151–52
Miller, Henry, 47
Mingdi, Emperor of China, 140
Ming dynasty, 129, 207n1
missionaries, 28, 36